Dynamic Approaches to the Understanding and Treatment of Alcoholism

by Margaret H. Bean, Edward J. Khantzian, John E. Mack, George Vaillant, and Norman E. Zinberg

Edited by
Margaret H. Bean and Norman E. Zinberg

THE FREE PRESS
A Division of Macmillan Publishing Co., Inc.
NEW YORK

Collier Macmillan Publishers
LONDON

The Free Press
A Division of Macmillan Publishing Co., Inc.
866 Third Avenue, New York, N.Y. 10022

Collier Macmillan Canada, Ltd.

Library of Congress Catalog Card Number: 81-65033

Printed in the United States of America

printing number

2 3 4 5 6 7 8 9 10

Library of Congress Cataloging in Publication Data
Main entry under title:

Dynamic approaches to the understanding and treatment
    of alcholism.

    Includes bibliographical references and index.
    Contents: Alcohol use, alcoholism, and the problems
of treatment / Norman E. Zinberg and Margaret H.
Bean — Dangers of psychotherapy in the treatment of
alcoholism / George E. Vaillant — Denial and the psy-
chological complications of alcoholism / Margaret H.
Bean — [etc.]
    1. Alcoholism—Addresses, essays, lectures.
I. Bean, Margaret H. II. Zinberg, Norman Earl
            [DNLM: 1. Alcoholism—Congresses. WM 274
D997 1978]
RC565.D9   616.86'1   81-65033
ISBN 0-02-902110-3   AACR2

First the man takes a drink,
Then the drink takes a drink,
Then the drink takes the man!

Edward Rowland Sill,
An Adage from the Orient

Contents

Preface and Acknowledgments

This book developed out of a symposium on alcohol use and alcoholism* sponsored by The Cambridge Hospital/Harvard Medical School, Department of Psychiatry. All five of the contributors are psychiatrists, already psychoanalysts or in training to become psychoanalysts, and active teachers of psychiatry. Anyone familiar with the field of alcoholism will realize at once how rare it is to have under the roof of The Cambridge Hospital/Harvard Medical School, Department of Psychiatry so large a group of psychoanalytically trained psychiatrists thinking together about these problems, which, as we will discuss later, are so frequently avoided by mainstream psychiatry.

All of the contributors use a psychodynamic model for direct patient care and for teaching. Yet when it came to a discussion of alcohol use, it became clear that there were important and consistent divergences of views and, further, that the divergences of views in this group seemed representative of the field. George E. Vaillant presents a direct view of the disease model of alcoholism and an A.A. (Alcoholics Anonymous) position essentially negative to ordinary psychiatric treatment for al-

---

*"The Nature of Alcoholism and the Care of the Alcoholic," March 4, 1978, Science Center, Harvard University, Cambridge, MA.

coholism and suggests a minimal focus on individual problems. Margaret H. Bean is less concerned with the overall philosophy of alcoholism than with the mechanics by which alcoholics and those around them are able to deny the condition. Norman E. Zinberg finds it of crucial importance to put alcohol use and alcoholism within their social perspective, while John E. Mack presents a coherent effort to understand the problems and effects of alcoholism as they are centered within the "self," also in its social context. And finally, Edward J. Khantzian presents a more traditional defense of psychiatric treatment for alcohol problems, directly in opposition to Vaillant.

For the implications of such divergent views from people with such similar backgrounds to be understood, Bean and Zinberg as editors felt it worthwhile to provide an overview chapter that spells out the complex levels of misconceptions and misunderstandings in the alcohol field. Thus the introductory chapter discusses an overall perspective on alcoholism, the problems presented for the "helping" groups, nonprofessional as well as professional, active issues in diagnoses and treatment, and some recommendations for the future.

One of the great problems in the field of alcoholism, which is discussed in the introductory chapter, is the paucity of thoughtful theoretical and practical communications from mainstream psychiatrists, particularly those analytically trained. It has been as if the field of alcoholism and those few psychiatrists involved in it have been segregated and seen as single-issue specialists. All of the contributors, in addition to being psychoanalytically oriented, work actively as teachers in mainstream medical school and psychiatric training programs. It is our hope that this volume, which contends that all psychiatrists and physicians generally must pay attention to alcohol use, will act as an opening for discussion and contributions from the entire field and not solely as another specialized contribution from psychiatrists with a distinctive interest.

Without the competence and commitment to continuing medical education of Douglas Jacobs, M.D., the symposium from which this book derived would never have taken place. In addition to the authors who contributed to this volume, other participants in that symposium were William Clark, M.D., Lee B. Macht, M.D., Peter E. Nathan, M.D., Henry L. Rosett, M.D., and Steve D. Stelovich, M.D. Their intellectual stimulation not only helped make the individual contributions to this volume more coherent but also aided the editors in developing the papers into a collection.

Ms. E. S. Yntema's creative editorial assistance in the preparation of the Introduction was invaluable. Without Miriam Winkeller's intelligent and thoughtful efforts, this collection could not have been completed, and Claudia Mary Cusani contributed valuably. Above all, we want to express our appreciation for the devotion of the staff, professional as well as nonprofessional, of the many alcohol treatment programs, in particular Hilma Unterberger, whose work permitted us to learn so much about alcoholism, and for the tenacity of those patients who appeared at such programs and made the painful effort to struggle with alcoholism.

Margaret H. Bean
Norman E. Zinberg

About the Authors

Margaret H. Bean is the Harvard Medical School Career Teacher in Substance Abuse at The Cambridge Hospital and a faculty member of the Harvard Medical School. She has published several professional articles on the use of intoxicants, in particular a series on Alcoholics Anonymous.

Edward J. Khantzian is Special Assistant to the Director, Department of Psychiatry, The Cambridge Hospital, and Associate Professor of Psychiatry at The Cambridge Hospital, Harvard Medical School. He has published a number of articles in the field of psychiatry and on the use of intoxicants, with particular emphasis on the inner psychological state of the user.

John E. Mack is senior staff member of the Cambridge-Somerville Mental Health and Retardation Center; Professor of Psychiatry at The Cambridge Hospital, Harvard Medical School; and Chairman of the Executive Committee, Harvard Medical School Departments of Psychiatry. In addition to publishing numerous professional articles and textbooks in the field of psychiatry, and on the use of intoxicants, he is the author of *A Prince of Our Disorder*, a psychological study of Lawrence of Arabia, for which he was awarded a Pulitzer Prize.

George E. Vaillant is Director of Training, The Cambridge Hospital, Department of Psychiatry; Professor of Psychiatry at The Cambridge Hospital, Harvard Medical School; and Director of the Study of Adult Development, Harvard University Health Services. He has published many articles in the field of psychiatry and on the use of intoxicants, with special attention to long-term follow-up studies, as exemplified in his recent book, *Adaptation to Life*.

Norman E. Zinberg is Co-Director of Training, Department of Psychiatry, The Cambridge Hospital, and is on the faculty of the Harvard Medical School. He is a former Fulbright-Hays Senior Lecturer and Guggenheim Scholar, and is the author of several books and many articles in the field of psychiatry and on the use of intoxicants.

Introduction: Alcohol Use, Alcoholism, and the Problems of Treatment

Norman E. Zinberg
and Margaret H. Bean

Perspective on Alcohol Use and Alcoholism

Public attitudes toward intoxicant use generally and alcohol use in particular are confusing and paradoxical. In one sense, people readily acknowledge that ours is a drinking society. But this comment generally carries with it the implication of excessive or abusive alcohol use. If asked what he meant by "a drinking society," the commenter would be likely to mention the auto accidents, criminal behavior, or interference with personal relationships and health associated with alcohol use, as if he did not know that the majority of American drink temperately and without causing problems for themselves or others. According to a 1979 Gallup poll:

> ... 69 percent of the adult population (18 and over), or nearly 102 million Americans, drink more or less regularly [and] only 5 to 10 percent overdo it. ... Contrary to his public reputation, the adult U.S. drinker is commendably moderate. In 1978 he consumed 3.01 gallons of distilled spirits, 3.035 gallons of wine, and about 34 gallons of malt beverages, chiefly beer. At first inspection, the figures seem high. But they reckon out to a daily consumption rate of less than one ounce each of liquor and

wine and a little less than one 12-ounce bottle of beer. . . . Among the
world family of nations, the U.S. ranks a respectable twenty-third in per
capita consumption of alcohol. [Koffend, 1979]

In fact, there are some who claim that moderate drinking is good for
you. It is remarkable and important not only that the enormous majority
of drinkers drink temperately but also how rarely in our current climate of
opinion this fact is remembered. Further on, we will discuss the major
issue of abstinence as a treatment goal. However, if one has not been an
alcoholic, abstinence as a way of life can be deviant in the sense that most
Americans cherish their right to drink. A requirement of abstinence im-
pinges on a person's freedom and often his self-esteem.

The difficulty in facing the facts about alcohol use extends to the other
end of the spectrum. Few people, professionals included, acknowledge
that alcoholism is treatable and that, given the chronicity and tenacity of
this addiction, the recovery rate is significant (Baekeland, 1977). It is as
if there were a consistent, unconscious cultural effort to make alcohol
even more fearsome than it is.

Yet at the same time, paradoxically, almost all subcultures have their
own myths that support the use of alcohol: Different drinks produce
different hangovers, so that if you avoid the wrong one, you will be all
right. Alcohol promotes sexual performance. A ''hollow leg'' shows
strength, power, and a capacity for control. Alcohol is good for shock and
freezing cold. Alcohol is good for what ails you, especially snakebite.
Frenchmen do not get drunk. Alcoholism is a vice (and a danger) mostly
for the very rich. On and on the list goes, including the oldest saw of all,
In vino veritas.

The reasons for the paradox are straightforward, if not simple. As
Zinberg points out in his chapter in this volume, drinking is far more
valued than most people in this culture care to admit: thus the myths that
support drinking. On the other hand, the social use of alcohol as a
euphoriant, disinhibitor, relaxant, or mild anesthetic has little to do with
alcoholic drunkenness, an experience which is painful in the short run and
damaging over time. Concern over this long-term destructive power of
alcohol and the accompanying, terrifying loss of control undoubtedly
perpetuates the cultural exaggeration of the hopelessness of recovery.

Later on we will discuss the extreme difficulty in making an early
diagnosis of alcoholism. It cannot be done from single episodes of drunkenness. Further, it is not made easier by the fact that it is hard to
understand drunkenness at all. Nowadays people rarely set out to get
drunk. They hope to get ''high,'' they say, and at times neglect to stop

when they should. There were historical eras when some people took periodic occasions to get drunk (Zinberg & Fraser, 1979).

Andrew T. Weil (1972) makes much of being high as a way of returning to the awesome vertigo of childhood twirling games. Perhaps drunkenness is the dark side of transcendence, a descent to a symbolic suicide and apotheosis. Who could doubt that we all share a tropism toward such darkness? If alcohol merely made slobs or fools of us, the self-care Mack stresses in his chapter in this book would be sufficient protection against its abuse, but there is a fine line between self-care that blocks action to reduce danger and self-care that soothes and permits one to relax. Many flirt with the boundaries. Anyone who has had the experience of drunkenness knows that the familiar white magic of alcohol has the potential of evil for the depleted self. What else is the addict's enthrallment to self and his rejection of reality but evil?

Evil is not, of course, a scientific term. It is used here only to convey the sense of horror that alcoholism and other addictions raise. That sense of horror underscores the tenacity with which alcohol use in general and alcoholism in particular is considered a moral issue. The moralistic view of drinking in the United States goes back a long way. And it is not just those abstinent or abstemious descendants of the temperance and prohibition movements who moralize about the use of alcohol. Alcoholics cling to a moral model and eschew a medical one. In his chapter in this volume Vaillant has written of their loneliness, which they accept as deserved. They prefer guilt to abstinence.

It can easily be argued that this moral stance deters only the most controlled of drinkers. It certainly deters alcoholics only briefly. Such a stance does, however, lead to the acceptance, though now less than formerly, of a criminal model for drinkers. (This does not refer to the criminal results of drunken driving or of any other crime committed under the influence.) If the out-of-control drinker is where he is either through lack of moral fiber or through an overt immoral urge to destructiveness, then why should he not be treated like any other criminal who takes the easy way out by stealing or what have you, who is, in other words, aggressively antisocial? If the drinker is bad, he should be punished.

This moral model of alcohol use directly opposes a disease model. A focus on the patient's experience may help to explain the fragmented picture of responses to the alcoholic. For example, the patient will, as a result of his drinking, have interactions with different pieces of the responding social system—a court, police, psychiatrists, or a hospital—depending on what his symptoms are (assaultiveness, depression, bleeding) and how these are interpreted by those around him. The patient is defined by a fragment of himself that interlocks with a particular responding unit. The central problem is how to turn that interaction into a situation in which the alcoholic has a large chance of getting help.

Because of the sin-illness muddle, the coping system is not clearly committed to the concept of alcoholism as a disease. The disease concept cannot be logically and definitively validated. It is a value position, proposing comfort and effective treatment. One acts *as if* the patient has a disease, and certain effects follow. The problem is that the patient often rejects his sick role and the responding agent is often not clear about the usefulness of pushing him to accept this role. Many participants in the responding system have had no training in effective work with alcoholics. They drift from moral to medical model and back, and vacillate between doubt and conviction in their intervention. The position to be taken, that the alcoholic is ill, is peculiar and not logically obvious. Patients say it is painful, but not harmful. Cummings (1979) states this in the following way: "Addicts do not come to us to be helped for their addiction. They come to us because they are about to lose something or have lost something. . . . The therapist must start with the full realization that the client does not really intend to give up either drugs or the way of life."

Certainly those knowledgeable about and experienced with the chronic nature of alcoholism would recognize any contact with a professional or nonprofessional group by an alcoholic as a beginning, a transitional step necessary before any extensive reclamation work can begin. That the first steps are usually tentative, halting, and full of denial is recognized and accepted. However, if the people in the responding social system are not experienced with alcoholics, they are bewildered by clients-patients-applicants who love their "disease" and want more than almost anything in life not to be parted from it. Much of the confusion over the shift from the criminal to the medical model has to do with the slow transition to an understanding that the alcoholic is not fully in control and purposively destructive. The mechanism of loss of control is not at issue here. It could be physiological or unconsciously psychological or of some other nature. But any disease model posits some such event as loss of control as the basis on which the patient is seen as sick, not bad. Psychosis underwent this transmutation to disease status around the turn of the century. Alcoholism is painfully undergoing it now.

The medical model can subsume a broader definition than "disease." Three of us use it freely: Bean uses it to describe the stages of alcoholism and their relationship to denial, which is seen not just as a defense in strict psychiatric terms but as a symptom, a chemically promoted consequence, and a perpetuation of the alcoholism. Khantzian assumes some kind of ailment, since all his cases "have it." Vaillant insists upon a strict disease definition as a practical basis for correct treatment and a protective umbrella against the patient's overwhelming guilt. For Mack the medical disease definition is antipsychiatric because it exempts the patient from responsibility and partly disqualifies us from understanding alcoholism by understanding alcoholics. But his psychiatric model, in which the process can be explained as partly psychological but not conscious and so not in voluntary control, is equally forgiving of the patient. The use of the disease definition is unfortunately restricted because distorted reporting, which sees only advanced alcoholism as sick, has given alcoholism literature (which colors public attitudes) a limited notion of the disease which we find specious. Alcoholics are rarely seen for alcoholism per se, and if seen, are otherwise diagnosed or labeled until the advanced stage. By then, as Bean usefully shows, the disease has taken over their lives; their perceptions, behavior, and motivation are distorted, and they usually have physical symptoms.

Most confusing of all is the extent to which alcoholics, early in their condition and increasingly even after they have symptoms of all sorts, are able to deny their loss of control over drinking and the effects of it. Their loss of control and the damage that it is causing are so obvious to outsiders that nonalcoholics often think of the denying alcoholic as crazy or, if not, as infuriatingly obtuse. All the chapters in this volume deal with this complex and basic mechanism, which, more than any other single factor, fuels the continuation of the drinking. We will not treat it extensively here. Suffice it to say that the understanding of denial is crucial not only to the understanding of alcoholism but also to the understanding of the responses of others, professional and nonprofessional alike, to the alcoholic.

Social and Professional Problems with Alcoholism

Before we address the subtle problem of diagnosing the alcoholic and the perplexing problem of treatment, we will sketch the problem as it appears to the milieu in which the drinker exists. First of all, it must be remembered that for everyone in the milieu, coping with alcoholism is no minor issue. The out-of-control drinker is deeply psychologically threatening to the huge majority of controlled drinkers. Many wonder, "Could it be true that there but for the grace of God go I?"

But the threat of the drinker in a modern technological society goes far beyond age-old social and psychological description. In the old days "the horse knew the way home"; today alcoholics drive cars. "The excessive use of alcohol," in historical terms only recently called alcoholism,* "annually presents society with a staggering bill: somewhere between $25 billion and $40 billion, in terms of lost labor productivity, health and medical costs, highway carnage, criminal procedures, treatment, and welfare. Alcohol abuse is a factor in 40 percent of all traffic fatalities, accounts for 50 percent of criminal arrests, and fills one of four general hospital beds. By the most benevolent estimates there are at least 5 million chronic drunks in the United States" (Koffend, 1979). This sort of "linkage" reasoning is loose by scientific standards, but what the lawyers call substantiality—the necessity to believe your own eyes— makes it permissible in this area.

When alcoholism was seen as a private misfortune and not a public health problem, long-suffering families took much responsibility and bore the burden. Via burgeoning auto insurance rates, health costs, and taxes—since control of alcoholism is vested not only in the treatment system but in courts, schools, the armed services, management, and labor unions—the burden is borne by all of us, and, gradually we begin to see, the responsibility as well.

Families, friends, teachers, co-workers, clergymen, physicians con-stantly are presented with early alcoholism but often cannot "see" it. It is no small matter to stigmatize someone as an alcoholic, and in this society that is still a fair way to describe what happens. As we will see in the discussion of diagnosis, it is hard to be reasonably sure which is the controlled heavy drinker and which the early alcoholic. But leaving aside for the moment the fear of making a mistaken diagnosis, consider the other issues. The alcoholic himself refuses to acknowledge that his drink-ing is out of control. Not only does he deny the problem but he consis-tently, with primitive cunning, obstructs any interference with his be-loved evil. Drunks deserve their reputation for being able to manipulate their families, friends, and other aspects of their social environment. They may not be able to see what is going on in themselves, but their ability to bully, wheedle, charm, or otherwise elicit the misplaced kind-ness of some form of cooperation from others is remarkable.

Remarkable but understandable. Families of alcoholics see them-selves as stigmatized by association, as do friends. There is guilt aplenty. Few of us are immune to the concern that had we done or not done this or that, the friend, sister, husband would not have gone off on a toot. Worst

*The word "alcoholism" was coined in 1852 (Onions, 1952).

of all is the sense of helplessness and uncertainty: just what to do, when and how to do it. Afterward, when things have deteriorated pathetically, it is easy to say that the family should have pushed harder or gone to Al-anon or a professional themselves. But earlier in the game the fear of making a bad situation worse, the hope that it is not as bad as feared, the sensitivity about one's own place in the community, and the terrifying degree of one's rage at the drinker combine with ignorance and misconception about available help and its effectiveness to immobilize us.

Under these psychological conditions many families, friends, and work associates join the alcoholic in his denial. A number of friends and family join him in his drinking as well. This is hardly surprising. Having threatened, persuaded, cajoled, and reasoned with him with no effect, they become increasingly disorganized. Alcoholism, as far as the drinking is concerned, may not be truly contagious, but its secondary problems affect everyone around the drinker (Jackson, 1962).

There was a time when, under these circumstances, the next part of our social environment's response system to be involved would be a clergyman. Today it is far more likely to be a physician. For one thing, physicians see alcoholics because they feel or look ill. For another, one of the most acceptable things people in the social environment can persuade a drinker to do is "have a checkup." If family, friends, or other associates accompany the drinker to his appointment and say they fear he has a drinking problem, at least the physician has something to go on. But usually, because of the designated patient's denial of his alcoholism and his antagonism to his family's and other's concerns about his drinking, he comes alone.

That leaves it up to the physician to pick up the clues, and sadly, he is ill prepared to do that, both because of his lack of training in the area and because of the nature of usual doctor-patient interaction. A recent national survey of medical education on alcoholism, that was funded by the National Institute on Drug Abuse (NIDA) and the National Institute on Alcohol Abuse and Alcoholism (NIAAA) (reported by Pokorny et al., 1978) studied medical and osteopathic schools. In 105 of the 117 schools, the percentage of total required teaching hours devoted to alcoholism varied from zero to 3.1 percent, with a mean of .6 percent and a median of .4 percent. Elective courses were not offered in one-third of the schools, though where they were, the enrollment figures suggested "substantial student interest." Only 17 of the 105 schools had any continuing education programs; almost half had no substance-abuse teaching for residents. The authors comment that "students who have completed medical education in the U.S. during the past few years do not feel prepared to deal with alcoholism and drug abuse. They frequently emerge from school with negative attitudes and an unwillingness to treat addicted patients.''

At most medical schools, students' instruction about alcoholism is mostly in the classroom, though there are exceptions, such as the University of Minnesota, where all second-year students get ''supervised tutorials'' (Harris & Westermeyer, 1978). There is more teaching about substance abuse where faculty includes participants in the NIDA/NIAAA Career Teacher Training Program in the Addictions, established in 1971.

In the Macy Foundation survey of 1972, it was concluded not only that addiction problems should receive more curriculum time (Stimmel's ideal curriculum) but also that ''departments of medicine [should] bear the primary responsibility for substance abuse teaching,'' in contrast to departments of psychiatry, which take most of the responsibility at present. Remarkably, the American College of Physicians 1979 recommendations for a library for internists ''contained no specific references on alcoholism and drug abuse'' (Novick & Yancovitz, 1979).

In an article written for general physicians, Burnett (1978) concludes that ''failure to treat seems determined more by a failure to diagnose . . . than by desultory attitudes of health professionals toward alcoholics,'' and that ''the prevalence of alcoholism as seen in general office practice is usually estimated as exceedingly low.'' Since the National Council on Alcoholism (NCA) criteria (1972), the subject of his article, were widely distributed in 1978, the continued ''failure to diagnose'' can be ascribed to faulty education in history taking and, if not to a desultory attitude, then at any rate to a pessimistic or denying one. The low prevalence of perceived alcoholism can be partly accounted for by the fact that ''most programs of medical education have continued to focus on alcohol-related disease without considering either the etiological significance of alcohol to specific illnesses or the importance of a drinking history to medical diagnosis and treatment'' (Straus, 1977). Many doctors prescribe alcohol-interactive drugs because they do not diagnose alcoholism. Even among psychiatrists ''only a handful,'' Zimberg (1978a) found, were ''willing and able'' to give office-based therapy to alcoholics.

Not only are most physicians not trained to diagnose or encouraged to treat alcoholics, but what training they do receive is on the most far-gone and deteriorated addicts. Another survey of medical school teaching on alcohol and other addictions (Zinberg, 1976) found an emphasis on extreme cases where the diagnosis was never in doubt and the treatment was absolutely necessary and relatively clear-cut. These case studies, usually from a psychiatric ward or an alcoholism or addiction center, are no help in identifying cases of early alcoholism and, in fact, interfere with the investigation of less clear-cut syndromes by giving medical students and physicians in training the erroneous impression that they know what an alcoholic is when they see one.

Given the average physician's lack of background and training in recognizing anything but these extreme cases, it is quite understandable that the physician is uncomfortable with intrusive personal questions that go beyond the ostensible presenting complaint. Many physicians will ask a patient about his ethanol intake but will accept the patient's response without further question if it is innocuous and if the physical condition is not yet so severe as to brand the answer automatically as evasion. In many respects, the physician unconsciously colludes in the denial of alcoholism. After all, usually his patients work with him to ferret out a problem, not to obscure it, and he treasures that model. Also, as in most human interactions, he wants to be able to accept people, including patients, at their own estimate of themselves. Stirring up difficulty that is not presented almost feels like making trouble, and, usually correctly, physicians adhere to Osler's first rule of medicine: "Don't give the patient anything he didn't have before" (Osler, 1928).

In addition, the physician does not want to damage his relationship with the patient by appearing to be suspicious of him and thinking "ill" of him. Even acting as if one were *about* to label another person an alcoholic would weigh heavily on a relationship where cordiality and good feeling are valued. One can add to that, without in the least questioning the physician's ethics but merely admitting his humanity, his desire to hold on to the patient and not do things that would drive him away.

Overshadowing all else, however, is the painful question of what exactly to do with the patient if one does suspect alcoholism. How to find out "for sure," and then what? One bugaboo that appears immediately is the problem of confidentiality. Usually family members are aware of a patient's drinking problem, but the patient may be very reluctant to bring this issue to them. Should the physician simply tell the patient what the diagnosis is and let him decide whether to act on it or not? Or does the physician have a greater responsibility to the patient? That is, should he see that someone responsible is informed?

In this day of third-party payments and employee assistance programs, the problem is even stickier. How sure does the physician have to be before he reports a diagnosis of alcoholism? One need not look further than the physician mentioned by Vaillant (1977) who accepted brain surgery rather than a diagnosis of barbiturate addiction to appreciate how socially catastrophic such a diagnosis still seems to many people.

Another issue alluded to by Vaillant is less frequently named but very real. Alcoholics often are not nice patients. They telephone at unreasonable times; they make promises and break them, leading to embarrassment and disappointment all around. Their pain after a drinking bout and their potential physical deterioration are very real, so that the physician feels he must do something, but what to do with this uncooperative person remains confusing.

Psychiatric referral is high on the list, but this too is not a clear-cut recourse. Just as physicians see alcoholics because they feel or look ill, psychiatrists see them because they feel or look depressed, upset, or guilty. Here we return to a central theme in this volume. Does an emphasis on these emotional symptoms act to increase the difficulty in recognizing alcoholism, as Vaillant states unequivocally,* or does this psychiatric approach offer a way to begin with hard-to-reach patients, as Khantzian contends? The physician is hard put to know. Few psychiatrists want alcoholics as patients—even Khantzian would acknowledge this— and few, if they see such patients, do very well with them. Most of the training issues discussed apropos physicians apply equally to psychiatrists, and if general physicians' schedules cannot cope with the uncertain and erratic nature of contacts with alcoholics, psychiatrists are even more rigidly scheduled.

Active alcoholics find accommodating to such schedules difficult if not impossible. They are hard put to be interested in themselves and their pain. When they are drinking, they care only about the drinking; when between bouts, they care about the suffering from the drinking and how to prevent it, not about the intricacies of their personality conflicts. To a certain extent, social work has moved in to take up the slack in many areas. Social workers are professionally trained, schooled in patience, and likely to have more flexible schedules than psychiatrists. They too, however, run into the same problem of inadequate training for dealing with the complexities of this patient group.

Under these social circumstances professional approaches to alcoholism have lagged until recently, while A.A. has flourished. A.A. ingeniously avoids many of the professional pitfalls. It begins by presum-

---

*"In a recent survey, 23 percent of a random sample of psychotherapy patients seen in a large metropolitan mental health center were suffering either from addictive problems or from emotional problems substantially exacerbated by alcohol or drug abuse, and only 3.5 percent of these were so identified by their own therapists" (Cummings, 1979).

ing a disease concept of alcoholism which is quite different from the medical model but carries many of the same implications. The alcoholic is considered to be in the grip of disease and therefore unable to deal with his drinking. Changing the concept of alcholism from one of vice, weakness, or lack of will power or judgment to one of disease makes the "treatment" more acceptable socially and helps to alleviate his guilt. Though insisting that alcoholics have to become abstinent to recover from their disease, A.A. is not prohibitionist. It prescribes abstinence only for those who cannot handle alcohol as most others can.

Most observers agree that the alcoholic's denial of his problem is the greatest obstacle to his recovery (Bailey & Leach, 1965; Bean, this volume). A.A. has no magic but many techniques to approach this psychological block. When a drinker contacts the organization, members work patiently to show him that his symptoms indeed indicate a disease called alcoholism. His increasing acceptance of this fact allows the new member ("pigeon") to talk about it openly as a speaker at meetings or in small groups. This discussion breaches a basic inhibition against self-awareness and often permits the new A.A. member to go still further. Once these matters, which had seemed so sordid, are talked about, the new A.A. member feels more comfortable. A member working through A.A.'s twelve suggested steps of recovery will see how the same type of defense mechanism, which limits self-awareness, may be operating in other aspects of his personality. The twelve suggested steps of A.A. are the following (Alcoholics Anonymous, 1977):

1. We admitted we were powerless over alcohol—that our lives had become unmanageable.
2. Came to believe that a Power greater than ourselves could restore us to sanity.
3. Made a decision to turn our will and our lives over to the care of God *as we understood Him.*
4. Made a searching and fearless moral inventory of ourselves.
5. Admitted to God, to ourselves, and to another human being the exact nature of our wrongs.
6. Were entirely ready to have God remove all these defects of character.
7. Humbly asked Him to remove our shortcomings.
8. Made a list of all persons we had harmed, and became willing to make amends to them all.
9. Made direct amends to such people wherever possible, except when to do so would injure them or others.

10. Continued to take personal inventory and when we were wrong, promptly admitted it.

11. Sought through prayer and meditation to improve our conscious contact with God as we understood Him, praying only for knowledge of His will for us and the power to carry that out.

12. Having had a spiritual awakening as the result of these steps, we tried to carry this message to alcoholics and to practice these principles in all our affairs.

A.A. retains the focus on the one issue, alcoholism, and leaves the rest of the personality alone. It recognizes, as many psychiatrists do not, that the job of stopping alcohol intake is a necessary underpinning for any further psychological understanding.

As an organization, A.A. offers the great benefit of fellowship to alcoholics, surely some of the loneliest people on earth (Trice, 1957). Those who have had the experience of alcoholism are suspicious of depending on others. Joining the fellowship of A.A. permits intensely personal relationships such as sponsorship—a close one-on-one apprenticeship for the process of recovery—and it also allows for more structured impersonal relationships such as those in large meetings.

The program is arranged so that every time a member calls for help, a different person can easily answer the telephone and take up the "twelve-step" work. The suggestion that a member remain in constant touch with the organization even when he is traveling answers his great need for company and minimizes his feelings of isolation and guilt. Perhaps even more important, twelve-step work provides a chance for those being gratified to gratify others and thus to make something positive out of the experience of alcoholism. This not only relieves guilt; it encourages self-esteem.

A.A. refers to itself as "the last house on the street." This means that the alcoholic who judges himself harshly and constantly and who correctly perceives that he is so judged by most of his peers has one place which will not turn him away, no matter how degraded or despairing he may appear. A.A. says that he need never be without help and that he will not be judged in that place no matter how often he succumbs to his "disease." He can always turn into the "last house" and find acceptance from others.

An important tenet of A.A., basic but little understood, is the view that an alcoholic is always recovering, never recovered. One is sober from minute to minute, from day to day; and because the next drink is always imminent, overconfidence is dangerous. An A.A. member may stay sober, but by his awareness of what he must overcome, he is always potentially a drinker.

Understanding that he has an abnormal response to any alcohol is a remarkable insight. The alcoholic may be biologically different, genetically or as a result of addiction, from moderate drinkers. He also has a highly ambivalent relation to alcohol; he loves and hates it intensely. A.A. recognizes that the alcoholic has two fears which are so strong as to be phobic: the fear of drunkenness and the fear of sobriety. These fears continue to appear all the way from detoxification to the last stage of recovery. The alcoholic, despite his pleas that he likes to drink, that drinking makes him feel better or better able to exist in his own skin as well as with other people, comes to loathe and fear his drunkenness. Will he once more defile and degrade himself physically, emotionally, and socially by getting and staying drunk? Even in the depths of alcoholic torment in a detoxification ward, he will frequently wish or even believe that some day he can become a controlled drinker. Will he be deprived of the soothing power of alcohol, the palliation of the sickness of withdrawal? Whatever drink supplies—imagined social ease, Dutch courage, emotional distance, respite from sorrow—it is much prized; to an alcoholic, life without drink is terrifying, even phobic (Zinberg, 1977).

A.A.'s method is to "allow" the imminent danger of drinking to continue as a fantasy-fear. This leaves the A.A. member with an ongoing desire for whatever value he obtained from drink as well as an awareness of his moment-to-moment conquest of the desire to drink. Thus the reality of early sobriety, which at first seems so frighteningly gray, is balanced by the stimulating fantasy of drinking. Unfortunately for the alcoholic, his drinking memories fasten upon that one moment when the ethanol-engendered glow allowed him to feel like a king and screen out the sullen, surly, deteriorated aftermath, whereas his view of sobriety focuses upon the moment when he felt most inadequate. In time, however, the safety, physical recovery, release from withdrawal, and social and psychological advantages of sobriety tip the balance toward abstinence; the experience of being in control of oneself and able to interact with people directly rather than through a boozy haze becomes reinforcing. Unlike the members of the straight world, to whom the advantages of sobriety are self-evident, A.A. does not underestimate the alcoholic's fear of being sober. Instead, by insisting that the alcoholic is always recovering, never recovered, it keeps the possibility of drinking always at hand but still a hand's breadth away.

A.A. in effect sees the patient as a whole person who has great difficulty in coping with a particular chemical. He is free and responsible,

but his conflict is experienced as overwhelming, and thus he turns to a
"higher power," in A.A. parlance, which many understand as another of
A.A.'s heuristic devices. There is nothing in A.A.'s view of a "higher
power" which is incompatible with psychiatric understanding. There are,
however, psychiatric points of view that see the patient somehow as
inherently defective—not physiologically, as one with an allergy to alcohol, but as having a defective or impaired ego or personality structure
(Knight, 1937b; Brill, 1919; Rado, 1933). That the most deteriorated
alcoholic can, at times, pull himself together for a special event or to get a
welfare check is usually ignored because these psychiatrists have moved
away from a conflict theory of human functioning. This defect theory has
profound implications for the psychiatric relationship. Having an ego or
personality defect or lack is far different from the notion of a physiological allergy or response to alcohol such as the flush that occurs characteristically in Orientals after alcohol is ingested (Ewing et al., 1974). Such
psychiatrists find it hard to point out to a patient that he is not making use
of personality or ego capacities available to him, for, in effect, they see
him as not having certain capacities. This theoretical position forces A.A.
toward an antipsychiatric stance and, in our view, makes it more important for the organization to present the disease concept as if the disease
were literally contagious rather than as a way of expressing what has
happened to the alcoholic.

Diagnosis

Many of the problems of diagnosis have already been mentioned.
Obviously the most difficult, as Zinberg's cases show, is differentiating
the heavy drinker, who manages his intake empirically and, in his view,
with more or less pleasure, from someone who is heading into difficulty.

Controversy surrounds the definition of alcoholism. "Drinking that
does harm" is a reasonable and usual rule of thumb, but it is often hard to
determine genuine dysfunction, which varies with amount, rate, purpose,
and practical circumstances. Drinking that would get an Italian-American
ostracized may be normal for someone of Irish background; what can
jeopardize a bus driver's job may pose no threat to a handyman's. It is not
just a matter of what alcohol abuse makes people do or how it affects their
relationships or whether they feel sick in the morning. If it were, more
people would react to drinking by identifying it as a problem and making

the intrusive effort to get the drinker to a physician, a treatment facility, or A.A.

It is much easier to say that someone drinks too much than to say he is an alcoholic. One can go simply by quantity, as in the former statement. But eliciting from the patient or client a history of frequent drinking to drunkenness, drinking that interferes with the capacity to function at work or to relate to colleagues, friends, and family, or long periods of memory deficits during drinking, known as blackouts, requires patience from all concerned and considerable alertness to and knowledge about alcoholism. To make a diagnosis of early alcoholism, such a history is necessary because many of the above symptoms usually precede the physical damage and deterioration characteristic of later alcohol addiction.

It is rare to get a straightforward history of such difficulties. Rather, the person seeking to diagnose alcoholism must go beyond such questions as "How much do you drink?" and "Does your drinking cause you difficulty?" He must go to questions designed to focus on the drinker's own concerns about control—"Do you ever decide before you go out just how many you can have?" and "Have you ever decided to stop drinking for a while?" and the like. Such questions, if answered in the positive, arouse the suspicion of alcoholism.

Differentiating between heavy drinking and early alcoholism is not the only diagnostic problem. Alcoholism must be differentiated from simple intoxication. A study of "serious events" (crime, accidents, and suicide) highly correlated to alcohol abuse suggests that in some events drinking is not so much the cause of trouble as a releaser of action in some symptom-prone people and a cause of impairment or disability in others (Diesenhaus, 1980).

Even well-advanced cases of alcoholism, which one would think easy to diagnose, can be problematical. Since the early 1960s there has been an enormous increase in the use of psychoactive drugs, both licitly, for medical and psychiatric treatment, and illicitly. As a result of the attention given to the potential of drugs to alter consciousness states for the better, many troubled people, sometimes entirely unconsciously, have experimented with drugs as self-medication for severe emotional disorders. Alcohol has been no exception to this trend, and with its powerful addicting potential some people who attempt self-medication end up with alcoholism which masks their original condition. This is exactly the reverse of the case Vaillant cites in his chapter in this volume where the severity of the alcoholism led to a mistaken diagnosis of psychosis.

Often attempts to distinguish the self-medicating alcoholic with an underlying psychosis or other serious disorder from the "straight" alcoholic occur when the drinker is withdrawing from alcohol, which is a serious complication. It may be necessary to distinguish ordinary alcohol withdrawal from withdrawal complicated by the physical illnesses common in alcoholics. Chalmers and Wallace (1978) say that the patient may appear psychotic, hallucinating, and frightened in early withdrawal. If he does not recover from these symptoms in the course of a few days, the differential diagnosis includes concurrent psychosis, continued withdrawal, and medical illness. "Continued withdrawal [may be] evidenced by such signs as tremor, agitation, sweating, illogical thinking, depressed mood, anxiety, and, on occasion, a sudden and unexpected delayed seizure" (Chalmers & Wallace, 1978). These authors add, "The therapist should be alert for such symptoms as persistent headache, dizziness, difficulty in breathing, cardiac arrhythmias, flushing, sudden drops in energy, difficulty in waking, memory deficits, complaints of abdominal pain, and poor appetite. These may reflect continued withdrawal, but they may also indicate chronic conditions and diseases of increased likelihood in alcoholics (e.g., hypertension, liver disease, gastritis, ulcer, carbohydrate-metabolism disorders, brain dysfunction, anemia, heart disease, polyneuropathy, emphysema, and stroke)" (Chalmers & Wallace, 1978).

In our view, making the diagnosis is the beginning of treatment; it makes possible movement toward a genuine therapeutic regimen for the condition. The next step, which is crucial to getting someone into active treatment, is conveying the diagnosis. This is an extremely difficult problem. First and foremost comes the question of whether the patient continues to drink. Until the drinker's mind is clear, hope for his acknowledging alcoholism is very small indeed. As we have mentioned, discussions with the family, while necessary because sometimes they are more willing than the drinker to talk with someone or go to Al-anon, result often in denial and a sense of helplessness.

It is not usually helpful to talk to the drinker while he is drinking, and even after he is no longer intoxicated, he will have some confusion and memory loss for a time. For many long-time drinkers the usual five-day detoxification period may not be adequate to allow the central nervous system to recover enough to enable them to have a rational and objective discussion. They may feel sick because of medical complications, but even if they are not yet physically disabled, they feel too poorly to make much sense about the future. Sadly, a longer hospitalization for medical complications is an excellent opportunity to discuss the diagnosis with an alcoholic, as a case of Bean's in this volume illustrates exactly. All too often the luxury of having the alcoholic drug-free long enough for some genuine clarity is simply nonexistent.

This is, of course, one more example of the painful and frequent dilemmas that make this group of patients so difficult for professionals in the field. A physician understandably wants to tell the patient what is wrong and what to do about it, which begins with "Stop drinking." If the patient feels sick, the physician thinks there is even more reason for the drinker to follow this excellent advice. It is hard for a nonalcoholic to understand that to the drinker the best "medicine" for his sickness is as close as the nearest bar. If the patient is actively drinking, he will promise anything just to get away from the doctor.

What professionals are gradually recognizing and what A.A. has known for a long time is that postponement is pointless. Bean points out that sometimes, although rarely, it is true, even a single confrontation can be significant. Usually it takes many encounters because alcoholism is a chronic condition replete with remissions and exacerbations. Preferable to the postponement and maintenance of denial would be for the drinker to seek the deep understanding of the thinking of the alcoholic from the inside, as it were—A.A. members or the sophistication of a general physician or psychiatrist trained in alcoholism who would bypass the denial of drinking and take up any area that seemed open. At any rate, the most important thing to remember is that once the diagnosis is made, the patient must be told and told again. This is difficult for most of us. The physician needs to believe that it is a *good* thing to talk to a patient about his drinking. This is not obviously true, because it is clear that the interaction is painful to the patient, and he tries to avoid it. If it were not so conflictual to accept the diagnosis of alcoholism and the treatment for it, patients would not be so resistant to hearing it. Nevertheless, entering the drinker's conflict on the side of his having a serious condition which is treatable is a basic therapeutic move and is too little recognized as such.

The Move to Treatment

Once the drinker begins to move toward the treatment system, whether professional or nonprofessional, what will generally happen is influenced by a number of factors: who made the diagnosis, whether the patient has insurance coverage, what facilities are available, and what treatment philosophy the staff subscribes to. The stage of the patient's alcoholism is obviously important. In the late stages care may be little

more than custodial. Different situations may require different treatment
approaches. What awaits the patient at home, if he has a home? Will the
family cooperate in treatment? Do they need help themselves? The diagnosis is likely to have been complicated by related factors of mental or
physical health, which will affect the caregivers' priorities for treatment.
The age of the patient makes a difference. For instance, "clinical depression and anxiety are not common problems in young, healthy male alcoholics" (Hamm et al., 1979). Sex also matters: young women alcoholics are more likely to be depressed (Tamerin, 1978). Social and
ethnic patterns will have an impact. Any previous attempts at treatment
and the degree of successful recovery in the past are also essential elements.

The greatest controversy about alcohol treatment services for almost a
half century has been about the primacy of professional services rendered
by physicians, psychiatrists, nurses, psychologists, social workers, and
the like in a variety of inpatient and outpatient settings and those services
made available by nonprofessional volunteers, chiefly Alcoholics
Anonymous. The phenomenal growth of A.A. since its founding in 1935
in Akron, Ohio, by "Bill W." and "Dr. Bob S." attests both to the need
for such a service and to its efficacy. Except for the treatment of direct
medical complications A.A. does not rely on other professional services,
and, as Vaillant shows in his chapter in this book, some members actually
regard many of them as deleterious to the treatment of alcoholism.

Whether because of the traditional reluctance of the professional
groups to treat alcoholism, the alien philosophy of A.A., the most successful treatment modality, the cultural insistence that alcoholism is a
moral dilemma, or because of a combination of all three, it is only in the
past decade or two that there has been a growth of professional interest
and investment in the treatment of alcoholism. At this time when there is
a moderate increase in the availability and effectiveness of alcoholism
treatment services (although not yet a commensurate increase in satisfactory objective studies to provide empirical data about various treatment
techniques and modalities), the alcohol field has been assailed by demands involving special populations, and this is creating a new and
tendentious conflict. Groups such as women, blacks, Hispanics, criminal
offenders, American Indians, the aged, and the unemployed have demanded special attention. While it can be argued that groups which have
common social, psychological, or legal characteristics may well have
intrinsic drinking patterns and problems of rehabilitation, there are growing questions as to whether such characteristic issues warrant separate
treatment situations in each case.

This controversy over the potential fractionation of treatment services heightens the contrast between various competing, often feuding professional groups and A.A., which, despite considerable diversity among different groups, retains its more or less monolithic reliance on the credo of the "Big Book" (Alcoholics Anonymous, 1939). Two other controversies, where empirical data are skimpy, plague emerging professionally oriented treatment services. First, many questions are raised about the efficacy of inpatient services, including inpatient detoxification, except for patients with obvious medical complications. As inpatient services are vastly more expensive than outpatient services, unless their superior efficacy for many cases can be demonstrated, any insistence on inpatient settings can be interpreted as an insistence on professional hegemony.

Second, the enormous increase in the use of both licit and illicit psychoactive drugs raises the questions of whether to treat alcohol and other addicts in the same facility and, of even great difficulty, what to do with those people who have another addiction along with alcohol. Both of these questions focus attention on an inherent difference between A.A. and professional services. Although the concept of alcoholism as a disease is essentially heuristic, in practice it suggests a segregation of those who suffer that disease. A.A. has uneasily accommodated people with dependence on other drugs, and it remains doubtful whether they have the same disease.

The usual professional approach, on the other hand, while acknowledging fully that alcoholism is a biopsychosocial condition, has been to treat chronic alcoholism as a psychological problem, except for active intoxication, withdrawal, and medical complications. Whether individual psychological problems are precursors to or the result of the alcoholism is of little practical consequence. What are of consequence are the family, job, legal, social, intrapersonal, and emotional difficulties concomitant to the long-standing dependence on alcohol. In a basic sense that is Mack's point in this volume. Approaching all these complex consequences of alcoholism from a psychological stance, in the absence of empirical data supporting this approach, requires considerable sophistication and training. That requirement has not been met. Hence most detoxification and residential treatment programs as well as most aftercare and employee assistance programs refer their clients to A.A.

The most recent estimates (Vischi et al., 1980) claim that 1.7 million people participated in formal treatment programs in 1977 and 671,000 participated in A.A. in the same year. There is considerable overlap in these figures as the huge majority of those participating in A.A. at one time or another had contact with a formal treatment program. No one has a clear idea of how many actual alcoholics there are, so there is no way of knowing what fraction participated in some form of treatment. The figure most often used for the number of alcoholics is 5 million, but as Zinberg points out in his chapter in this volume, the definition of an alcoholic or problem drinker decides who is called what, and some authorities who see anyone who drinks alcohol regularly as a problem drinker use a much higher figure, while those who insist that seeking some form of treatment determines alcoholism use a lower one.

Referral to Treatment

Obviously, the most desirable referral situation is self-referral. The drinker recognizes a problem, assumes the responsibility of seeking an appropriate therapy, and expects to cooperate. Membership in A.A. depends—initially and forever—upon self-identification as an alcoholic. "The only requirement for membership is a desire to stop drinking" (Alcoholics Anonymous, 1977). In medicine in general and even in much of psychiatry the self-labeling model is the rule, and while resistance and lack of compliance with a treatment regimen often occur, the conflicts take place within an overall alliance between therapist and client. In the early stages of alcoholism, this model is the exception. Not that self-referral does not occur, for it does. Most, if not all, alcoholics have at one time or another a distinct awareness that their drinking is out of control. In such lucid moments they may turn to a treatment situation. This is particularly true when the person has had previous treatment.

There is some indication (Diesenhaus, 1980) that if an active community mental health system is in place and easily available, self-referrals are more likely to occur. As near as can be told to date, based more on clinical experience than on hard data, these referrals tend to be like those from physicians and clergymen. The drinker does not necessarily go in and announce himself an alcoholic. The denial and pain at the thought of giving up alcohol are too great. But he does go to see someone and says that something is wrong. Hence it is necessary for the person or agency consulted to be sufficiently aware of the possibility of alcoholism to make the diagnosis and sufficiently well trained and sophisticated to steer the drinker to A.A. or a formal alcohol treatment service.

Another major referral source is families of alcoholics, usually after some participation in Al-anon. In the early years of A.A. Al-anon and

Alateen were developed by the wives and families of members, for people who cared about, or lived with, an alcoholic. They focus on direct alcohol education, understanding what factors in the family perpetuate drinking, and helping family members learn a set of techniques of interaction with the alcoholic that make continued drinking less likely and acceptance of treatment more so.

Even when the referrals come from families, clergy, or physicians, the element of coercion is far greater than with most other sorts of problems. Usually these referral sources do not begin by threatening but become more coercive when the natural assumption—once the drinker has been told of the damage to himself and to others, he will do something about his drinking—proves false.

Other referrals to any form of treatment are more coercive. The most coercive are police and the courts. Since the decriminalization of drinking, if alcoholics are picked up by the police, they are usually not jailed, but are taken to a detoxification center. Often they can be jailed because of something they did while drinking, and they are less likely then to be referred to treatment. All too often the handling of the drunk is left to the individual officer, and again the problem of the level of training and sophistication emerges. Sometimes a knowledgeable judge can use his power to get an offender into treatment. This has been particularly true in recent years with the existence of drunk-driver programs.

In the past the drunk driver was usually given a warning or two, and after another offense had the book thrown at him, with loss of license or jail. Today in many states judges on any driving-while-intoxicated charge will insist that the culprit attend a certain number of A.A. meetings, participate in an alcohol education course or an alcohol counseling program, or do some combination of these. This approach brings the drinker into some part of the treatment system.

The most important and effective use of coercion has been the development of employee assistance programs in industry that train supervisory personnel in dealing with drinking in the work place (Heyman, 1978). Drinking on the job, absenteeism, and poor performance because of drinking are common. In the past, and all too often in the present, employers offered the drinker a second chance unaccompanied by a recommendation of treatment. When the drinking recurred, their patience was exhausted and they fired the drinker. The growing concern of both employers and unions about this procedure, which offered no assistance to those in trouble, led to the acceptance of a coercive approach. The employee is faced with his poor performance and the assumption that this performance resulted from his drinking. The emphasis is on job performance and he is told that if his performance does not improve, he must enroll in a treatment program or be fired.

This procedure reaches an important segment of the population. Workers are per se a selected group; they are still actively employed and ostensibly value that employment. The threat of job loss is powerful coercion indeed. For this threat to be maximally effective, an actual employee assistance program should be in place or reasonably available. It is a great added advantage if families of employees can be included in these programs, and in more enlightened companies such coverage has been arranged.

The same model has been attempted by the armed forces, in particular the navy, with similar success. Other attempts, however, have not been so effective. Impaired-physician programs also offer a powerful threat, loss of medical license if treatment is refused, but the success of these programs is difficult to judge because of the traditional secrecy within the medical profession. Programs for incarcerated drinkers are also difficult to measure. Efforts of teachers and school health authorities to find young drinkers early and coerce them through their wish to remain enrolled apparently have been unsuccessful in making referrals that stick. Perhaps these questionable efforts have not found the right incentive.

Detoxification

If a patient has been drinking heavily, and is addicted to alcohol, when the alcohol use stops, he will go through the physiological symptoms of a withdrawal syndrome. The purpose of detoxification is to bring the drinker safely, and as comfortably as possible, through the sickness of withdrawal. Most drinkers go through withdrawal repeatedly without detoxification. Different types of detoxification procedures are available. They may be inpatient or outpatient, with drugs or without, with nonprofessional or with professional staff, usually both, with counseling offered toward the end of the period or not. They may be embedded in a larger alcohol program with aftercare and further treatment available, or simply in a free-standing center offering only detoxification itself or, as often occurs in hospitals, offering little but treatment of the complications of addiction, such as liver disease and trauma.

The decision about the type of facility often depends as much on what is available and the bias of the referring source as it does on a careful clinical decision. Reports in the literature do try to set some standards.

For outpatients, Imboden et al. (1978) recommend four or five days on central nervous system depressants, plus thiamine; the patient should be seen at least weekly and tranquilizers tapered off after two or three weeks. Many recommend a much shorter period—three days except in complicated cases.

Imboden et al. (1978), writing for the general physician, state that hospitalization is mandatory if there is disorientation, hallucination, the shakes, dehydration, fever over 101°, medical or neurological complications, or seizures in the nonepileptic patient. If d.t.'s occur, they say, patients "require a level of medical and nursing care comparable to that of an intensive care unit," since most cannot take liquids by mouth. Most alcoholics need a better diet, with large amounts of thiamine to offset their malnutrition.

Almost all acute detoxification procedures call for palliative psychoactive medication to ease withdrawal. Problems about medication arise because some symptoms of withdrawal can continue for months and years. It is understandable that the recovering alcoholic may ask for drug relief of these symptoms, and, as Tamerin (1978) points out, in office practice many are given minor tranquilizers. Among the writers in this volume Khantzian might agree with this procedure, particularly if the symptoms include prolonged anxiety and sleeplessness. Other writers in this volume—Vaillant, Bean, and Zinberg—agree more with the A.A. position except in certain cases. This clinical position holds that the prolonged use of such medication beyond the acute withdrawal stage acts first as an alternative to drinking, but soon is experienced as tantalizing and, especially as tolerance develops, invites a return to drinking for the full desired effect instead of the feeble alternative of low doses of tranquilizers. It is a difficult dilemma for both the caregiver and the recovering drinker, and probably in the long run more an issue for treatment than for the detoxification procedure; but the reason given for the prescription is often detoxification purposes.

Treatment

There is no generally accepted notion of exactly what alcoholism treatment is. It is worth saying quickly that while most people think of a medical model as specific—for example, prescribing penicillin for pneumococcus pneumonia—in fact for most conditions decisions about when to treat what and how to do it are far more diverse and conflictual than is generally acknowledged. Hence alcoholism treatment, with its enormous diversity and conflicts, can be seen as a paradigm for all of the biopsychosocial conditions. Thus far in this discussion we have indicated that treatment actually begins with the recognition of the alcohol problem by significant others or by the individual himself. If others, then the drinker must be made aware of the problem and referred to some professional or nonprofessional treatment situation. During that introduction to treatment, beginnings are made by the drinker; his family and his job, if he has retained one, are in a sense being prepared for treatment proper, which may take weeks, months, years, or, as A.A. believes, a lifetime. Probably most authorities on alcoholism would agree with that time frame. There may be some value, however, in separating treatment into periods which are not entirely dependent on duration. The first is the period of active treatment, where the drinker must face his destructive behavior patterns and learn to live without depending on alcohol, no matter how long that takes. The second is the time necessary for him to consolidate and integrate these changes into a life style and a personal view of himself not drinking, as Mack theorizes in his chapter in this book.

This generalized overview of treatment encompasses programs as diverse as the A.A.-oriented program described by Vaillant and the direct psychiatric treatment approach described by Khantzian in this volume. The pigeon in A.A. must find a sponsor, attend meetings, get the message about his destructive behavior patterns and learn to live without his dependence on alcohol. Whatever the vast difference in approach, the patient-neophyte-pigeon going the psychiatric or counseling route must find a therapist, meet with him regularly, and begin to understand about destructive behavior patterns and learning to live without his dependence on alcohol, so that at some level of consciousness these issues can be articulated.

In practice today most recognized alcoholics are referred to one of the 16,957 existing A.A. groups (Diesenhaus, 1980). A.A. members participate either as volunteers or staff at many of the active detoxification centers, and much of the counseling offered by non-A.A. members aims at getting the drinker into A.A. Nevertheless, as Baekeland (1977) correctly points out, even with the enormous growth of A.A. it still accounts for only a fraction of the alcoholics. Probably an equally small fraction spend a long span of time in active counseling or psychiatric programs aimed at working out the emotional issues associated with dependence on alcohol. Certain very specialized treatment concepts such as behavior modification probably account for a handful. Where are the rest?

To understand the apparent discrepancy between the number of alcoholics in treatment and the number of alcoholics requires an understanding of the disorder itself. As we have noted, many who would be classed by others as alcoholics refuse to see themselves that way and stay away from treatment. More central is that the above-mentioned figures of 1.7 million in formal treatment programs and 671,000 in A.A. are not a count of static groups (Vischi, 1980).

The recently sober alcoholic is terribly vulnerable. Most detoxification programs do not allow enough time for recovery, and many only treat the complication of withdrawal, without referral to treatment for the underlying drinking problem. "The rate of drinking relapse following inpatient treatment is discouragingly high, and of those who relapse, more than 80 percent do so within two months after discharge. Furthermore, the dropout rate from outpatient treatment is typically greater than 50 percent. On the other hand, it is known that if an alcoholic can remain abstinent for one year, his chances of remaining abstinent are excellent" (Chalmers & Wallace, 1978). Writing for the general practitioner, Imboden et al. (1978) utter a necessary reminder: "Alcoholism is a chronic illness and, as with any chronic illness, there may be relapses after varying periods of remission. The occurrence of a relapse does not mean that the treatment plan has been a total failure." But it does mean that the 671,000 people in A.A. in a given year or the 1.7 million in programs may represent many who, at least the first few times around, stayed only a short time.

Another factor, more encouraging, of which far too little is made, is spontaneous recovery. Studies by Waldorf and Biernacki (1978), Lemere (1953), and Kendall and Stanton (1966) on addiction show that this occurs far more frequently than has been acknowledged. The drinker who decides to stop often has a "reason" such as a religious revelation or a response to a death or illness, but investigation often reveals similar occurrences earlier that had no effect on the addiction. Study of spontaneous recovery is of great importance to any concept of alcoholism treatment because just as there are chronic alcoholic recidivists, so too are there many who respond surprisingly favorably—given the tenacious nature of alcohol addiction—to relatively brief treatment.

Vigorous programs that reach alcoholics before they are entirely in the most severe (gamma) stage (Jellinek, 1960) report excellent results. For example, the navy has a model rehabilitation program begun by Zuska (1978), with reported success at two years' follow-up of 84 percent for patients twenty-six and older, 50 percent for patients twenty-five and younger. Officers and enlisted men attend the same group therapy sessions; Antabuse is usually prescribed; and attendance at A.A. meetings is compulsory. Initiated quite informally by Zuska and a retired, sober alcoholic commander, the program at first met stiff opposition. Two witnesses to the navy's open-mindedness are the program's quick expansion (facilities to treat 20,000 men per year, if necessary) and the fact that petty-officer graduates have a slightly higher than average rate of promotion to chief petty officer. Certainly a study of such a program in the armed services that included the role of overt or covert coercion would be most interesting. Many active employee assistance programs report similar results.

Another factor which accounts for alcoholics not in treatment is access. Although, as stated earlier, all figures to do with alcoholism are highly suspect, several studies over the years indicate that the poor and particularly the poor of certain ethnic groups, such as blacks, Hispanics, and American Indians, have a disproportionately high percentage of alcoholics. These people have the least access to treatment. Zimberg (1978b) not only documents the existence of large numbers of black and Hispanic alcoholics who have never been in treatment, even briefly, but also discusses their responses to treatment programs, once even the most minimal demonstration projects have been established. He shows that the poorest alcoholics are more likely to be diagnosed psychotic or brain-damaged than alcoholic, which also deprives them of proper treatment. This is an important finding. In order for us to know how responsive they might be in treatment if it were more widely available, Zimberg's work deserves attention, for there is little documentation about work with this neglected and underserved group.

For example, Zimberg (1978b) describes a demonstration day-hospital program set up in Harlem (black) and in East Harlem (mostly Puerto Rican). The staff were recovered alcoholics from the area, plus social workers and a psychiatrist; the clinics gave "medical examinations and treatment, psychiatric evaluations and treatment, individual and group therapy, and disulfiram (Antabuse). Patients graduated from the day-care program to the more intensive treatments that were available. . . . '' The Harlem day program (black) gave alcohol education, provided social opportunities and outings, and so on. When patients had been sober for a reasonable time, they got vocational training and eventually jobs, at which point they became so anxious that some relapsed and all needed a great deal of support. If they stayed sober, there was a once-a-week follow-up, Antabuse if needed, urgings to go to A.A., and weekend clinics for support; they could come back any time.

The program for Puerto Ricans was a bit different: more family therapy, less A.A., less Antabuse. The men thought it manly to drink; the women were not supposed to drink, and if they did, they felt tremendous guilt; families were much closer. Of course, the staff had to be bilingual. Zimberg points out that if the drinker had nothing to lose by drinking, he would go on doing it, and that he had difficulty finding new or improved jobs for his recovered patients.

The most important recommendations about treatment for alcoholics have a high level of agreement. Such questions as whether to use A.A. or a professional and whether to see people individually, in a group, or in a family setting evoke strong conflicts, but observers agree that once sober, alcoholics prefer, as Wallace (1978) says, "a state characterized by a moderate-to-high activation level. Witness the enormous amounts of stimulating drugs, e.g., caffeine and nicotine, consumed by sober alcoholics. Even the so-called states of serenity of many sober alcoholics are intensely focused states of moderate-to-high activation rather than low. . . . The problem . . . is not to reduce obsessional energy, an often impossible task, but to switch the focus of the obsession."

This statement is as true of any A.A. meeting as it is of any professional detoxification center or day-care facility. Once the alcoholic is sober, his energy must be channeled into something that he can feel is worthwhile so that his life is meaningful. It is this that makes Zimberg's concern about the paucity of available jobs so poignant. Authorities agree that the time of newly won sobriety is a crucial period. A.A. advises the most tender care of oneself; Wallace (1978) says "self-centeredness" is useful and desirable. Once in A.A. or any other treatment, alcoholics increasingly learn to "surrender" their resistance. They acknowledge loneliness and dependency needs. Thus, as Mack and Khantzian say in this volume, they may not have too severe an impairment of the self, and it may be rebuilt.

Abstinence as a Treatment Goal

The question of whether alcoholics can ever drink again safely is one of the most emotionally fought battles in the field. Proponents of each view sometimes behave as if the answer will be settled by the group which can muster the largest numbers or be the most vocal, rather than by posing questions and doing research to answer them. Perhaps the intensity of the controversy will seem more comprehensible given a context. Many of the pro-abstinence group are A.A. members or steeped in the A.A.

philosophy. They have seen or felt the ravages of active alcoholism. They also know from vivid and repeated experience that almost all alcoholics wish with poignant intensity to be able to drink without harmful consequences. The wish is so intense that some are not able to acknowledge that it is a fantasy that they repeatedly attempt to bring about in reality, often with disastrous results. It is clear that for some alcoholics, the attempt to drink is dangerous, excruciating, or both. The amount of pain and destruction to life, job, self-esteem, and family from a relapse may be enormous.

This group tends to see anyone who says that an alcoholic may be able to drink safely as an ally of the disease and possibly a sadistic, deliberate saboteur of the alcoholic's comfort and safety. It is important to remember that A.A. has received little or no help from professionals at any time and that many alcoholics have received what they considered poor treatment at the hands of professionals, such as being given drugs that provoked craving and precipitated a relapse or established a second addiction. Understandably, they are self-protective and suspicious.

Many of the proponents of moderate drinking as a possibility for alcoholics are professionals with research backgrounds. They see themselves as genuinely curious about objective reality, with no ax to grind, and with the intention of working to provide real information about the nature of the disorder, with the hoped-for consequence of improved understanding and care of alcoholics.

When some of these researchers announced their findings that some alcoholics could return to moderate drinking, at a press conference prior to publication of *Alcoholism and Treatment,* the so-called Rand Report (Armor, et al., 1976), they were naively appalled to find themselves vilified and attacked. The Rand Report suggested that "some alcoholics can return to controlled drinking, and in fact that for one group—men under 40 who are not yet 'highly dependent' on alcohol—those who returned to social drinking were less likely to relapse into alcoholism than those who abstained," and that "alcoholics who attend A.A. are not more likely than others to be freed of their dependence." The study was conducted by the Rand Corporation for NIAAA, whose directors rejected the report and continue to insist that abstinence is "the most important goal" and that alcoholics who can return to social drinking may never have been real alcoholics anyway, which takes us back to the inevitable question of the definition of alcoholism. Much other research, as Gitlow (1979) points out, tends to support the possibility of a return to social drinking. But ambiguities in methodology, the unspecific qualifier "some alcoholics," and the disastrous results when some alcoholics try to drink socially raise questions. Many authorities insist that any sober alcoholic who wants intensely to drink, even "socially," may be about to relapse. The controversy leads to flat polarized statements of each point of view.

For all practical purposes, at the present time abstinence is considered the goal in the treatment of all alcoholics. Zimberg says that "alcohol is not necessary to life, and it is quite possible to live and even be happy without consuming alcohol" (1978a). More wryly, Gitlow says, "I must confess to some surprise that we have spent so much money and time during the past decade to realize that some alcoholics can drink alcoholic beverages some of the time" (1979).

If these comments seem harsh on those who advocate some return to drinking, it should be noted that they respond to the points of view of those who have felt virtually destroyed by alcohol. Some recovering alcoholics believe that many advocates of a return to social drinking are nonalcoholics who unconsciously wish to protect and justify their own controlled drinking. It is extremely difficult for the alcoholic, whether recovering or not, to conceive of the importance to many controlled drinkers of moderate drinking. The alcoholic, whether he admits it or not, and many do, may see moderate drinking as too little to do much good and too much to allow an independent life.

We take the position that this view is probably right. Some alcoholics, probably those with shorter histories of alcoholism, few symptoms—less than seven or eight positive answers to the twenty-six NCA questions (National Council on Alcoholism, 1975)—and little or early addiction, may be able to resume social or moderate drinking, though often by reliance on external devices such as tallying drinks (National Council on Alcoholism, 1975). But other alcoholics appear from clinical experience to lose control of their drinking if they try this and should be expected to need to be completely abstinent. All of the authors in this volume stress the importance of abstinence, Khantzian at the outset of treatment in particular. He goes on to emphasize an approach that considers the possibility that therapist and patient can work together toward a resumption of controlled drinking.

Though a life of abstinence seems unimaginable and unattainable to many alcoholics at the outset of treatment, the work is usually less harrowing and easier for both therapist and patient if abstinence is established at the start. For practical purposes, most of us take the position that it is a mistake to let the possibility of controlled drinking in the future come into question until late in treatment (one of us, Bean, may suggest that the patient wait five years before considering it, and by then it is rarely an issue). Perhaps the best way to deal with it, unless and until the patient is deemed ready to choose, is to say, "We don't know, but we doubt it." "An issue as critical as controlled drinking for alcoholics requires extensive, rigorous, ecologically relevant, and methodologically sound research. Laboratory studies of drinking behavior lack ecological relevance (Mello, 1972)" (Wallace, 1978). Recent research on the existence of naturally occurring substances such as the endorphins raises questions about what unknown physiological changes may result from prolonged addiction that would leave an individual with quite different capacities to tolerate a particular substance. "Anecdotal reports (Davies, 1962) and recent large-scale survey research methods on treatment outcome (Armor et al., 1976) lack methodological rigor" (Wallace, 1978). Moreover, these studies are addressed principally to the separate issue of spontaneous remission. "While controlled drinking remains a theoretical possibility for some unknown number and equally unknown type of alcoholic, it has no practical application in alcoholism treatment at the present time" (Wallace, 1978).

Where Do We Go from Here?

As we hope to have conveyed, there is no tight blueprint, no Manhattan project, to direct future work on alcoholism; nor, in our view, should there be. Alcohol use and its sometimes destructive consequences are themselves too intertwined for a clear path to emerge. Obviously, what we and everyone else would like to see is a direct assault on the destructive consequences of drinking, without assaulting the cultural assessment of the usefulness of drinking. All too often in the past, both in this country and in other parts of the world, the assaults have been monolithic—prohibition—and unsatisfactory.

The development of social policy ignores at its peril the ancient and obvious fascination of Western culture with drinking. No topic, except perhaps sex and, in the past, religion, has so large a slang vocabulary as drinking; and slang coinage is a folk art of sorts, a way of manipulating import, ascribing meaning, evoking—or modulating—emotion, aggrandizing or minimizing, veiling awe, mocking fear, touching taboo. Consider the Bacchae, the Orphic mysteries, superstition, and Christian sacrament. Some kind of magic is certainly involved, and it survives (even now it is thought unlucky to offer a toast in water).

Drinking songs have long abounded in this culture, but most, rather than invocations to intoxication like "Lucy in the Sky with Diamonds," are formal poems like "Anacreon in Heaven," the original words for

"The Star-Spangled Banner" melody. This too suggests the extent to which this culture is in transition. While in all probability the startling growth in the number of people who regard themselves as "born again" indicates that the death of religion was announced too soon, this culture has secularized its most profound fascinations, including sex and drinking. They are "studied" nowadays, though the studies are still hobbled by superstition and anxiety, suggesting that the transition has some way to go.

"Higher authority" is no longer an article of belief; and with it has gone the sustaining trust in an afterworld, where one had counted on discovering at last, and if need be restoring by atonement, the worth and the meaning of one's life under the divine plan. The only "plan" we can gloss takes place in the mortal inner world to whose richness and riotous conflict we were directed by Freud. This brings us down to Mack's concept of the self, in which social interactions, as they serve, by back-and-forth mirroring, to define the individual, are not merely a surround or matrix, but an essential part of the self; down, moreover, to his perception of A.A.'s "higher authority" as fulfilling a profound need of the impaired, alcoholic self.

Certainly A.A.'s willingness to place that higher authority in the context of "God as you understand Him" makes it possible in many chapters to separate A.A.'s notions from more formal religious views of God. A.A.'s entire tradition of volunteer service, anonymity, and acceptance of suffering humans, no matter what their condition, is compatible with modern evangelical practice and strengthens A.A.'s authority. In A.A. an alcoholic contracts for the rest of his life "to atone for his failure—to combat his disease" (Alcoholics Anonymous, 1939; Alcoholics Anonymous, 1955). This reliance on a moral core is far too little understood by most of the "self-help" organizations that have attempted to copy one or another aspect of A.A., many of which, while using words like "anonymous" in their titles, are profit-making ventures.

The economic aspect cannot be overemphasized in its implications for the future. Just as we must attempt to protect moderate alcohol use while we struggle against alcoholism, so must we protect A.A. while we attempt to upgrade professional services which need greater financial support. Everything we hope for from the future will cost money. The development of employee assistance programs, the integration of alcoholism services into the general medical system, the improvement of detoxification and follow-up services for the indigent, the inclusion of alcohol problems in third-party payments, and, in particular, the expansion of special services for special problems such as those of pregnant women, minorities, and non-English speakers—all these can be reliably expected to save money in the long run but require initial major investments.

That alcoholism services save money in the long run is no illusion, and this is not only true of industrial and military programs which reduce absenteeism and other costly lapses. Zimberg (1978b) notes the economics of a program for "the treatment of chronic alcoholics in a hostel-type alcoholic rehabilitation program compared to the involvement of the patients with the criminal justice system through arrests for public intoxication. This study was carried out by graduate students in Monroe County, New York.* The study determined that the alcoholism rehabilitation program generated a benefit of $147,556 greater than the cost of the program through the patients' increased productivity, work-program operation, jail-costs savings, reduced judicial caseloads, and increased public services. . . . Adding variables related to the social, health, welfare, and criminal-justice system costs of no treatment can demonstrate that alcoholism treatment for the poor can have major economic impact for society beyond the help for the particular patient in treatment."

For the investment to be made, the public and various official agencies must be sufficiently aware of the problems of alcoholism, what it does to our society, and the grounds for cautious optimism about its treatment. To create such awareness requires, of course, an initial investment. We cannot in this chapter delineate all of the educational and research efforts that we believe will encourage such awareness, but we would like to mention a few that might be crucial.

In so many respects the role of physicians is critical. There is ample evidence that when a career teacher or a career researcher operates within a medical school, the space in the curriculum for that person's specialty expands. The NIAAA program in this area should be expanded, and efforts to recruit people into this heretofore unpopular field need thoughtful attention. If our previously presented finding is taken seriously—that courses about alcohol use usually present only obvious cases, so that the range of issues is hardly understood by the students—a whole change in the philosophy of this teaching will be accomplished.

Certainly the increased involvement of health care professionals should not be limited to physicians and certainly not to psychiatrists. Nurses are a crucial group and must not be neglected. Williams (1979) reminds us that nurses dislike alcoholics even more than the general

---

*Monroe County, New York, has one large city, Rochester, population about 350,000, and is otherwise fairly wealthy and suburban.

public does, and there is little doubt that in part this is due to the paucity and poverty of the training they receive in this field. The training of nonprofessional vocational and occupational workers and counselors recruited from both recovering alcoholics and nonalcoholics is absolutely necessary.

Some of the best work in the health field is being done by psychologists, sociologists, social workers, biostatisticians, and even anthropologists. But education must go beyond the health care workers and the professional disciplines to reach the general public. The National Commission on Alcoholism, which began its work in February 1981, will have much to say about this central goal. Such education goes beyond simplistic warnings about harm to the greater sophistication of ways to manage alcohol use responsibly, abstinence being only one of those ways. There is little doubt that one of the Commission's recommendations must be for greater cooperation between the public and private sectors.

Research will require similar levels of cooperation. Medical research is usually ambiguous in this field because it is so difficult to set up controlled studies, because baselines are difficult to determine (what is a "normal" drinker?), because one cannot induce disease in humans in order to study it, because "informed consent" is a peculiarly tricky matter, because pathologies do not come singly, but in clusters (and in alcoholism the clusters can include almost anything), and because socioeconomic factors are always present and difficult to evaluate. In addition, alcoholism is hard to define (Zinberg's chapter), self-reports are suspect (Vaillant's chapter), and physicians know very little about experimental design and statistical techniques.

Physicians are often forced to rely on anecdotal reports—e.g., alcoholism-linked zinc deficiency in exactly two patients (Williams et al., 1979). Moreover, though clearly the number of reported alcoholics is very large (though not in proportion to the population), as we pointed out earlier very little is known about spontaneous remission. In any case here are a few general suggestions for research:

1. Prospective studies of predisposition to alcoholism, including genetic, physical, social, emotional, ethnic, and racial factors
2. Studies of untreated alcoholism and "spontaneous" recovery
3. Epidemiological, cross-cultural, psychological, and sociological research on the natural history of alcohol use
4. Studies of special subgroups of alcoholics—e.g., psychotics, children, women, and families—including initial presentation, rates of

progression, types of clinical courses, and different stages and types of disturbances

5. Studies of efforts to refine the NCA criteria and other classification systems in order to allow more accurate predictions
6. Studies of different treatment methods, including the treatment of different types and stages of alcoholism, and studies of the process by which different patients-clients select or are matched with different types of treatment
7. Studies of selected examples of successful intervention, e.g., A.A., behavioral, psychiatric, and psychoanalytic studies of the recovery process
8. More and better studies of the abstinence issue

One final caveat. The suggestions we offer for education and research are fairly specific and indicate that broadening our knowledge base and promulgating our information about alcohol use and alcoholism will afford better prevention and treatment of problems and safeguard formal and informal social controls over use. In the field of the study of intoxication there are overwhelming imponderables. The years 1962 and 1963 are usually given as the beginning of the drug revolution (Weil, 1972; Zinberg & Robertson, 1972). The general classes of drugs such as psychedelics, cannabis, opiates, and cocaine have been available for many years, but despite occasional bursts of social concern, their use in this country before 1962–1963 had been sharply limited to small, usually deviant groups.

Since the early 1960s very large numbers of people have tried many of these drugs: perhaps 50 million have tried marijuana, 10 to 15 million, cocaine. In the early to middle 1960s psychedelics were the rage, then cannabis; then we had a heroin "epidemic," and now cocaine is in the forefront. When the wave of preoccupation with one or another of these drugs has passed, the use of that drug continues. Perhaps not many of those now caught up in the quick spurt of stimulation from cocaine care much about psychedelics (although most of them have used marijuana), but there is a legacy of interest in psychedelics that continues in this culture. The folklore about its use remains alive, and there are flurries of revival of interest. A case can be made that these waves of use of different intoxicants and the residue of users are an inchoate social effort to test the impact of a variety of intoxicants on our social structure and learn how to integrate and institutionalize such use.

If this is so, then this effort must be in a very early stage. Except for a brief period in the 1960s when "heads" (marijuana users) put down alcohol use except for a little wine, and "juicers" (alcohol users) were violently opposed to marijuana use, all of this drug use has been accompanied, sooner or later, by alcohol use. It is very hard to guess what effect increased drug use will have and in particular what the integration of the use of other drugs will have on alcohol use and the development of alcoholism. Predictably, most attention and concern have been directed to the potential for the development of dual addictions. It is our hope that studies of the social synchronization of these factors in our culture will not limit themselves to the damaged end products alone.

Finally, it is possible that novelists and poets may give us access to the inner experience of the alcoholic, as the last century's *poètes maudits* and the popular singers of the 1960s did for the drug addict. As the critic Alfred Kazin (1976) has noted, it was not until this century that alcoholism became an occupational hazard for creative writers. If today's creative writers write more about their experience of it than they have so far, then their productions will put into words necessary information about the changing influence of alcohol on our culture. The use of alcohol has been with us for millennia, but its influence in degree and kind constantly changes and requires constant monitoring.

Dangers of Psychotherapy in the Treatment of Alcoholism

George E. Vaillant

This chapter is organized in three parts. First, I review the evidence for viewing alcoholism, not as a symptom of emotional illness, but as a disease analogous to hypertension or diabetes. Second, I present a heuristically useful case history. Third, I focus on some of the specific issues that render psychotherapy actually counterproductive in individuals actively struggling with the disease of alcoholism. In doing so, I suggest an alternative model for its care.

But how can alcoholism be called a disease? Indeed, there are at least six reasons for *not* considering alcoholism analogous to medical disease. These objections need to be examined.

First, alcoholism conforms to no Koch's postulates, and there is no known underlying enzymatic defect. Rather, it is multiply determined and the determinants are different in different people. *But* the same can be said of diabetes and hypertension. My thesis is that the continued use of alcohol once an individual has lost the capacity to control how much or how often he drinks is both a necessary and a sufficient cause of the syndrome that we label alcoholism. In the majority of cases, before patients lose control of their use of alcohol, they are no different from the general population. Once abstinence from alcohol is achieved and a suitable convalescence has passed, they are no longer "ill." Thus the term "disease" conveys the point that the etiology of alcoholism is uncontrolled drinking, that uncontrolled drinking is not symptomatic of some underlying disorder, and that for most alcoholics return to controlled drinking lies outside an appeal to reason or to a dynamic unconscious. Like the hypertensive or the diabetic, the alcoholic cannot usually cure himself by will power or insight alone.

The second objection to using the medical model in conceptualizing alcoholism is that there is no clear line that separates the alcoholic from the heavy drinker. With diseases, you either have them or you do not. Diagnosis should depend upon signs and symptoms, not upon value judgment. But again consider hypertension or diabetes. We regard them as medical diseases, albeit ones of diverse and often poorly understood etiologies. There is no fixed point when we can decide that "normal" variation in blood pressure has evolved into "abnormal" elevation. Rather, in early stages, the diagnosis of hypertension and diabetes is relative. The more numerous and severe the signs, the more certain the diagnosis. Value judgment is always involved. So it is with alcoholism; normal drinking merges imperceptibly with pathological drinking.

The third objection is that alcoholism is affected by so many situational and psychological factors that the disorder must often be viewed as reactive. Some people drink uncontrollably only after a serious loss or when they are in a specific situation. Again, some alcoholics, by an act of will, return to normal drinking. But these observations are equally true of hypertensives and diabetics. Avoiding specific living situations and exerting will power over salt and caloric intake are sometimes enough to cause the "disease" of diabetes or hypertension to disappear.

The fourth objection to using the term "disease" in the treatment of alcoholism is that for remission alcoholics must learn to assume responsibility for their own drinking. If they were led to believe that alcoholism was a disease, would they not see this label as an excuse to drink or as a reason why they could not be held responsible for their own recovery? *But* in seven years I have suggested to hundreds of alcoholics that their alcoholism was a disease. To my knowledge, not one either was disheartened or used this as an excuse for the next binge. In Alcoholics Anonymous (our staff is required to attend once a month) I have listened to scores of alcoholics discuss their remission. Most of them subscribed to the concept that their alcoholism was a disease *and* that they were responsible for its treatment. Once again, diabetes is a disease, but one for which the individual must assume primary responsibility.

The fifth argument against calling alcoholism a disease is the most compelling. Uncontrolled, maladaptive ingestion of alcohol is not a disease in the sense of biological disorder; rather, alcoholism is a disorder of behavior. According to this argument, there is no more reason to subsume alcoholism under the medical model than to include compulsive fingernail biting, gambling, or child molesting in textbooks of medicine. Alcoholism reflects deviant behavior that should best be classified by sociologists and treated by psychologists skilled in behavior therapy. I would agree *but* for several problems. First, there are insufficient behavior therapists available to even begin to care for the problem of alcoholism; and even if they were available, most alcoholics at present do not possess the social set to seek them out for help. Second, unlike stopping gambling or fingernail biting, stopping alcoholic drinking often requires skilled medical attention during the period of acute withdrawal. Third, unlike gamblers and fingernail biters, most alcoholics as a result of their disorder develop secondary symptoms that require medical care. For example, an estimated 20 to 40 percent of all general hospital patients have a drinking problem, and alcoholism plays a major role in the four leading causes of death in men aged twenty to forty—cirrhosis, suicide, homicide, and automobile accidents. Finally, unlike gambling and fingernail biting, the behavior disorder known as alcoholism leads to such mistreatment of those whom the alcoholic loves that enormous guilt results. As a result, the behavior disorder model (conveying as it does the concept of misbehavior) generates far more denial in the alcoholic than the disease model (conveying as it does behavior outside of voluntary control). In short, in order to understand and study alcoholism, it behooves us to employ the models of the sociologist and of the learning theorist. But in order to *treat* alcoholics effectively, we need the models of the medical practitioner. In order to be treated, alcoholics require a label that will allow them unprejudiced admission to the emergency rooms and access to medical insurance coverage, to paid sick leave, and to the willing care of medical practitioners—all of which are denied to compulsive gamblers, to child molesters, and currently to a majority of alcoholics. In other words, using the term *"disease"* rather than *"disorder"* becomes a useful device to persuade the alcoholic to admit his alcoholism and a semantic ticket to guarantee the alcoholic admission to the health care system.

The sixth objection to the term "disease" is our deeply ingrained belief that alcoholics are premorbidly different from other people; that alcoholics have personality disorders; that alcoholics have had unhappy childhoods; and that they drink because they are depressed, lonely, and anxious. In short, the sixth objection is that alcoholism is but the tip of the iceberg, a symptom of underlying psychiatric disorder, and that its proper treatment (at least for the rich, well-educated, and highly motivated alcoholic) should be via dynamically oriented psychotherapy. It is to this last objection that this chapter is addressed.

Alcoholism as a Disease

First, if alcoholism is a symptom, there should be an underlying disorder. For example, prospective study of heroin users has suggested that a majority of these individuals have come from relatively disrupted homes and that premorbidly they have been poly-drug abusers (Vaillant, 1966; Robins, 1974). In contrast, there is no good evidence to suggest that heavy cigarette smokers (cigarette abusers) are very different from the general population, at least in their psychopathology. Is alcoholism more like tobacco or heroin abuse?

Retrospective studies have supported the latter view. In the eighth edition of his textbook on psychiatry, Lawrence Kolb writes, "In spite of the conviction of most alcoholics that they would be quite normal if they ceased drinking, psychologically well-adapted personalities are seldom found during periods of sobriety" (Kolb, 1973, p. 205). The majority of retrospective studies suggest that alcoholics are premorbidly passive, dependent, latently homosexual, sociopathic, "oral-dependent," and fearful of intimacy.

At the present time, however, there are at least five prospective studies of alcoholics which suggest these positions are untenable. First, there is the study by Kammeier et al. (1973) of thirty-eight University of Minnesota graduates who were later admitted to Minnesota detoxification centers. At the time of hospitalization for alcoholism this group had significantly pathological MMPI profiles, with the highest elevations on the scales reflecting depression and sociopathy. However, ten years earlier, when the thirty-eight men were in college, their MMPI profiles were quite normal.

Both Lee Robins and the McCords followed up samples of children at high risk for delinquency and found that, not surprisingly, the alcoholics in these samples had many of the premorbid characteristics associated with predelinquent children; however, the investigations found that the alcoholics' childhood character did not differ dramatically from that of the antisocial nonalcoholics in the group (McCord & McCord 1960; Robins, 1966).

There have also been two prospective studies of premorbidly normal subjects. The first, carried out at the Institute of Human Development at Berkeley, found that premorbidly prealcoholic youths were more active, impulsive, independent, and heterosexual than their high school classmates who on long-term follow-up did not abuse alcohol (Jones, 1968). I reviewed the lives of 268 men from their sophomore year in college until age fifty (Vaillant, 1977). In this study differences were not found that distinguished the premorbid character of alcoholics from the character of nonalcoholics. If anything, the alcoholics were premorbidly more assertive, extroverted, and comfortable with the heterosexual role than nonalcoholics.

Second, if alcoholism is but a symptom of underlying emotional difficulties, we should expect alcoholics to have had more difficult childhoods. This did not seem to be the case in either the study from Berkeley or in my own follow-up studies. When clinicians blind to the future examined the childhoods of the college sophomores who later became alcoholic, they could not distinguish them from those of nonalcoholics (Vaillant, 1977).

Finally, if alcoholism is just a symptom of emotional distress, we might expect alcohol to be a good tranquilizer. Alcohol should achieve what the alcoholic maintains it achieves: it should raise self-esteem, alleviate depression, reduce social isolation, and abolish anxiety. However, work by Mendelson and colleagues suggests that despite what alcoholics say, objective observation of drinking reveals that chronic use of alcohol makes alcoholics more withdrawn, less self-confident, more depressed, and often more anxious (Tamerin & Mendelson, 1969).

Thus it seems fair to state that what alcoholics tell us and what actually transpires are not congruent. In *retrospect* the alcoholic's use of alcohol seems symptomatic of disordered personality, childhood pain, and the need for a chemical anodyne. But when studied *prospectively,* the loss of control over alcohol comes first and the alcoholic's explanations seem like mere rationalizations. In short, alcoholism may be conceptualized as a disease in the sense that the disordered drinking patterns are for all intents and purposes out of conscious control, and that uncontrolled alcohol ingestion is both a necessary and a sufficient cause for much of the psychiatric disability associated with so-called "alcoholic personalities."

If alcoholism is merely a symptom masking underlying conflict, psychotherapy ought to be the approach of choice. But if disordered drinking patterns are the primary problem, if the conflict of which the patient tells us is an unconscious effort to mask his acknowledgment of that problem or "disease," what then? Might not psychotherapy be plagued by false assumptions? Would not treatment be like treating a patient with hypertensive headaches for unacknowledged anger? One of the great strengths of psychoanalysis is that it has taught us that the past is not always what the patient tells us. If we were to treat a school phobic by trying to unravel what the child found frightening at school, we would be badly misled. We would never discover that a function of school phobias is to displace attention from conflicts at home. Too often psychotherapy of the alcoholic is like taking a phobia literally. Its roots in displacement are forgotten. Let me present a case history. (Certain details are altered to preserve anonymity.)

Case History

1962

When James O'Neill presented himself to a Philadelphia general hospital, he was a 41-year-old economist for a large industrial firm. He said he had suffered rectal pain on moving his bowels for four days, a complaint he had treated primarily with whiskey. His family history revealed a mother who died at sixty-two of abdominal cancer (untrue) and a father who died at sixty-one of a myocardial infarction. His own past history revealed excellent health except for an eight-month hospitalization in 1957 for "anxiety neurosis." For the past two years he had been in psychotherapy. He was noted to smoke two packs of cigarettes per day and to have "excessive intermittent alcohol ingestion, ? amount." Review of systems revealed tachycardia and hypertension for several years and the fact that he vomited following excessive drinking. His pulse was 120, his blood pressure was 154/102, his liver was down two finger breadths. He had a bilateral inguinal hernia and a rectal abscess. The discharge diagnosis was ischio-rectal abscess and anxiety neurosis. He was to return next month for hernia repair.

When Mr. O'Neill returned, his pulse was 88, his blood pressure was 160/110, and he was described as quite labile. This time the discharge diagnosis was bilateral inguinal hernia and neurogenic hypertension. Significantly, throughout his hospital course, his blood pressure remained 120/80.

1957

Perhaps the details of his 1957 psychiatric hospitalization would cast light on O'Neill's problems. At that time his hospital chart revealed a thirty-six-year-old man, a father of four and a former assistant professor of economics, who was admitted to a Philadelphia psychiatric hospital for the first time. He complained of being a ''failure at his marital and professional responsibilities because of drinking and missing teaching appointments.'' His admission note added, ''Present symptoms include excessive drinking, insomnia, guilt and anxiety feeling,'' and the diagnosis was ''behavior disorder, inadequate personality.''

Over an eight-month hospital stay, the following history was obtained: ''According to the patient's statement, his drinking and gambling began in the summer of 1948 when he became depressed because he did not do well on his Ph.D. generals and was refused entrance into a fellowship organization. At this time his roommate from college did make the fellowship on what the patient described as less merit. The patient at this time began to drink during the day, and to miss teaching appointments; however, he continued to teach and to keep his family together.''

He obtained his Ph.D. without difficulty, and in 1955 he transferred from the faculty of Berkeley to the University of Pennsylvania. During the next year and a half he was very unhappy because of ''the strict regimentation.'' He was dismissed from Pennsylvania with six months to go on his contract and spent the next nine months until admission doing a great deal of gambling and spending long hours away from home.

One month after O'Neill's admission a psychiatrist contributed the following note to his record: ''The patient was glad to see me when I dropped in on him at the hospital 2 weeks ago. However, he did not show up for his appointment . . . and I called him at the hospital to find him sound asleep on his bed. He gives the excuse that it's a little difficult to get a pass. . . . He showed little feeling, although he clearly expressed his suspicions and anger through the people he talked about. [In other words, he showed both passive-aggressive and paranoid trends.] His pattern of drinking, sexual infidelity, gambling and irresponsible borrowing led him to recognize from his reading that it adds up to a diagnosis of psychopathic personality—especially since he's experienced no real remorse about it. Since he gave some books to his son to sell, and among them were four books from the University library, he was accused of stealing books and shortly afterwards was discharged for moral turpitude. He claims he did not sell University books knowingly.

''He states emphatically that he is not an alcoholic, but his rather florid face belies this claim. Since he's discontinued his teaching duties, he says he's been drinking every day and has never been more than half an hour away from a shot of whiskey. Even while teaching he would be in a barroom by the middle of the day. In support of the statement that he's not an alcoholic he points out that he's been taking only one or two drinks each weekend [on weekend passes] since his admission to the hospital.

"During all the time that he was frequenting bars, contacting bookies, and registering in hotels to philander, he always used his own name. It's interesting that when he was carrying on his nefarious pursuits, he got considerable satisfaction out of it being known that he was a professor. There is a difference between his relationship with women and his relationship with men. First of all, when his mother died in 1949 he felt no remorse. He did not remember the year of his mother's death, and in view of the fact that he dates his extracurricular activities as beginning about 9 years ago, this confusion is probably significant. He speaks warmly of his three sons, feeling that they like him although he's not been much of a father. His oldest son has none of his Boy Scout badges, because he's not been able to come to his father for help."

The following history was taken from O'Neill's hospital chart: "The patient is the only child of parents who were in their thirties at the time of his birth. The patient is at the present time married and has four children. His wife is living and well. The patient's mother died in 1949 at age 57 of carcinoma of the uterus. [In fact, the mother had had her uterus removed in 1938.] The patient's mother in the last four or five years of her life refused to allow doctors to attend her because she had turned to the Christian Science faith, although she was an R.N. [So we perceive this alcoholic's mother as eccentric; the real facts, as we shall see, suggest otherwise.] The patient's father is living and well and is a retired Army officer.

"On admission the patient was placed in group therapy twice a week. During his 8 month hospital stay the patient was taken into individual therapy 3 times a week. In therapy the patient was able to work out a great deal of feelings towards his family, in particular towards his mother and also towards his wife. The patient felt quite hostile and anxious about the fact that he was an Army brat and never had a normal childhood, that his parents were always very cold and grown-up towards him. He harbored many feelings of hostility towards his wife who he feels does not appreciate the fact that she's married to such an intelligent college professor, and all she wants is to have money and bigger homes."

The discharge diagnosis was "anxiety reaction manifested by feelings of ambivalence about his family and his parents and his work." The precipitating stress was considered to be "the death of the patient's mother and a long history of drinking and gambling and going into debt." He was considered to have suffered from "an emotionally unstable personality for the past 20 years."

1962–1968

Between 1957 and his hospitalization for rectal fistula O'Neill had received over one thousand hours of psychotherapy, months of inpatient treatment, and no real appreciation of his alcoholism by patient or clinician. After 1962 he was fired from three jobs, and then this Berkeley Ph.D. spent the next three years up to 1968 unemployed and living off his wife. Once again, in September 1968, he was admitted to a Philadelphia psychiatric hospital. On admission his chief complaints were "I'm angry at the world, angry at my wife and the kids' resentment, I'm no damn good." His record revealed, "Since he's returned to Philadelphia he's been drinking heavily, about a quart of whiskey per day. The patient had a history of heavy alcohol intake for the past 20 years. He began to experience auditory and visual hallucinations, paranoid ideas, suicidal thoughts, and he sought hospitalization. The patient also wrote some checks using a bank account that he doesn't have and is fearful about the consequences. The patient claims to have marital difficulties and he's been separated from his wife on and off. The patient had a history of a previous psychiatric hospitalization. During the course of hospitalization the patient was treated with chemotherapy and intensive group psychotherapy and assigned to milieu activities."

After a few weeks of hospitalization he was discharged as "not depressed, not suicidal, and with no active psychotic ideation." He was discharged on 300 mg of chlorpromazine a day and 50 mg of amitriptyline. His discharge diagnoses were "schizophrenic reaction, paranoid type" and "chronic alcoholism."

1940

Fortunately, this man had been part of the already mentioned prospective study of men chosen as college sophomores for psychological health (Vaillant, 1977). Thus there was in existence a prospectively gathered investigation of James O'Neill. In college he had undergone several psychiatric interviews, psychological tests, and a home interview of his parents by a family worker. Unfortunately, none of this information was ever obtained by his hospital psychiatrists. Psychopaths cannot be expected to belong to studies of healthy male development.

A child psychiatrist in 1974, blind to O'Neill's future after age eighteen, was asked to compare his childhood with those of his peers. She wrote that she would predict that "the young student would develop into an obsessional, hardworking, non-alcoholic citizen, whose work would be related to law, diplomacy, and possibly teaching. He would rely on his intellect and verbal abilities to help in his work. He would probably marry and be relatively strict with his children. He would expect high standards from them." She summarized the raw data given to her as follows: "The subject was born in a difficult delivery. The mother was told not to have more children. He was bright and learned quickly, he was inquisitive. He played with older children. His attachment to his parents was demonstrated by his difficulty separating from them to go to camp at age 11. He returned home after two weeks. His parents were reliable, consistent, obsessive, devoted parents. They were relatively understanding; their expectations appear to have been more non-verbal than explicit. The father was characterized as easy to meet, the mother was seen as more quiet; no alcoholism was reported. Warmth, thoughtfulness and devotion to the home were some of the comments. The subject spoke of going to his father first with any problems, and of being closer to his mother than to his father. His peer relations were reported to have been good, and little or no conflict with his parents was reported."

1940–1950

O'Neill's prospectively gathered college record revealed the following: When he was twenty-one, he married his childhood girlfriend. He had been in love with her since age sixteen, and now, six years after they got married, the marriage still seemed solid. Between 1940 and 1950 other observers summed him up as follows: The dean's office of his college ranked his stability as "A." The internist of the college study described him as "enthusiastic, whimsical, direct, confident, no grudges or chips, impressed me as an outstanding fellow." The social investigator saw him as "hearty, hail-fellow-well-met, describes life as happy, describes home life as happy, and united." The psychiatrist was initially greatly impressed by his "combination of warmth, vitality and personality," and put him in the "A" group. Later the same psychiatrist commented that the subject was "not too sound, showed mood fluctuations and hypomania." However, upon graduation the staff consensus was that he should be ranked in the top one-third of this group of sophomores already preselected for psychological health. In health, the psychiatrist wished to place him in the middle third. When O'Neill was twenty-three, his commanding officer in the army wrote the following efficiency report on this future "psychopath" and "inadequate character": "He is able to recognize problems and arrive at sound expeditious solutions." He was thought to give "superior" attention to duty, and the officer wrote that he "particularly desired" his services.

After ten years of prospective observation the study staff's consensus was that they would "place him in the unqualified group in terms of ethical character," and the director of the college health services described him as a "sufficiently straightforward, decent, honest fellow, should be a good bet in any community."

1972

In October 1972, thirty-two years after he entered the study of normal development and twenty-two years after he lost control over his use of alcohol, I met James O'Neill in his one-room efficiency apartment in an expensive Manhattan neighborhood. By the neatness of his grooming, by the number of well-sharpened pencils on his desk, and by his careful ordering of facts, O'Neill impressed me as an orderly man. There were many expensive accessories in the room that suggested that he had been as prosperous over the past two years as he had claimed.

In appearance he was balding, sported a distinguished mustache, and wore elegant, if worn, clothes. During the interview at first he had a lot of trouble looking at me and seemed terribly restless. He chain-smoked, walked back and forth, lay down first on one bed and then on the other. In avoiding eye contact of me, however, he was still seriously aware of me as a person, and I felt that he was always talking to me. He behaved like a cross between a diffident professor and a newly released prisoner of war, rather than a person truly frightened of human contact. I never got the feeling that O'Neill was cold or self-absorbed. If anything, he suffered from hypertrophy, not agenesis of the conscience.

Nevertheless, he described himself to me as having been "a classical psychopath, totally incapable of commitment to any man alive." I felt much more he was a lonely but a kindly man. His mental status revealed an energetic man who kept a tight rein on his feelings. As he put it to me, "I'm hyperemotional; I'm a very oversexed guy. The feelings are there, but it's getting them out that's hard. The cauldron is always bubbling. In A.A. I'm known as Dr. Anti-serenity.''

His mental content made frequent reference to Alcoholics Anonymous, which, besides his wife, was clearly the dominant object in his life. I asked him what his dominant mood was, and he said, "Incredulity. . . . I consider myself unspeakably lucky; most people in A.A. do.'' He told me of his thousand hours of psychotherapy and said that "the net effect was zero.'' Since over the course of therapy his diagnosis had deteriorated from inadequate personality to schizophrenia, I felt that he was probably not being too harsh.

Several revelations emerged from our interview that seemed important to understanding alcoholism.

First, he brought me up to date on his own view of the precipitants of his alcoholism. He said that he had failed to win a coveted fellowship in April of 1948, his son had been born in November in 1948, and his mother had died of cancer in January 1949, after a year of chronic illness. "I watched her die; I visited her daily; I'll never forget the stench." This sequence of traumatic events, he asserted, led to his alcoholism.

However, from the prospective record, the facts were that in 1948 he had accepted the loss of his fellowship philosophically; to give birth to a son, if you have been well loved yourself, is hardly a psychological disaster; and his mother did not die until August 1949, of an acute perforating ulcer of four days' duration. She allowed herself to be adequately cared for in a hospital. Prior to that, as a registered nurse, she had embraced Christian Science; but she suffered from amyotrophic lateral sclerosis of many years' standing, and for a nurse to become a Christian Scientist in order to cope emotionally with that diagnosis is hardly to deny herself the wisdom of the medical profession. It was only in retrospect that O'Neill reconstructed his mother's death as the result of cancer in the uterus that she had had removed eleven years before. This is not to deny that his concern over his mother's growing paralysis did not affect his drinking, but merely to underscore the fact that alcoholics reorder traumatic events to justify their drinking and that psychotherapists believe them.

From the prospective record it was also possible to record a more accurate sequence of O'Neill's feelings about his mother's death. The child psychiatrist of the prospective record had called their mother-child relationship among the best in the study. In 1950, six months after the loss of his mother, a study observer had said that the subject felt the loss of his mother deeply. At the time his mother's physician had remarked that the subject "was devoted and helpful during the illness." It was only seven years later, during his admission to a Philadelphia psychiatric hospital, that O'Neill reported having no feelings toward his mother and maintained that his parents were always very cold toward him.

Second, O'Neill brought me up to date on the progression of his alcoholism. He had begun drinking heavily in 1948, and by 1950 he had begun morning drinking. By 1951 his wife's uncle, an early member of Alcoholics Anonymous, had suggested the possibility of alcoholism. However, the same year his own university's health services diagnosed him as having "combat fatigue," and his wife had insisted that he was not alcoholic. He admitted that between 1952 and 1955 he had written his Ph.D. thesis while chronically intoxicated and that he had regularly sold university books in order to support his drinking. By 1954 his wife began to complain about his drinking, and by 1955 it was campus gossip, although in his hospital admissions in 1957 and 1962 the diagnosis was not made. During the same weekends in 1957 when the psychiatric hospital had recorded him as having only a couple of drinks, "with my wife on welfare I would go out on weekend pass, get drunk, and gamble," O'Neill told me in 1972. After he was discharged from the hospital in 1968, O'Neill returned to binge drinking over the next fifteen months and finally in February 1970 went on a binge where he drank a case of scotch in five days; he was hospitalized for two weeks, and came into contact with A.A. for the first time. For the next thirty months he had remained sober, except for one three-week lapse. The fact that he was a sophisticated Ph.D. did not prevent him from being the chairman of a blue-collar A.A. group. It is significant that both his self-detrimental gambling and his extramarital affairs stopped as soon as he stopped drinking.

O'Neill's wife, who had become used to taking on a lot of responsibility over twenty years, told me that in 1972 she still found it hard to see him as a functioning husband. His own perception was that the disagreements between him and his wife could at last be talked about. He cast the current tragedy of his life in terms of not knowing his children and of them not knowing him. "I was a parasite on the whole household for twenty years," he told me. Thus sobriety does not abolish old wounds, it merely permits the healing process to begin.

Third, a final sequence of events was a shift in O'Neill's attitude towards religion. At nineteen he had said, "I think that the Bible is the best code of morals there is." He did not have a personal God but thought Christianity should be expressed in active commitment to others, not in reflective worship. At age twenty-eight he wrote that he did not go to church but that in his distance from religion "I regret an important type of deeply personal experience which I've never known." After a decade of drinking he never went to church and wrote, "American Protestantism seems barren and bigoted . . . Church means very little.'' In 1972 he had returned to church membership and took an active role in its function.

Fourth, upon leaving his apartment, I noted several books related to gambling on his bookshelf and wondered if this remained an interest. He said that he had now sublimated that interest into becoming a consultant to a state government that was setting up a state lottery, a considerably more profitable occupation. In other words, with the remission of alcoholism his ego functioning had matured. Instead of acting out his compulsive gambling, he had harnessed that interest in a socially and personally constructive way.

In closing, O'Neill told me he could not agree with Alcoholics Anonymous in calling alcoholism a disease. ''I think that I will the taking up of a drink. I have a great deal of shame and guilt and remorse and think that's healthy.'' I heartily disagreed; I hypothesized that his shame had facilitated his denial for two decades.

An Alternative to Psychotherapy

My thesis is that the patient who tells us that he drinks because he is depressed and anxious may in fact be depressed or anxious because he drinks. He may draw attention from the fact that it is painful for him to give up alcohol. The alcoholic's denial may be simultaneously at a conscious, unconscious, and cellular level. In no other mental illness is the deficit state so clearly a product of disordered chemistry and yet the secondary conflicts and associations so dynamically fascinating to psychiatrists. The greatest danger of this is wasteful, painful psychotherapy that bears analogy to someone trying to shoot a fish in a pool. No matter how carefully he aims, the refracted image always renders the shot wide of its mark.

Consider the scenario of *Who's Afraid of Virginia Woolf?* We see George and Martha locked in a sadomasochistic marital struggle. Drawing on his protagonists' childhoods, Edward Albee fills his audience in on the complex roots of their current conflict. The therapists in the audience may speculate that if George and Martha could come to terms with their parental introjects and learn openly to love each other through psychotherapy, their need for alcohol would vanish. But let us look at that scenario more closely. In fact, the sadism between George and Martha rises parallel to their rising blood alcohol. People mindlessly torture each other—and their therapists—because they have a disease called alcoholism far more often than people misuse alcohol to punish those they love.

Let me approach the problem from a different tack. Once compulsive drinking is established, any excuse justifies a drink. Consider well-analyzed training analysts who chain-smoke. Despite their access to previously repressed parental introjects and despite deep understanding of their oral needs, analysts continue to smoke. Do they do it from an unconscious death wish or from intractable habit? There is reasonable evidence that premorbidly many alcoholics are no sicker than many heavy smokers. To formulate their habit in terms of their *retrospective* accounts of parental derpivation or psychological conflict would be a grave error.

At this point, I shall describe the Cambridge Hospital program for treating alcoholics. The administrative control of the program is in the Department of Medicine and in its own nonpsychiatric community board. A cornerstone of this program is to avoid sustaining therapeutic alliances with alcoholics so as to avoid transference; and, it is hoped, thereby to avoid the lion's share of the ensuing countertransference. The staff has been deliberately recruited from the psychodynamically naive. The reason for this philosophy is that even if alcoholics can learn to tolerate their transference, therapists of alcoholics seem to have extraordinary difficulty in tolerating theirs. For example, for years I was associated with two psychoanalytically oriented, sophisticated, humane community mental health centers. In both there was an unwritten sign over the entrance to inpatient and outpatient services. The sign said, "Alcoholics need not apply." This stemmed from senior staff's countertransference, not from the needs of the community.

In contrast, if the Cambridge Hospital alcohol program shuns psychotherapy, if it phobically avoids transference, it also treats more alcoholics than any other program in Massachusetts. It has a walk-in service sixteen hours a day, seven days a week; patients are seen without appointment. The staff has learned to accept, not reject, the twenty-time repeater; to offer hope and experience to the ten-time repeater; and to offer education and treatment to the one thousand alcoholics who are seen each year for the first time. Alcoholics' needs for welfare, shelter, detoxification, and referral are met day and night. Getting alcoholics to return for subsequent visits is not a problem.

However, when an alcoholic comes for a return visit, he sees whatever counselor is on duty. This could be any one of ten individuals. Even group leadership is on a rotating basis so that patients will come to groups to work on their problem of alcohol, not out of alliance to an individual. Again, on the detoxification unit, a patient is welcome to return as many

times as he needs detoxification. but on every admission the patient is
assigned a new counselor. The focus of the program is to produce alliance
first to the institution Cambridge Hospital and from there through stepwise progression to encourage the patient to move on to an alliance with
Alcoholics Anonymous. This organization, by its very emphasis on
anonymity, strives to avoid sustaining individual alliances. A member is
taught to ally himself with his peers' ego strengths—not with those of his
therapist.

Let me explain this unusual approach: Why does it help treatment to
regard alcoholism as a disease, not a psychiatric disorder? Why does it
help to violate the usual principles of doctor-patient alliance?

First, alcoholism is a disorder with unexpected relapses and intense
needs for help at unexpected times. The alcoholic, like the unconcious,
has little sense of time. Unexpected relapses tend to be destructive to any
ongoing relationship, and this includes the most selfless therapeutic alliance. The patient literally is not under his own control. One of the
advantages of a walk-in clinic, a hot line, and A.A. is that they do not
expect the patient to be in control. If we treat alcoholism by trying to
sustain a therapeutic alliance, we expect the alcoholic's symptoms to be
dynamically determined, controllable through insight, and affected by the
state of the transference. However, once we feel that there is a dynamic
relationship between our response and the patient's drinking, we develop
superstitious and magical ideas about our powers, and this leads to hyper-
vigilance, then mistrust, and finally rupture of the alliance. It is no accident that the first step of Al-anon, as well as A.A., is "We admitted we
were powerless over alcohol." Rather than engender therapeutic
nihilism, the Cambridge Hospital program paradoxically has this motto as
its cornerstone. Our treatment staff are asked to attend Al-anon regularly.
The whole treatment philosophy is designed to alleviate the enormous
staff guilt generated by the seemingly inexplicable failure of some alcoholics to recover. Teaching staff to "let go" of patients when they
leave allows them to welcome those who may return.

Similarly, we try to involve the closest family member of every patient admitted. But the task of family therapy is not just to view the
patient's alcoholism in the context of his ongoing family relationships but
also to view his ongoing familial battles from the perspective of the
"disease," alcoholism.

The second reason for avoiding psychotherapy is that if the onset of
alcoholism is facilitated by object loss, it is even truer that alcoholism
causes object loss. There is probably no group of people more exquisitely
lonely than chronic alcoholics. They have replaced virtually every mean-

ingful person in their lives with inanimate bottles. The temptation of the sensitive therapist to step in and try to fill that loneliness leads to overwhelming demands, e.g., crises on weekends, Christmas, or in the early hours of the morning. The therapist withdraws, and the alcoholic's misperception that his loneliness is too great to bear is confirmed. So, again, it is important to avoid therapeutic relationships leading to intense transference and countertransference.

The third reason for the Cambridge Hospital's philosophy is a paradox of alcoholism. Dynamic treatment can serve to increase, rather than lessen, the patient's denial that he has a problem with alcoholism. For if alcoholism is regarded as a symptom, then misunderstood relapse only increases the patient's guilt toward his therapist. If alcoholic sadism is regarded as dynamically, not chemically, engendered, shame is immense. But if the patient's rages and relapse to alcohol are a symptom not of his unacceptable ambivalence, but of his matter-of-fact illness, then the patient's guilt is reduced and he can keep his alcoholism in consciousness. Not only can he remember that his marriage and childhood were *allegedly* intolerable; also, he can see as intolerable the *fact* that he now truly has difficulty controlling his drinking.

The fourth reason for avoiding psychotherapy is that alcoholism is sometimes preceded and is always followed by profoundly low self-esteem. By definition, a sustained therapeutic relationship and its accompanying transference present the therapist as a powerful and reliable figure enhancing the alcoholic patient's low self-esteem and exacerbating his contempt for his own incomprehensible unreliability. Alcoholics learn to displace this rage at self to contempt for the reliability, the tolerance, and the sobriety of their long-suffering therapists. A therapist can only experience this as ingratitude. In response, the patient can only conclude that his ego strengths can never be allied with his therapist's.

In contrast, the anonymous peer groups in Alcoholics Anonymous ask only that the patient accept help from those who are as vulnerable as himself; and equally important, of course, A.A. allows him to help in return. An alliance is forged and self-esteem goes up. True, A.A. has a system of "sponsors" and "pigeons," but one definition of a pigeon is "someone who keeps the sponsor sober"! Thus we have another paradox. Psychotherapy asks that the patient admit helplessness to his doctor, encourages him to say how little he has to be grateful for, but insists that he be independent enough to pay for that privilege. A.A. costs the patient nothing but shows him that he is independent enough to help others and encourages gratitude for the smallest blessings. That such an approach involves denial of emotional suffering is true; but research into serious medical illness is slowly teaching us that selective denial can be lifesaving.

Fifth, there is also evidence that a small group of alcoholics have been so profoundly deprived in childhood that the reliving of early rejections in psychotherapy may be unbearable. If most alcoholics are not premorbidly sociopathic, a very high percentage of sociopaths are alcoholic. Thus a significant fraction of alcoholics *have* had early childhoods similar to those of severe delinquents and poly-drug users. Some alcoholics *have* suffered early maternal neglect which may impair their capacity to care for themselves. However, the yearnings involved make their appearance in the transference, and *that is where the danger lies*. The fact that the subject never had an adequate mother becomes amplified by the transference rather than relieved. Psychoanalysis helps us love the parents that we have had but does not provide the parents that we never had. Doctors, wishes aside, are not mothers, and the analyst's couch is no bassinet. There are times in life when the affects associated with early abandonment may best be left alone. And the period during which an alcoholic gives up alcohol is one such time.

Indeed there are precious few ways that adults acquire sustaining parental introjects. There are few ways that an adult can truly find a mother substitute. One way is by loving group membership, for example, in A.A. or the church; another is becoming a mother substitute himself, for example, being a matron in an orphanage or a twelfth-stepper in A.A.

The sixth and final justification for the Cambridge Hospital philosophy is the worthy psychodynamic goal that alcoholics must be taught "the inviolable unity of their own selves." I think that to achieve that goal, alcoholics must learn that their drinking behavior is *not* a reflection of their dynamic unconscious, but just the reverse. Often what emerges in the therapy of an alcoholic is psychological confabulation in order that the patient can continue his chronic addiction. The chief complaint "I drink because my wife left me" masks the fact that "my wife left me because I drank," and the self-loathing that derives from the secret belief "My wife left me because I am bad because I could not stop drinking" hides the more bearable and admissible fact that "my wife left me because I could not stop drinking because I was powerless over a disease."

Psychotherapists encourage and focus upon the affects of anger and sadness, but in chronic alcoholism interest in the patient's "poor me's" and "resentments," instead of uncovering old wounds, merely brings forth reflex confabulation to explain unconsciously conditioned relapse to alcohol. But as the case history illustrates, without prospective study appreciation of this fact is immensely difficult and the alcoholic's anger and depression become major foci of psychotherapy.

To conclude, once an alcoholic has achieved stable sobriety, he will have the same needs for and capacity to benefit from psychotherapy as would any other member of the population. But bald facts from the lives of 268 men, prospectively followed from their sophomore year in college until age fifty, underscore the theoretical points of this chapter. Twenty-six of these men at some point lost control over their use of alcohol. One-half sought psychotherapy and on the average received about two-hundred hours of psychotherapy. With time, one-half of these men have achieved stable remission from their alcoholism—usually through abstinence. In only *one* case did psychotherapy seem to be related to the remission; in many cases it seemed to deflect attention away from the problem.

Denial and the Psychological Complications of Alcoholism

Margaret H. Bean

It is not yet possible to predict of individuals whether they will or will not become alcoholic. Once dependence is established, however, its consequences are predictable, though patterns of development vary.

This chapter will describe the psychic disruption that results from the experience of alcoholism. It will attempt to trace linkages between the physical experiences of repeated loss of control and intoxication and the emotional consequences of being alcoholic. What develops, concurrently with mild central nervous system impairment and a system of defenses based on denial, is a clinical state which has been called the alcoholic personality and often assumed to antedate the alcoholism.

The chapter will suggest that the so-called "alcoholic personality" is partly a complication of alcoholism. By "alcoholic personality" I mean the distortions in personality functioning commonly seen in drinking alcoholics such as impulsivity, self-centeredness, self-destructiveness, irresponsibility, poor judgment, regression, irritability, labile mood, and the defense system based on primitive denial, rationalization, projection, and minimization.

I will argue that substantial personality dysfunction is directly caused by both physical events and the experience of being alcoholic, and will attempt to show how. Once the dysfunction has developed, it sustains and entrenches the alcoholism. When the alcoholism is in remission, many of the personality disturbances recede as well.

This approach differs from those of Mack and Khantzian in this book, who try to define what deficit in psychic structure produces the alcoholism. Although, as they show, psychopathology may antedate or contribute to the establishment of alcoholism, this chapter ignores etiology, and describes what happens after alcoholism begins.

The personality disruption described does not replace the character of the sufferer. Rather, it overlies and may partially obscure the original personality, which will reemerge when the alcoholism is treated, with two other developments possibly added. The alcoholic may have permanent or temporary personality destruction on a neurological basis, and he may have massive repair and relearning to do to restore his psychic integrity after the devastating experiences that occur in the lives of alcoholics, much as a stroke victim or concentration-camp inmate will be affected by his experience.

The experience of being an alcoholic is complex and extremely painful to the sufferer. It begins gradually. The person rarely realizes that he has symptoms of early alcoholism. Instead he is likely to be both bewildered and frightened.

Social and medical myths about the disease intensify fear, shame, and isolation. People with alcoholism face prejudice and contempt. Families and employers are bewildered and angry with them. Many doctors and health professionals are not trained to diagnose or treat them and instead react with avoidance of diagnosis or confirmation of despair and rejection of the person.

The disorder may begin subtly but moves along and usually worsens over time along three channels. The first is loss of physical health, safety, and comfort. The second is psychological damage. The third is resulting losses and destruction of the things the person loves in his life: relationships, career potential and achievement, economic status, and legal identity as a citizen in good standing. These events, quite characteristic in alcoholism, cause intense and increasing suffering. As any such process occurs in a person's life, he reacts to it.

The idea of psychopathology produced by trauma during adulthood is not new. It has been described in life-threatening and crippling disease, and a range of human catastrophes such as knowledge of impending death (Becker, 1973; Kubler-Ross, 1969), combat (Brill & Beebe, 1955), natural disasters (Lindemann, 1944; Rangell, 1976; Titchener & Kapp, 1976), and incarceration in a prison camp (Frankl, 1959). Just as it is possible to generalize about the psychology of disaster or concentration-camp victims despite the obvious fact that each has a unique personality and defensive style and might react to the trauma in idiosyncratic ways, with alcoholism there will be wide variation according to what the person brings to the experience, but the experience is so powerful that it is possible to describe a general response to it.

In all these other events the painful process is experienced as unavoidable and overwhelming. There seems to be no explanation for it and no help for it. The psychological reactions to these traumas usually include a period of shock, decompensation, and regression. Then the person makes a variety of efforts to control, master, cope with, and later to bear, understand, and transcend the suffering. That a person faced with the experience of alcoholism would react like other human beings faced with trauma seems obvious. That such a psychology of response to suffering must be understood to work effectively with alcoholics also seems clear.

It is practical to speak of the "phases" of alcoholism, which can be identified as early alcoholism, with such experiences as blackouts and loss of control of drinking; a middle stage, with growing psychological dependence; development of tolerance to alcohol, and then frank addiction and withdrawal; remission and relapse; and finally deterioration. It is natural to discuss these phases in a chronological order, though individual alcoholics may not progress predictably from phase to phase. Reversal of direction, telescoping, and skipping phases are common. Each phase may be complicated by psychological disruption and the consequences of impaired function on social, economic, legal, and physical wellbeing.

This concept of alcoholism borrows from many other thinkers in the field (Jellenik, 1952, 1960; Goodwin, 1971; Goodwin et al., 1973; Eddy et al., 1965; Seevers, 1968; Wikler, 1970; Nathan & Bridell, 1977; Rado, 1933; Glover, 1928, 1932; Simmel, 1948; Hartmann, 1935, 1951; Krystal & Raskin, 1970; Wurmser, 1974; Ablon, 1976; Calahan & Cisin, 1976; Chafetz and Demone, 1962; Chafetz & Yoerg, 1977; National Commission on Marihuana and Drug Use, 1973; Pattison et al., 1977; Kissin, 1974). Though some models clearly acknowledge the importance of subjective factors—"motivation," "craving," and "psychological dependence"—in the *establishment* of abnormal drinking patterns, many of them cease to interest themselves in the behavior and psychology of the drinker *after* the development of alcoholism, in the response to what is happening, how the alcoholic acts, and the way he or she seems to feel.

In the development of alcoholism, different physical and psychological factors are paramount at different stages. I have not found it practical to discuss these factors separately, in isolation; for treatment purposes, it is more useful to examine them in interaction. Other chapters of this book discuss drinking as a social phenomenon, the vulnerable personality, and the applicability of psychoanalytic methods in treatment. All these subjects have bearing on mine, but my central purpose is to link the alcoholic's subjective experience with the way he presents clinically.

However we may refine upon it (Keller & McCormick, 1968; Keller, 1977), alcoholism means repeated harmful drinking. As a working definition of harm I will use "serious problems related to drinking in any of these areas: physical, emotional, social, vocational, financial, or legal." A working *description* of alcoholism, since research in the field is spotty though extensive, and since patients' own perceptions are distorted, must draw on other fields of experience. To know "what it feels like," for instance, it is useful to compare the experience of alcoholism to other traumas, to look at brain-damaged patients and refer to drug addiction. A few vignettes, rather than formal case histories, have been drawn from clinical work with patients.

I admit to a strong positive bias. Alcoholics can get well, even on their own. Studies exist, though of small samples, that show a recovery rate for untreated alcoholics of from 17 to 24 percent over a two-year period (Imber et al., 1976; Kendall & Staton, 1966; Lemere, 1953; and Orford & Edwards, 1977), suggesting that over a lifetime recovery rates are much higher.

Alcoholism treatment programs including A.A. have differing assumptions, though much understanding could be shared. Some patients enter the treatment system more comfortably via their physician or psychotherapy than via A.A., but their drinking is often neither understood nor addressed. People are often fearful and depressed about entering A.A. or an alcoholism treatment program, but get more reliable help in staying sober there. They may not be able to learn how to take care of their disorder until their minds clear. They may require a period free of alcohol to begin to understand how to go about recovering.

A part of the alcoholic's resistance to treatment has often been the negative and rejecting reaction he encounters among caregivers who, themselves pessimistic, are apt to collude in his denial. Just as the diagnosis of alcoholism is painful to accept, so it is painful to make without therapeutic optimism, as in the following story:

Katharyn P. aged 60, came into my awareness with a family history of nearly every member being alcoholic. The patient herself had drunk nearly continuously for over thirty years. When I was called to see her, she had chronic liver disease, lung disease, and heart disease, and had been in a confused state with mild disorientation and inability to remember more than two of five objects at three minutes for the eight weeks she had been in the hospital. Fortunately, her neurological impairment eventually cleared. During the three years preceding our contact, her need for medical admissions for pneumonia, head trauma, and fractures from falls due to drinking had doubled every year, until in the year before I saw her she had had a dozen admissions. Her physicians had meticulously cared for the complications of her alcoholism without seeking treatment for the alcoholism itself. The reasons they gave for this were doubt that there was any treatment for alcoholism, uncertainty about how to find it, and a strong if misplaced sense of tact. When they attempted to bring up the matter of her drinking, she became upset, and since she seemed unable to bear to talk about it, they usually avoided the subject of alcoholism.

When I confronted her about her drinking and how it was endangering her, she was embarrassed and furious. She hated me, for I had humiliated her beyond endurance by lifting off her defenses and exposing her to the life she had to look back on of years of drinking. Shame was intense even though she had been a quiet, generally secret drinker who had her liquor sent to her home and drank it there, offending no one except her own conscience. The humiliation, depression, and guilt unleashed by breaching her denial were more than she could stand, and as soon as she could, she signed herself out against medical advice from an attractive, kindly alcoholism rehabilitation unit. She rejected A.A., but she was willing to come to see me weekly and to attend an occasional rehabilitation program meeting and has not had a drink for over 3 years. During this time she has required hospitalization for her frail medical condition, but only for a total of a few weeks per year, as opposed to seven months of the year previous to the beginning of her alcoholism treatment.

For many years this woman did not get help for her alcoholism. It was not that she did not realize what was happening to her. She did. She simply, understandably, could not bear to face it without help, and the process of helping her face it was an excruciating and demanding therapeutic event. In this case her problems were compounded by the fact that her numerous medical caretakers shared in her denial.

It seemed to me that this sixty-year-old woman, in breaking the addiction, the habit, and indeed the way of life that had been entrenched for thirty years, showed extraordinary strength of character. As her mind cleared, her stubbornness and tenacity came to the fore. The obstinacy of her fight against me could be channeled into the fight against her craving for alcohol, a fight which initially she had to carry on at every moment of every day. Whatever may have been her original reasons for drinking, they had long since receded into forgetfulness, and she was able to see that the craving was outweighted by the dire consequences of drinking. It was possible to divert her thinking into envisioning the possibility of recovery. She liked a fight, and she liked winning it.

Eventually, she simply summed herself up as "one of those people who just can't drink." She needed no deeper psychological insight. "From the first drink," she said, "I guess I was an alcoholic." Since she had usually drunk alone, it is clear that she did not drink for ordinary social reasons. Possibly she was vulnerable to alcohol from the beginning; her family history did suggest both inherited and environmental predispositions.

As a background to the description of the development of alcoholism, we will look at healthy and heavy drinking.

Healthy Drinking

Although it is not simple to define healthy drinking, we may briefly say that it is usually drinking in company, and that its extent is defined by each culture and established by custom, influenced by age and the availability of alcohol. Generally, behavior is consistent with self-esteem and does not produce trouble in the drinker's health, his relationships, or his economic and legal status; it does not cause pain and deterioration in his mental life. Drinking is within range of voluntary modification or self-control. And some healthy people choose not to drink at all.

Healthy adolescent drinking in our culture is usually motivated by curiosity, a wish to become adult, and peer pressure; adult social drinking, at least partly, by the pleasures of conviviality. The simple act of pouring and holding a drink has a symbolic significance, like changing to slippers after work: a cue to relaxation. Though the taste is often an acquired one, alcohol tastes good to most people, smells good, feels warming. Subjectively, in healthy drinkers its effect is to produce relaxation, regression, decreased inhibition, and euphoria. These are cheerful effects: pleasure that can be deliberately sought and unfailingly obtained.

Heavy Drinking

It is striking that most adults drink moderately, while only a small fraction become heavy drinkers or alcoholics. Some healthy drinkers can ingest relatively large amounts with no resulting trouble. Some healthy drinkers drink alone; some heavy drinkers drink only socially. Most healthy drinkers have at least once or twice become drunk; some heavy drinkers never have (Some drinkers become alcoholics overnight; some heavy drinkers continue for a lifetime without ever becoming alcoholics.) Drinking to avoid pain is more common to heavy than to healthy drinkers.

Heavy drinking is defined by quantity, not by its dangerous effects. We classify this group as not alcoholic because the drinking does not produce harmful consequences. The person may be on a continuum moving toward alcoholism, and some heavy drinkers will probably become alcoholic. But despite increasing amounts of alcohol taken, increasing frequency of drinking, more frequent drunkenness and hangovers, and perhaps some blackouts, the diagnosis of alcoholism does not yet apply (Bacon, 1973).

A drinker may drink to calm his anxiety or to conceal it, and may find the alcohol "works" so well that he comes to resort to it before, or in, any threatening situation or at any time when painful feelings surface. Or he may drink only during a period of stress or loss, such as divorce.

Control factors may include ethnic patterns of moderate use or abstinence. Families may act as models for healthy or abusive drinking or may protect the drinker from the consequences of his drinking (Ablon, 1976; Calahan & Cisin, 1976). After the unpleasant experience of hangovers and perhaps some blackouts, the drinker may moderate his intake or stop.

Alcoholism is partly a learned habit, with reinforcement producing and maintaining the drinking. Many independent factors reinforce drinking. One is the psychological effect of the act itself separate from the chemical effect. This is analogous to a repetition compulsion, and is seen in alcoholics who drink despite taking Antabuse, who know that if they drink they will experience not the usual chemical effect, but instead dangerous sickness. Another factor is direct oral gratification from drinking, tasting, and swallowing. This resembles compulsive eating. Probably most important is the pharmacological effect of alcohol on the brain with its corollary change in sensory and emotional experience.

Heavy drinking may begin as a symptom, to mute conflict or get rid of intolerable affect. But as often as the symptom is repeated it produces reinforcement, so that it is powerfully learned.

Another reinforcing characteristic of alcohol use is its value as a defense in avoidance learning. Just as a rat will press a lever to prevent shocks, an anxious shy person may drink before a job interview to reduce anxiety. The reinforcement is that the interview is then less painful. This learning is particularly resistant to extinction because it is never tested. There may also be a positive operant conditioning learning pattern in people who drink to produce pleasure or get "high."

The psychological factors related to heavy drinking will include the factors that characterize any behavior. Alcohol use, like eating, is likely to have meanings and uses according to individual psychological style and pathology. The neurotic may use alcohol as a chemical equivalent for a psychological defense (see the chapters by Mack and Khantzian in this book, and Khantzian et al., 1974). A person with a hysterical personality may use it to reduce conflict during a sexual experience. The abuse of alcohol in depressions of all kinds is well known. The depressed person may use alcohol for anesthesia and relief, or to express self-destructiveness or devaluation. In a person with oral character traits alcohol may, like food, be used in place of people as an object for satisfaction and comfort. A schizophrenic may incorporate alcohol into a delusional system. One man became convinced that the "Greater Power" relied upon in A.A. to maintain sobriety was forcing him to drink against his will. Or the heavy drinker may use alcohol to mask unacceptable feelings or to get in touch with inaccessible ones. Some schizophrenics appear to attempt to ward off psychosis with alcohol.

The Distinction Between Heavy Drinking and Alcoholism

This is a partly psychogenetic model for heavy drinking, but not for alcoholism. The question remains why some heavy drinkers become alcoholic, and others do not. Psychopathology can contribute to abnormal use of alcohol and heavy drinking, as described above. There are clear situations in which each choice to drink is a response to a separate feeling state or conflict and is chosen. Like other symptoms, such drinking is designed to relieve the conflict or pain. This situation may be in effect in heavy drinking, but in alcoholism, as in heavy cigarette smoking, *these rules no longer apply*. Once alcoholism begins, each drink is not a separate choice in response to a feeling state. When there is physiological dependence, drinking may be determined by the length of time since the last drink, not unresolved oral needs or unconscious suicidal tendencies. Even before the establishment of physiological dependence, psychological dependence and the establishment of a learned habit of drinking may augment or supplant classical symptom formation in the production of drinking.

In alcoholism drinking becomes an epicycle which is self-sustaining. In order to interrupt it, it is not enough to remove the factors which led to excessive drinking. For example, treatment of depression which may have preceded the alcoholism is necessary but not sufficient. The autonomous cycle of addictive drinking must also be broken. A psychogenetic model of symptom formation is clearly active at some points in some drinkers and is clearly buried under and superseded by other factors at other times. Clinicians need to know when it is making a contribution and when other factors are paramount.

A causal link between alcoholism and some forms of mental illness may be established. There is evidence for at least association in some genetic studies (Goodwin, 1971). But prospective studies have not clearly demonstrated a "prealcoholic personality" (Vaillant, 1980 and in this book). Early reviews of research studies which tried to determine a set of character traits typical of the alcoholic or "causing" alcoholism found few reliable characteristics (Lisansky, 1967; Sutherland et al., 1950; Syme, 1957).

More recent studies using more sophisticated methods have shown some subtypes among alcoholics (Skinner et al., 1974; Whitelock et al., 1971; Williams, 1976), but since the studies are retrospective, these findings might equally well support the hypothesis argued here, that there are differences between alcoholics and nonalcoholics, but some of these may be *produced* by the disorder and not found before its onset.

Several studies suggest that psychopathology follows the onset of alcoholism. In a prospective study of a group some of whom later developed alcoholism, general maladjustment and especially depression, health concern, and guilt increased between the original testing and the alcoholic stage (Hoffman et al., 1974).

Another prospective·study of the causal relation between drug abuse and psychiatric disorders followed a group of drug abusers for six years. Initially there were no significant symptom differences between the groups. At six years eight of fourteen depressant users had serious depression, five of eleven stimulant users had psychoses, and the twenty-six narcotic users showed no change in psychopathology. It is possible that different preexisting personality disorders determined drug selection, but at the beginning of the study symptom levels in all three groups were low (McLellan et al., 1979). The study did not specify whether alcohol was one of the drugs the depressant group used, and it would be important to study alcohol separately, but the clear intergroup differences are provocative.

Every alcoholic has a character structure which may be predisposing *or not* before the alcoholism, but whoever experiences alcoholism will undergo characteristic psychological damage. This damage will be grafted on to the original psychological organization and intertwined with it. The alcoholic will then present clinically as more or less psychologically impaired depending on stage and complications of alcoholism as well as on initial strengths and weaknesses of character.

Early Alcoholism

Heavy drinking may persist indefinitely, maintained by familial and social forces, by psychological factors, or as a learned response. But in some drinkers and perhaps even some people picking up their very first drink, another set of developments occurs.

This group is distinguished from the group I have called heavy drinkers because the drinking, whatever amount, causes harm. The person is alcoholic. The symptoms vary, but many include blackouts, hangovers, solitary drinking, morning drinking, and sneaking drinking, antisocial acts while drinking, and experiences of loss of control (Bacon, 1973).

The patient may have come to this stage down any path, over any length of time. He may have begun to drink regularly to the point of stupor, or he may not always or even very often drink to excess. But his "meter" is out of order. When he decides not to drink, he may find himself drinking anyway; when he does drink he doesn't know what will happen, how much he will drink or how he will act. After a few blackouts, hangovers, and embarrassing recollections, he will try to control his drinking, will almost certainly fail, and will try again repeatedly. Should he be seen clinically, he will probably not be correctly diagnosed.

Unless he has been drunk very recently, he has no physiological symptoms. He may be well dressed, satisfactorily employed, and entirely presentable. No one wants to admit that he is out of control, and few doctors want to confront a patient with such a suspicion. It is easier to assume that loss of control is an unusual event than to inquire searchingly about previous episodes. Early alcoholics who have prepared themselves to ask for help with their drinking may thus find themselves subtly discouraged. Of all alcoholics early ones are the most neglected, least understood, most frequently undiagnosed, and easiest to treat. It is unusual for them to seek help, but if they do, a single interview may begin recovery, though they need more help than that.

The early alcoholic has little or no impairment in his physical functioning, except for the memory loss of blackouts and the discomfort and slowed thinking of hangovers. He has no withdrawal symptoms, though his drinking has unpleasant consequences, such as upsetting people who care about the drinker.

He may be aware of his unusual drinking, anxious about it, and ashamed and depressed when he drinks too much. But what may be evident to outside observers is often opaque to him. He has little idea that he has an abnormal response to alcohol, or what that means.

What he notices is that he repeatedly loses control of his behavior. He realizes, and others realize, that this is not like social drinking. Why does he not act on this knowledge and stop?

Instead, he does two other things. He does not accept his loss of control as fixed. He does not give up hope that he can drink socially and safely. Like a child learning to walk, he tries over and over again to master the drinking. He begins a determined, doomed struggle against his loss of control. He continues to lose control. His thinking begins to shift in reaction to these repeated experiences. Denial, rationalization, and projection appear in relation to drinking.

The next case shows how denial appears in relation to drinking:

Peter L. is a 30-year-old professor of design raised in many countries by diplomat parents. He first came to treatment with me after his wife separated from him because of his drinking. He was referred by a physician, his prep school roommate, who had been worried about his drinking for several years; he had always refused treatment until his wife made good on her threat to move out.

He was young, gifted, rich, handsome, and depressed. He wanted psychotherapy for his depression. He denied having any difficulty related to drinking. He gave a history that he sometimes drank too much at parties, only drank on social occasions, never at work or in the mornings, had no severe hangovers, and denied memory blackouts. He did not drink every day. He found the idea that he could not control his drinking infuriating and stigmatizing.

He saw me as a judge who, if he could figure out how to conciliate me, would benignly allow him to drink, or who, threateningly, might deprive him of his drinking. He had intense feelings about alcohol. He thought that if he was alcoholic he was degraded and defective. Coming to therapy was proof of his defect, and was regarded as punishment, and penance. He distracted attention from his shame by fighting about scheduling and about the fee. He had trouble accepting the idea that his decision to drink or not was an issue of his safety and comfort. He felt that if he could not drink socially he was morally inferior.

I told him I was not sure he was alcoholic, since he had no addiction or withdrawal symptoms, but that he reported damage to his relationships and to his self-esteem from drinking, and his wife and friends were concerned. He now admitted to blackouts, but felt he chose to get drunk.

He desperately hoped that if only we could treat his depression, he would be changed in some way and would then be able to drink. He was sure his drinking was out of control because of some psychological disturbance. (This much longing for alcohol is not characteristic of social drinking and indicates that he was psychologically dependent.)

He was determined to prove that he was not alcoholic. He stopped drinking altogether for three weeks. As soon as he stopped drinking, he spent much less time in therapy arguing that he was not alcoholic. His depression lifted. He talked about the comfort of knowing that if he did not drink, he could not get into danger. He was amazed at his previous insistence that he could control his drinking, and appalled at the risks he had taken with his career and marriage. Sober, he was soon talking about what happened to him when he drank, telling me that he had nearly weekly blackouts, insulted and assaulted friends at parties, drank much more than his friends, and spent time with a couple he neither liked nor respected but enjoyed because they were very heavy drinkers, probably alcoholic. That is, sober, he was able to talk about the frightening and painful aspects of drinking which he previously denied.

After several weeks the desire to drink returned. He began to feel that he had proved he was not alcoholic and to deny trouble with drinking. He came to an appointment half an hour late, saying that he didn't want any more treatment, that it made him depressed. By the end of the session he acknowledged that he had started drinking again and did not want to feel bad about it, which would happen if he came to treatment. He denied being worried or guilty, but protested too much. Because of his distress he decided to continue therapy.

The next few weeks he avoided the topic of alcohol and denied that he was having trouble. He insistently defended his right to drink and his self-respect, threatening to break treatment if I continued to ask about the drinking. One day he came in depressed and full of self-hate. He had lost control of his drinking and while drunk and in a blackout had driven a carload of friends into a post. Some of them were injured. He was furious with me, saying that if I had not undermined his self-confidence, he would not have lost control and drunk too much in the first place. Now full of remorse, he described the previous few weeks in which his daily alcohol consumption had been slowly rising, from two drinks to six or more. Because of his shame, he had needed to lie about this in therapy. As the guilt and embarrassment about his blackout episode overwhelmed the denial, he described real damage caused by his drinking. He was able to make the causal link between his pain and his drinking.

He was also able to make a plan to get sober. He stopped drinking again, and this time he was depressed and angry about not drinking. He reluctantly agreed to go to A.A. He returned from one meeting feeling that he was different from the people in A.A., that he was superior. He was confirmed in his belief that he was not alcoholic. But he was possessed and pursued by craving for alcohol, wrestling with the desire to drink at parties, dinners, and business lunches. He was as preoccupied as a dieter longing for chocolate, and hopeless about the craving ever abating.

He stayed sober five weeks. During this time his wife moved back in. His spirits rose and he started drinking immediately. He drank attempting to control it but in increasing amounts and with increasing denial for eight weeks before he had another episode of loss of control. This time he got drunk at a party for the chairman of his department, destroyed a room, and had to be arrested, spending the night in jail. His wife moved out again. He had an acute "cure." Miserable, full of self-reproach and remorse, frightened about endangering his career, furious with me that I had not taken away his alcoholism, he stopped drinking again. He joined A.A. and this time he loved it. He fervently followed instructions, went to many of the meetings, and felt it was better than therapy, which only caused depression. He left treatment. Two days later he went on a three-day bender, which ended when he smashed up another car. He came back to therapy tired, sick, disgusted with himself, humiliated, and admitting, with gritted teeth, that he was alcoholic.

His experiences illustrate graphically what a painful process it is to accept the diagnois of alcoholism, a process which is necessary to begin recovery. Now, with his denial collapsed, he admitted that in the past he had had alcoholic hepatitis and had several arrests for drunken driving.

He has been sober in A.A. nearly a year. He goes to A. A. meetings every week, a brief period of daily attendance. His depression is improved, and he has reduced therapy to check-in visits though he may return for more treatment later. His wife, who had come in to talk a few times, goes to Al-anon occasionally, and they are together. He is not obsessed with the question of whether he can control his drinking. He finally "let go" the struggle for control and once he realized he could not drink safely had little trouble staying sober. He overcame a block to his creative production at work which had lasted for most of this year of treatment, and recently won a travel fellowship.

This patient has early alcoholism. He had the entire system of denial, psychological dependence, rejection of diagnosis, attributing pain and danger to other causes, and fight for control. He was not yet completely demoralized and hopeless about recovery. He was hopeful instead that he could drink safely. He hated his disease and diagnosis. Once he could give up the denial, he could choose whether he wanted to drink or not. Weighing the risks against his love of the idea of drinking, he chose to stop. He is typical in that when he was drinking and fighting to control it, he needed denial; when he stopped, he could acknowledge the painful consequences of drinking, soften his rejection of diagnosis, and make use of treatment.

Denial of alcoholism was present before addiction had developed and drastically decreased within a short time whenever he stopped drinking. While it might be argued that this obsessive denial was always present, he and his wife say that it began when he started drinking heavily and only occured around the issue of drinking. He can describe how as he begins to want to drink his thinking twists in order to allow him to do so, and how the denial is decreased when he is sober, and he cannot understand how he could have been so self-destructively irrational. He now knows how he must think to take care of his drinking problem.

I was not sure at first that this patient was alcoholic. He had no physical addiction, and his denial was very convincing. We initially decided to wait and see if he had any more dangerous and humiliating blackouts and losses of control. These did not occur immediately after he started "controlled drinking," but in each case he ended by loss of control. This, combined with his intense denial related only to drinking, made the diagnosis.

His alcohol problem had been worsening steadily over several years, and while one cannot predict what would happen to him next, if he continued drinking, he would appear to have been at very high risk of addiction and other complications. In A.A. people describing their early drinking often report similar experiences. His behavior and reactions are nearly universal among alcoholics. In A.A. newcomers are told, "Identify, don't compare, and sooner or later you'll hear your own story."

The "Middle" Phase

As the early alcoholic continues to drink, tolerance develops, so that he needs more alcohol to achieve the same subjective change. Even if he increases the dose, the desired relief may elude him. This, in fact, is what alcoholics frequently report: "It just didn't work the same way any longer"; and the observational studies likewise describe in drinking alcoholics an increase in psychic pain, depression, and anxiety (Capell & Herman, 1972; Mendelson et al., 1964; Tamerin et al., 1976; Vanicelli, 1972; Warren & Raynes, 1972; Mendelson & Mello, 1979). Insofar as alcohol was used as a pharmacological defense, it is no longer effective. So other defenses must be substituted to protect the ego from being overwhelmed.

One would think that by this time the alcoholic would surely want to stop. He wants to want to. But if he *really* wanted to, he thinks, why then of course he could control the drinking: this, he has to believe. One may ask whether the unconscious or repressed knowledge that he is, in fact, helpless to control the drinking may not underlie the clinging, dependent behavior so commonly seen in alcoholics at this stage and thereafter.

They experience intense need for people, though people are offended or feel rejected by their destructive behavior, rationalizations, and growing childish self-centeredness. At this phase, alcoholics are less likely to stop or try stopping, risking another failure, than they are to become passive. Cognitive changes result from repeated failures. Negative self-perceptions which are relatively inaccessible to corrective feedback lead to giving up (Kovaks & Beck, 1978). The person learns that his efforts are useless, and he stops struggling. Treatment from this point on must not only point out the harm from drinking. It must help to reverse the learned helplessness (Seligman, 1975).

Often the alcoholic has or finds reason to seek help, however; the complications of alcoholism can mimic almost any form of mental illness, leading him to think he needs a psychiatrist, or a fall or accident may give him an acceptable cause to present himself to a general physician. He both seeks and fears intervention with his alcoholism. He often cannot relate his pain to drinking. Whenever the diagnosis is suspected, the physician must aggressively pursue it since the patient can rarely make it for himself.

Alan T. was a middle-aged, red-faced, well-dressed white-collar worker with a bluff manner who came to the clinic complaining of depression, anxiety, sleeplessness, and inability to concentrate on his work. He denied any problems with drinking. His family also doubted that he had an alcohol problem. He had no signs of endogenous depression. He complained of increasing difficulty getting work done over about eighteen months. On close questioning about the nature of his difficulty at work, he admitted to confusion and lethargy. Further neurological examination gave no more information, but finally, on repeated concerned questioning about the confusion, he admitted to drinking at work. When it was explained that sometimes people felt bad about their drinking and found that they could not tell the whole truth about it at first, he readily admitted drinking a quart of bourbon a day by himself plus heavy social drinking, for three or four years. His denial was countered by empathy.

After about an hour of ventilation, support, reassurance, clarification, and intensive alcoholism education chiefly consisting of suggesting that his depression might be caused by the alcohol, that I thought it was, that I could help him with this, and that we could not tell if he needed psychotherapy or other help until he had been sober for a while, he agreed to attempt to stop drinking, see me weekly, and try A.A. Here denial was opposed by hope and information. He attended his sessions regularly, had no physical withdrawal or craving when he stopped drinking, and invested himself increasingly in A.A. At the end of the twelve-week period without alcohol which I had asked him to complete, his depression and sleep disorder had remitted completely, though he still had difficulty making himself do his work. At this time he related this to not liking his work and not wanting to work at all rather than to the confusion, lethargy, and guilt that crippled him when he was drinking. He has continued A.A., contacts me from time to time, and has been sober for several years.

Since this patient was able, with help, to admit how much he drank, and was able to countenance the thought that drinking in itself might be doing him harm, his denial system was in an early flexible stage of development.

Writings on Denial

For the practical purpose of this chapter I will use "denial" in the broad colloquial sense to include all the alcoholic's defenses which have a denying quality, or serve to protect his drinking behavior or his self-esteem. This is clearly different from the word's strict and careful use in psychoanalytic thinking, which will be described below.

Psychoanalytic studies of theories of defense, including studies of denial, scarcely mention alcoholism; psychoanalytic studies of alcoholism have little to say about denial (Glover, 1928, 1932; Rado, 1933; Simmel, 1948).

The literature on the psychology of the alcoholic is voluminous, and has been reviewed elsewhere (Armotang, 1958; Barry, 1974; Blane, 1968; Sutherland et al., 1950; Syme, 1957).

The papers that mention denial in alcoholism make some interesting points. Alcoholism is a chronic behavior that cannot be maintained and supported without organization and work (Paredes, 1974). Denial in alcoholism serves as a kind of functional deafness, the keystone of the pathological defense system of the alcoholic. It is reinforced by rationalization and defends against profound insecurity and low self-esteem (Twerski, 1974). According to Tamerin the appearance of denial is associated with active drinking (Tamerin & Neuman, 1974). In contrast, Hartocollis (1968, 1969), Gomberg (1968), and Vaillant (1976) treat denial as a character trait of the alcoholic, noting that denial of personal problems may precede alcoholism and be shared by the whole family. They do not specify how the onset of alcoholism was determined, and this would be important because denial is one of the early symptoms or complications of alcoholism, beginning well before the establishment of addiction, but consequent to symptoms of early alcoholism, as in the case on p. 65.

Psychoanalytic Papers on Drug Abuse

The scarcity of psychiatric writing on the psychology of alcoholism contrasts with the situation with drug abuse. Psychodynamic understanding of drug dependence generally assumes that the role of physiology in maintaining drug use is minimal. This is not true in alcoholism.

This work may be particularly helpful in understanding the relapse in an alcoholic who has been sober and for whom, at this point, withdrawal and confused thinking are not paramount.

Wurmser's (1978) is a fascinating discussion. He begins by casting aside the early psychoanalytic literature on the subject. He believes that drug use is psychically determined and that drug dependence has little physical basis.

He describes drug use as a defense against the problems produced by the ego defect of affect defense. Drug use is an attempt at self-treatment, an artificial defense against overwhelming affects, rather than a wish fulfillment or escape. The defense is against internal rather than external threats. The affects that cannot be tolerated are rage, shame, and hurt or abandonment. Wurmser believes that intense craving for the drug after withdrawal is related to upsurge of these affects, with a kind of narcissistic decompensation and ego fragmentation, which the drug reverses. That is, the drug is used as a replacement for a defect in psychological structure. He expands the characterization of the dynamic functions of drug use to help with several other converging problems—superego pathology, rudimentary ability to form symbols and use fantasy, archaic passive dependence, self-destructiveness, regressive wishes, and narcissistic crisis.

Krystal and Raskin's (1970) work is along the same lines, saying that the drug user is grappling with affects which have never been moderated or neutralized, so are dedifferentiated, archaic, and excruciating. They also emphasize the disturbance in object relations in drug-dependent people, their need for supplies and for object substitutes to take in. Drug users inevitably fail to achieve lasting satisfaction, with intense disappointment and rage, the ambivalence being handled by ego splitting and impoverishment. In any case, the use of drugs is seen as an effort to adapt and survive in the face of these serious problems.

Denial and Mechanisms of Defense

Defenses are processes which are a function of ego organization, and which regulate instincts and serve the integrity of the ego. The intention of the defense, to decrease pain and avoid anxiety, should be distinguished from the results of the use of the defense, which may be destructive to the ego, for example when denial of illness blocks treatment (Hoffer, 1968).

Freud's most extensive discussion of denial is in *An Outline of Psycho-Analysis*. He saw disavowal of external reality as the first stage of psychosis, and opposed it to repression, a rejection of the internal demands of the id. Denial, or disavowal, was the primal defense mechanism against external reality (Freud, as noted by Laplanche & Pontalis, 1973).

In his paper on fetishism (1927) he noted that in denial two contradictory elements occurred simultaneously, one taking account of reality and the other denying it, instead expressing a wish. He clarified that perception was intact, and that what was denied was the significance of the perception.

Anna Freud did not include denial in her list of defense mechanisms in *The Ego and the Mechanisms of Defense* (1966). She defined defense mechanisms as the means by which the ego wards off pain and anxiety from internal sources and controls impulses and affects. She continued Freud's distinction that denial was used against external rather than internal threats to the ego.

> The method of denial upon which is based the fantasy of the reversal of real facts into their opposite, is employed in situations in which it is impossible to escape some painful external impression. [A. Freud, 1966, p. 93]

Denial is a normal mechanism early in development, a preliminary stage for maturer defenses, from which it is distinguished by the fact that denial is not entirely intrapsychic since it protects against experience of real external danger (A. Freud, 1966).

Jacobson clarified how denial could occur when the distinction between internal and external was lost. This could take place if the ego regressed to the point where self and object, internal and external, were treated in the same manner. The process was regression, not projection (Jacobson, 1957).

Denial places two ego functions, the defense and the ability to test reality, at odds. During normal development it can be limited and gradually relinquished in favor of reality sense and maturer capacities to delay, deflect, regulate, and master tension (A. Freud, 1966).

In alcoholism denial is used in exactly the same types of conditions which Anna Freud described to evoke it in the first place, situations of helplessness against painful reality from which the person cannot escape.

Semrad and Vaillant have observed that recovery from schizophrenia and drug addiction reversed regression with sequential substitution of maturer defenses. Primitive projection, denial, and distortion are followed by affective, then neurotic, and finally healthy defenses (Semrad, 1967; Vaillant, 1971).

Recently some have abandoned S. and A. Freud's clear usage and employ the term "denial" in a less clear expanded way to include rejection not only of external perceptions but also of unacceptable internal reality, painful affects, and even instinctual drives (Moore & Rubenfine, 1969). Despite this semantic problem, their descriptions of the clinical uses of denial are helpful.

Denial has its origins in early attempts of the organism to obtain relief from painful external stimuli or the painful affects generated by them. The painful stimuli include objects evoking aggression, hence threatening object loss, and events which threaten the ego with danger. The denial mechanism, effective at first in conserving objects, in used later against painful percepts of the self, external trauma, and the punitive superego (Moore & Rubenfine, 1969).

Denial may be both adaptive and pathological:

> The adaptive function of denial is the avoidance of painful affects evoked by percepts which arouse signal anxiety basically related to the continuum of threats encountered by the developing ego: danger of loss of object, danger of loss of love, castration, superego disapproval, and loss of self esteem. [Moore & Rubenfine, 1969, p. 33]

In situations of extreme danger denial may be the most adaptive defense mechanism available, in temporary adaptation protecting the ego from being overwhelmed. The person accurately perceives the trauma and appreciates its implications, but maintains an unconscious unrealistic idea that the trauma has not taken place; then he gradually, stepwise, resynthesizes the ego split. Pathology results only when the ego split is not repaired, though denial may also be associated with more severe pathology. The ego split may be maintained by a fantasy, for instance of invulnerability, or specialness, which allows the person to disregard his perceptions (Trunell & Holt, 1974). The equivalent in the alcoholic is the fantasy that he can drink normally, moderately, and in a controlled way. This is one of the major obstacles to recovery.

Denial may be used to attempt to secure instinctual gratification as a special function of the pleasure ego important in id factors and wishes (Moore & Rubenfine, 1969). This is of special note considering the role of denial in alcoholism to preserve drinking.

Other defense mechanisms may be used to reinforce denial (Jacobson, 1959). Threat of breakthrough of denied material may lead to marshaling of adjunctive defenses, or acting out. These are invoked to protect the ego from being overwhelmed by the task of adapting to a loss too great to bear. Failure of adjunctive defenses along with the original denial would lead to experience of the pain which the defenses had been used against, such as depression, or other symptoms.

In alcoholism this occurrence of denial in association with clusters of related supporting defenses is very common, and bears testimony to the extent of the threat to the integrity of the ego.

How Denial Is Understood by Alcoholism Specialists

Denial is defined for psychoanalytic usage as a defense, a psychological mechanism to protect against pain. When contemporary alcoholism workers use the concept of denial, they mean something quite different. It is used broadly to mean the denial of obvious reality, but also to cover a whole range of alcoholic tactics to justify, hide, or protect drinking, to block treatment, and to deny responsibility for the consequences of behavior.

Denial as a Response to Trauma

The "denial system" in alcoholism is a set of psychological changes that occur as a reaction to alcoholism, a sort of psychological complication. The cases show the maladaptive effects of denial, especially the defensive resistances which block recovery and access to treatment.

What generates the psychological position which the drinker takes? The person who develops an addiction is faced with a strange subjective experience. Addiction is an organic assault on the physical and psychological integrity of the person.

He has repeated experiences of painful consequences of drinking. He ought to make the terrifying discovery that he cannot control his drinking, but he resists and denies it. He realizes that a catastrophe is afoot, and is bewildered and afraid. But he does not know what has happened to him. He does not say, "I drink because I have no control over alcohol use, withdrawal makes me sick, and drinking has been repetitively reinforced." He instead explains his experience in ordinary psychological terms, like the hypnotized person who closes the window and then rationalizes his action. He says, "I drink because my wife doesn't understand me" or "I drink when I feel depressed."

His usual intellect and judgment are not available to help him understand what is happening to him because alcohol has often impaired them.

When the alcoholic begins drinking, he does so in response to social and psychological forces. In alcoholism drinking shifts partly out of voluntary control, though it can still be modified voluntarily to an extent. The shift occurs without announcement or explanation, so it is experienced as continuing under voluntary control, while in reality it is not.

The impact of this experience cannot be overestimated. It is like the loss or reversal of the person's mastery and maturation in the acquisition of bowel and bladder control. These functions were originally under automatic physiological regulation and with development were brought into voluntary and social control. (This is not to specify the nature of alcoholic loss of control, which I do not claim to understand, but it is a good metaphor for the *experience* of loss of control.)

Because of the experience of loss of control, the despair that he cannot stop, the lack of understanding how to stop, and the terror of the consequences of stopping, the alcoholic sets up an elaborate psychological protective structure to preserve his drinking, a system of denial. His creative efforts to explain his experience to himself and master it, while they have disastrous consequences, are extraordinary and fascinating.

The alcoholic begins to react, by fighting to regain control, and to explain to himself and others why he is behaving so badly. Repeated attempts to recover control repeatedly, predictably fail. This gradually destroys hope. Alcoholism destroys the person's belief that he is a normal, worthwhile person, for he finds himself repeatedly behaving destructively. Self-esteem deteriorates. The experience forbids the normal social wish to be able to drink socially. The alcoholic becomes guilt-ridden. He is demoralized in his attempt to solve his problem with drinking, although alcoholics almost invariably make repeated constructive efforts before they give up in despair.

He does not respond to his failures by saying that he needs help because of denial, shame, fear, and confusion. The failures humiliate him, and he is afraid that if he talks about what is happening to him he will be stigmatized and his despair will be confirmed. Most people experience a diagnosis of alcoholism as a tragedy. By the time someone makes it, their hope is usually gone.

Growing helplessness, like the neurological effects of alcohol, engenders regression. Efforts at mature grasp of the situation and problem solving fail and are given up. The alcoholic no longer believes in the possibility of a solution, and he retreats to the undifferentiated responses of regression, avoidance, magical thinking, and denial.

As drinking increases, complications extend and intensify, efforts to control drinking fail, and simultaneously the alcoholic realizes that he cannot stop drinking; he becomes frightened and hopeless, and even more dependent on drinking. He is terrified of stopping, knowing that he would be faced with emptiness and sickness from the loss of drinking though he would also be relieved and feel better. He would also be faced with his shame and guilt, which are so intense that they are hard for most nonalcoholics to comprehend, and faced with the ruin of part of his life and other consequences of his drinking. When he does want to stop, which occurs when his contact with reality, and hence level of pain, is high, and occurs because of his self-respect and wish to recover, he does not think he can, and does not know how to.

One of his choices is to continue to drink while admitting that his drinking is bad, out of control, hostile, destructive, disgusting, and dangerous. To the alcoholic this appears untenable, like embracing the gutter, though there are some alcoholics who assume this attitude. Another of his choices is to give up drinking, which may be all that he feels that he has, and while its gratifications are not what they were when he started drinking, his need for it, symbolically, symptomatically, as an overlearned pattern, and to stave off withdrawal, is intense and unremitting. He does not believe that he is able to stop. He feels that this option is closed to him.

He chooses, instead, a third alternative, which to nonalcoholics appears incomprehensible, but in view of this discussion is seen to have a compelling internal logical necessity of its own. He denies his alcoholism. If one is alcoholic and denies it or fails to "know," realize, or acknowledge it, one is spared the staggering blow to self-esteem of the stigma of alcoholism, and one may drink, not because it is safe or acceptable, but because one can then rationalize that it is. He increasingly centers his attention on alcohol and dedicates his whole thinking to explaining, justifying, and protecting his drinking and attempting to compensate for the catastrophic problems in his life that result from drinking.

Denial of illness in this situation is different from anosognosia, denial of illness based on neurological defect, and different from psychotic delusion, though it borders on this extreme. Delusion is a positive created belief substituted for reality. In alcoholism denial is more like a rejection of reality or clinging to an old, wished-for reality than a creation of alternative reality.

Clinical Examples

Here is a case of a man who had never had treatment and had no hope. Jimmy R. was an elderly man, terrified, lonely, terribly sad, and full of self-hatred. "I'm nothing but a bum." But he made a valiant effort to pretend that he had no alcohol problem. He blamed the beginning of his problems on his service hospitalizations and the resulting bills. He did admit to memory problems, but they were "from working with carbon tetrachloride in World War II." He vomited in the morning, but that was "from nerves," which also rationalized his having to have a drink in the morning. He got rolled on the street, but that was "because kids have changed today." He was "anemic" but not alcoholic.

His life today is very sad. Scarcely anyone cares about him. He feels hopeless about getting any help from anyone. He believes that he is dying, having "lived three score years and ten," and is extremely isolated. He has health problems but "not a booze problem."

This man has a dual system, with excruciating reality acknowledged on one track and simultaneously denied on the other. He refuses to, or is unable to, bear the horror of his life, so he uses denial extravagantly in the face of obviously contradicting reality. It would seem that his denial of his alcoholism, while admitting all these other tragedies, is used here to protect the last tenuous shred of his self-respect, and that in this man denial is part of a primitive desperate scramble to protect himself against desolation and despair of towering proportions. Denial of his alcoholism may also serve to protect his drinking, but it had the feeling of a pathetic and ineffective attempt to preserve his last shred of dignity as a human being. He might be a bum, but he was not an alcoholic.

As a general formula, this holds: the greater the pain and the less the hope, the more rigid the denial, and thus, as Moore and Murphy (1961) point out, the less likelihood there is of successful treatment. This patient used massive astonishing denial to try to protect against despair, but without success. When denial is so dysfunctional, it must be regarded as almost psychotic.

Adjunctive Defenses

Denial is only effective temporarily. Work must constantly be expended to sustain it in the face of contradicting reality. The alcoholic fights to keep his distortions separated from realistic perception.

The methods include avoidance, delaying, minimization, projection, and rationalization. In avoidance, the person removes himself from situations where he will be confronted, or diverts attention or changes the subject. In delaying, the alcoholic denies facts despite knowing that information to prove him wrong is close at hand. A temporary stalling tactic, it is not based on long-term hope of convincing anyone to the contrary, but avoids for the present moment some painful realization or admission. In minimization, the person cannot stand to tell the whole of what he is doing, but is able to hint or tell part. Projection and rationalization externalize responsibility or make the drinking seem plausible.

Suppose the person has been denying his drinking to his child, who then says, "But I saw you." Defensively the parent has several options. He can continue to use denial, matching his story against the child's by saying "No, you didn't, I wasn't drinking." Or he can take one step backward, acknowledging the reality of the child's perception but defining himself as innocent of the action, since it was caused by evil outside himself. "Well, what do you expect with a bunch of stupid yelling kids? That's the only way I can ever get any peace around here." This is a case of a shift to projection, externalizing responsibility for the *motivation* while acknowledging the *act*.

Or he can acknowledge the reality of the action, and not blame others for it, but redefine the action as harmless, or himself as not alcoholic. "Yes, but it was only a short one, and one little drink never hurt anyone. Besides, I can control it." In this case he has chosen denial, rationalization, and minimization.

The literature of Alcoholics Anonymous abounds with clinical examples and ways to relinquish these defenses. Anyone interested need only look in the index of "*As Bill Sees It,* published by A.A. (Alcoholics Anonymous, 1967), under "rationalization," "honesty," and "alibis" for examples. For instance:

> The perverse wish to hide a bad motive underneath a good one permeates human affairs from top to bottom. This subtle and elusive kind of self-righteousness can underlie the smallest act or thought. Learning daily to spot, admit, and correct these flaws is the essence of character-building and good living. [Alcoholics Anonymous, 1967, p. 17]

And there are pamphlets such as *Alcoholism: A Merry-Go-Round Named Denial* (Kellerman, 1969) and *Dealing with Denial* (Hazelden Foundation, 1975).

All of these subordinate techniques in the alcoholic are usually directed toward the same two major goals as the use of denial: justification of continued drinking, and restoration of self-esteem in the face of the destructive consequences of drinking.

Organic Factors in the Psychology of Alcoholism

> It is faulty in principle to try to make a distinction between so called organic and functional diseases as far as symptomatology and therapy are concerned. [Goldstein, 1952, p. 245]

To be drunk is to suffer impairment of the central nervous system, which gradually is reversed as the hangover wears off. Staying drunk, or getting drunk repeatedly, may eventually produce permanent damage to the brain. A model of neurological dysfunction cannot be applied without modification to explain the findings in alcoholism, both because the brain injury in alcoholism is characteristic and different from other forms of injury and because it coexists with numerous other factors which make the clinical picture more complex. But the literature on brain damage, most importantly Kurt Goldstein's classic paper (Goldstein, 1952), is useful in explaining the alcoholic's psychological experience, responses, defenses, and restitutive efforts.

Post-Detoxification Dementia

The active alcoholic repeatedly enters an intoxicated state with alteration of consciousness, to the point of stupor or coma, disturbed sensorium and affect, and impaired memory, both in the form of "blackouts," periods during drinking when the person was able to function but for which he or she has either partial memory or none at all, and in the form of recent memory difficulties persisting after the intoxicated episode.

In addition to acute intoxication and post-detoxification delirium (d.t.'s) there is a separate and clinically important disorder—post-detoxification dementia.

> For a few days to weeks after their last drink patients who had been drinking heavily will exhibit a mild dementia or "wet brain." This condition can be distinguished from the memory defect of Korsakoff's psychosis because in mild dementia the memory and orientation defects are relieved by offering the patient clues. [Vaillant, 1978, p. 574]

This state may be chronic and mild but it is very important, since it reduces the individual's ego competence, self-protectiveness, and ability to respond to treatment.

The handling of affect is markedly changed. There may be loss of affective regulation, with intense waves of feeling often disconnected from external causes, fleeting and labile. Extremes of feeling follow each other unpredictably.

Clinical findings of mood lability, irritability, and dulled affective reactivity may be explained by damage to areas around the ventricular systems at the base of the brain, where drugs producing dependence, including alcohol, tend to accumulate preferentially (Rankin, 1975).

Several other types of affective disturbance are seen in alcoholism. The affective changes of withdrawal are regular and characteristic. The person is in an agony of physical sickness, ashamed, guilty, remorseful, fearful, and depressed. In addition to the physical component there is usually a reactive depression. Even if the alcoholic represses and denies the discovery that his life is out of control, some awareness of this breaks through, causing depression. And the frequent coexistence of affective disorder and alcoholism suggests that some depressed alcoholics may have major affective illness in addition to alcoholism.

Even more striking than the impact on affect is the change in the operation of the personality. This is not universal. It may be mild, and may only be clear-cut in advanced alcoholism. What is seen is a deterioration in the highest capacities of human functioning. Judgment, planning, abstract reasoning, and ethical concerns are all impaired. Memory is usually affected in special and separate ways. Use of language becomes more concrete and rudimentary. Emotional preoccupations show the intense self-absorption of the very small child, or the senile person. The personality regresses to an infantile id-dominated level of functioning with pronounced impulsivity and use of primitive defenses such as denial and projection. During drinking the person is overwhelmed and preoccupied with inner experience. Ego functioning is primitive and ineffectual. The person looks, feels, and acts helpless. The superego also regresses to a primitive punitive archaic mode. The person experiences intense guilt and simultaneous loss of effective impulse control.

Research on neuropsychiatric measures of subclinical brain damage in alcoholics shows two major findings. Alcoholics lose the abstract attitude, and complex perceptual-motor abilities are impaired (Kleinknecht & Goldstein, 1972; Rankin, 1975). "There is considerable electroencephalographic and pneumoencephalographic evidence of prolonged brain impairment and damage in alcoholics" (Parsons & Freund, 1973). "Perhaps individuals with a strong susceptability to blackouts may have a subclinical, very mild form of Korsakoff syndrome which may or may not progress with further drinking and time" (Goodwin et al. in Edwards et al., 1977, p. 109).

Premature Aging

The physical findings resemble premature aging (Illis, 1973). Alcohol can produce brain cell death or injury such as accumulation of "wear and tear" pigment and vascular lesions (Roizin et al., 1972). Cerebral atrophy in alcoholics has been demonstrated by pneumoencephalography and computerized axial tomography (Brewer & Perrett, 1971; Roizin et al., 1972; Tumarkin et al., 1955). During active drinking, delta wave sleep is decreased, as it is in older persons, a finding considered to represent diffuse cortical damage (Smith et al., 1971). Fronto-limbic and nondominant hemispheric functions may be impaired (Edwards et al., 1977; Parsons, 1975).

Extreme events, such as frontal lobe atrophy and Korsakoff's syndrome, though infrequent, may occur in deteriorated alcoholics. Such damage is permanent. Though there is controversy about these findings, some of the damage caused by alcohol may be reversible after substantial sobriety (Plum & Posner, 1966; Adamson & Burdick, 1973; Rankin, 1975; Kapur & Butters, 1977; Albert et al., 1979).

Nutritional deficiencies (Victor et al., 1971), hepatic dysfunction, and sleep deprivation, especially of REM sleep (Freedman et al., 1975) are complications of alcoholism which affect the brain. Nor can one ignore remoter physical complications, such as concussions, broken bones, and other results of alcohol-induced falls and accidents (as with the woman described on page 58).

While these conditions are likely to be marked and severe in chronic deteriorated alcoholics, it is important not to neglect their effect in early alcoholics. It may be difficult for a person without alcoholism to grasp that this disordered state with disturbed consciousness, arousal, affect,

memory, confusion, irrationality, and helplessness is a repeated prolonged experience in the drinking alcoholic. Some form of it, attenuated
or severe, may totally dominate his conscious experience.

What is the meaning of this for alcoholics? The alcoholic's experience
is equivalent to what it would be like for healthy people to have partial
general anesthesia to the point of stupor regularly several times a week,
and be expected to function normally, for example go to work, drive, and
so on, a few hours afterward. This explains some of the abnormalities in
the mental status of the active alcoholic, even when briefly sober. The
repeated failures at work and in social situations are likely to produce
humiliation and anxiety, and it is characteristic of the alcoholic, as of the
patient with brain damage, to produce defensive thinking and behavior.

In the early stage alcoholics, like other patients with depressed cortical functioning, may not be aware of loss of function, but instead experience mood swings, a sense of inadequacy, and a sense of increased effort
required for work. They may complain that too much is expected of them
and feel overwhelmed. They may lose interest in cultural, intellectual,
and aesthetic matters and show coarsening of interpersonal relations,
outbursts of anxiety, anger, and excessive need to be reassured and cared
for (Gardner, 1975; Redlich & Freedman, 1966).

At a more advanced stage, failure to complete a task evokes excuses
or alibis, a refusal to see failure. The person avoids challenging situations. Further deterioration produces more obvious inefficiency and failure, and more excessive emotional compensatory devices.

Both alcoholics and brain-damaged people show clinically not only
the organic deficit but the person's feelings in response to the deficit
(anxiety, distress, frustration, and regression) and efforts to adapt to the
situation such as social withdrawal, and use of rationalization and denial
(Goldstein, 1952).

Alcoholism has physical and neurological components. It makes
people sick, helpless, and out of control. The prognosis is generally
thought to be poor. It is terrifying. The person's response to it shares
much with the response to dreaded physical disease.

Many writers have pointed to the use of denial of illness by patients
with serious illness, impending death, and brain damage (Becker, 1973;
Dudley et al., 1969; Fulton & Bailey, 1969; Hackett & Weisman, 1969;
Kubler-Ross, 1969; Weisman, 1972).

Weinstein and Kahn (1953) point out that denial is used more in
stroke than in cancer or heart patients, whose sense of self and adequacy
is less at stake than in stroke victims, and suggest that this may be related
to the inability to think, use language, and control feelings, which can be

as devastating even as bodily pain, limitation of function, and fear of death. This would apply in alcoholism.

Levine & Zigler (1975) extend this idea that denial is related to the psychological impact of the disability or illness. They noted that the greater the threat to the self, the greater the refusal to come to terms with the illness. They examined denial that there was any difference in the real and ideal self before and after illness, and suggested that patients could choose one of two paths in this dilemma. They could use successful denial, inflating the real image back up to match the ideal, or they could lower their aspirations for themselves as stroke victims often seemed to do. Alcoholics tend to use both of these mechanisms. The first is denial that anything is the matter. The second is noted in A.A. in the phenomenon of "settling for less," or lowering expectations or aspirations.

The brain-damaged person, who is prevented from grasping his plight because of his impaired capacity to abstract, or disordered perception of his defect, is faced only with the situation of frustration and distress when he cannot perform an expected task. Other persons with defects such as stroke, or expressive aphasia, or drunkenness in alcoholism, are faced not only with the experiences of their impaired functioning but also with its meaning for them: that they are impaired or diminished persons. They are faced with the problem of restoration of their profoundly threatened psychological integrity and self-esteem.

Physical Dependence

Addiction is the final common path which results from repeated high doses of alcohol, taken for whatever reason. The neurons acclimate to the presence of alcohol, and when it is removed, the acclimated neurons rebound to overactivity. This appears clinically as withdrawal. While drinking no longer makes the alcoholic feel good, stopping makes him sick.

Psychological dependence on alcohol increases with physiological dependence, or frank addiction. With advanced alcoholics, the clinical picture increasingly shifts toward withdrawal symptoms as producing the wish to drink; the importance of drug effect as a pharmacological defense becomes less, as does the symbolic psychodynamic meaning of the agent or the act of using it.

The alcoholic reports that he is depressed and drinks in response to this. The psychic state results from physical withdrawal and perhaps a reactive depression. Drinking does relieve the distress, but this feeling and his action bear little relation to psychological factors leading to drinking.

Episodes of drunkenness before and after development of addiction appear confusingly similar. Both the heavy drinker and the addicted one say they are tense or depressed before they drink. The fact that a profound and dramatic change in regulation or control of drinking has occurred is obscured by its subtle and gradual development, by the fact that the drinker still experiences his behavior as psychologically controlled, and by his denial. The change is not appreciated because the shift is never formally announced. Failure to grasp this central point about the regulation of drinking in alcoholism has led to all manner of mismanagement and misunderstanding of the alcoholic.

A Clinical Example

Most of the patients described in this chapter have been middle-aged or elderly people, poorly able to envision a future without alcohol—depressed, guilty, and afraid. "Mental health is not dull" (Vaillant, 1977), though mental illness and alcoholism, which has succeeded syphilis as the great mimic of emotional disorder in every form, have been absurdly romanticized. Though the patient in the following story led a life of B-movie intensity, she never for a moment was able to escape her own unhappiness and sense of futility, her feeling that nothing added up. Given her youth, her intelligence, and her extravagant good looks, given that she should have felt equipped in every way to enjoy life, we at first suspected that some emotional disorder, probably borderline personality organization, must account for her long self-destructive history.

Marcia S., aged twenty two, came to the hospital after a moderately serious overdose of pills which she took at the height of a fracas with her boyfriend, with whom she had had a long, stormy, mutually torturing relationship.

There was no history of alcohol abuse, though the patient did acknowledge social drinking and heavy recreational use of drugs. She was coherent and oriented in mental status with no evidence of thought disorder, hallucination, or delusion. Although there was no press of speech, flight of ideas, or hyperactivity, she did complain of racing thoughts and confusion. She showed rapid, somewhat tumultuous shifts in affect from tears to guilt to self-hatred to rage to anxiety. Though she complained of difficulty sleeping, mostly restless sleep with no early morning waking, she had no appetite disorder. She was admitted to the hospital for evaluation of her depression and suicidal ideation.

Her last ten years had been tumultuous and chaotic with impulsive decision making, abusive drug use, much self-destructive behavior, dropping out of school, and a long history of psychiatric treatment of both conventional and counterculture styles.

During her evaluation, because of some discrepancies and evasions, drinking history was taken several times. She persistently denied difficulty with drinking. Suddenly she left the hospital, leaving the staff a note to inform us of her decision. A champagne bottle was found in her room.

When she turned up again, it was once more with complaints of depression due to trouble with a boyfriend. As before, she was anxious and desperate, complaining of trouble marshaling her thoughts, and denying difficulty with drinking. Her drinking histories varied with different questions, and she began to acknowledge that she was drinking heavily. She still considered her symptoms to be psychological in origin. She was contemptuous and repelled by the idea that she had a drinking problem. She was too young, vividly goodlooking, and streetwise to have alcoholism.

I told her that we could talk weekly regardless of the cause of her troubles, but that we could not be sure of the cause unless she could stay sober for a while. It seemed likely, I thought, that alcohol might be causing some of her pain: alcohol alone could do this to people. If that was the case, stopping drinking would make her feel better, besides strengthening her to cope with any other problems. If there was no change, she could drink again. After six weeks of explanations about alcohol, she made several attempts to get sober. To her panic and astonishment she could not. She was addicted and had withdrawal. With considerable urging and support she signed into an alcoholism treatment facility. She stayed five days, euphoric about how much better she felt physically. She now had the answer, needed no more treatment. She remained sober for a couple of months "on her own." She felt so much better, she couldn't believe it had been as bad as all that, and she was convinced that she could control it. So she began drinking again.

Shortly after she started, she appeared for an appointment, angry and reproachful, saying "You've spoiled my drinking," but it took several more attempts to stop on her own before she was willing to return to the treatment center. This time she was slightly depressed, sad about not being able to drink but too committed, too hopeful, to need to resurrect her denial. She became actively involved in several aspects of the rehabilitation program and A.A., quit her job in a liquor store, and made some sober friends. She did not return to see me for several months.

When she came, there was no more confusion, poor judgment, lability, anxiety, or sleep failure. She was still dramatic and charming and vulnerable to depression. She was furious to have alcoholism, embarrassed, and reluctant to engineer a total revision of her former jazzy lifestyle. She was living in a stable situation, had friends, a carpentry workshop, a garden, and a boyfriend who was a sober alcoholic. She was generally "pretty comfortable with myself for the first time in ten years." This time she could clearly see that when she drank she became depressed, impulsive, confused, regressed, helpless, and prone to desperate clinging relationships. When she stopped, her mood lifted and her controls improved; when she drank again her impulsivity and depression returned. She repeated this cycle several more times before she finally stayed stably sober.

In A.A. she found people who could help her make sense out of her chaotic experience. She described her blackouts to them, and they recognized and explained them to her. Alcoholics often think they are losing their minds and seek psychiatric help, and she found that more than half the A.A. members in the group she joined had seen at least one psychiatrist, often several, who missed the diagnosis of alcoholism. One of her psychiatrists had diagnosed her blackouts as hysterical amnesia. Another had called the tremulousness and insomnia of withdrawal anxiety neurosis. Another had noted her impulsive self-destructive behavior while she was drinking and concluded that she was character-disordered. Her other four psychiatrists added borderline personality organization, major affective disorder, depressed, with hypomania, and adjustment reaction of adolescence. None diagnosed her alcoholism. These were not poorly trained psychiatrists. Most had teaching appointments at prestigious medical schools. They were not incompetent or negligent. The diagnosis of alcoholism is often elusive and difficult to make.

Ten years, seven psychiatrists, several other therapists, six diagnoses: she had been in psychiatric treatment for half of her life and no one made the diagnosis of her most life-threatening difficulty. No wonder she was skeptical when I recommended further therapy after she had established sobriety and begun healing safely from the turmoil of repeated drunkenness. That she had alcoholism does not exclude the possibility of coexisting emotional disturbance. The most dangerous disorder should be addressed first, and when the patient has been abstinent for some time, psychiatric status can more easily be assessed.

This patient's denial obscured the diagnosis. So did my reluctance to accept her having addictive alcoholism barely out of her teens. It was easy to interpret her symptoms as psychological, but in fact she was, in terms of her age, surroundings, and general personality functioning, a typical alcoholic. Her denial system, in its obduracy and ingenuity, was characteristic of the addictive phase of alcoholism, a natural and predictable set of defenses.

If this girl had continued to drink much longer, her awareness of loss of control would probably have become less accessible; as it was, her denial struck me as to some extent conscious. Even in more deteriorated alcoholics, the "self" is always present, however submerged. Whether she would not or could not acknowledge her condition, she felt as helpless at realizing she was out of control as if she were paralyzed or incontinent, humiliated and shocked, demoralized and disorganized. Alcoholism threatens the sufferer's core sense of physical integrity and mastery.

With this patient, denial served principally to protect her self-esteem. Her reaction to the diagnosis of alcoholism had more of shock and injured vanity, I think, than fear. Since she didn't "know" that she couldn't live without alcohol, she did not dread the thought of sobriety, and the diagnosis was more of an insult than a threat. She did not foresee the miseries of withdrawal: the weakness, sickness, agitation, and insomnia she would feel as her depressed central nervous system rebounded, the longing for the alcohol that had always disposed of these symptoms before, and the painful, unanesthetized guilt and humiliation that would flood her as her consciousness cleared. When she relapsed after two months, she reinvoked denial to protect her self-esteem, and extended it to protect her right to drink; but the system never became entrenched and could not prevail against her hope.

Working with Patients Who Deny Their Alcoholism

This patient is typical: with further progression, with loss of hope and damage done, denial is strengthened, varied, and extended. The alcoholic's remarkable ingenuity in protecting his drinking is well countered by A.A., whose members clearly recognize the tactics of denial, rationalization, minimization, etc., and know when to confront, emphathize, or compare from their own experience.

They explain to the alcoholic that much of his subjective distress is "part of the disease" or "from drinking." They label these painful affective states "resentments," "the poor me's," "the fears," or "the remorse." In this way they are able to acknowledge the alcoholic's psychological experience as real and painful, but do not allow it to distract from the task of getting sober. These feelings they see as potentially dangerous excuses for drinking.

Alcohol workers know the dangers of traversing the swamp of a recently drinking alcoholic's psychology without beacons and guideposts. They have chosen, by and large, to select and simplify by some sensible rules what they will focus on and what they will ignore, contradict, and play down. Therefore they tend to minimize or confront rather than explore the alcoholic's moods, dynamics, and defenses. A whole massive area of the alcoholic's personality functioning must be discounted. They leave aside large areas of the alcoholic's experience as unworkable, or worse, seductively distracting attention from the fight against drinking into blind alleys of rationalization. They simply ignore some sources of affective distress, since they know from experience that much of it will abate if the alcoholic only stays away from alcohol. They succeed in using this simplified map of alcoholic psychology because they have grasped the combined physical and psychological nature of the phenomena they are grappling with.

But in so doing they reject the content of the alcoholic's experience and psychology as though it had no meaning and interest. His special griefs are not directly addressed. Little attention is paid to the use of the denial system as a defensive construction generated to protect against fear, pain, or psychological collapse. This is practical, but makes it difficult to understand the alcoholic fully, and to follow what is happening to him as his disorder develops, or during recovery.

The failure to empathize with the entire experience of the alcoholic and respect it as having meaning may contribute to failure to *engage* the alcoholic in treatment in the first place, though it facilitates working with him once he is engaged.

Progression

Surprisingly, addiction is usually not the end of the development of alcoholism. Further processes ensue, produced by physiological dependence and acting to reinforce and sustain the drinking. Although some alcoholics progress no further and others improve, these processes in some alcoholics produce complications and the phenomenon of deterioration. This is what is known in Alcoholics Anonymous as "progression."

Deterioration

In addition to the dementia and personality impairment, alcoholism may be complicated by loss of social, legal, financial, and emotional resources. The alcoholic may lose friends, family, marriage, job. He may be arrested, lose a license or repeatedly find himself in a detoxification center or mental hospital. At a time when the alcoholic most needs the pleasures and rewards of sobriety to oppose his drinking, these are progressively demolished.

A Clinical Example

Mario P., an elderly immigrant man with a forty-year history of drinking lived with his daughter, who protected him from the consequences of his drinking. He was rarely admitted to the hospital alcohol center, and when he was admitted, he readily acknowledged that he had alcoholism but denied that there was any reason for him to stop drinking. He was guilty and worried about his daughter's anger at his alcoholism—"She's right; I'm wrong"—but he felt drinking was not bad for him, and he saw no reason to stop. At this stage he used denial only to protect his drinking, not to deny that he had alcoholism.

Suddenly he began to appear frequently at the center. This turned out to be a result of his daughter's marriage and her move to another state. He was now evicted, living on the streets, for which he was totally unprepared and unskilled, and in serious difficulties with his health.

At this point he totally denied his alcoholism, or any difficulties from it. This apparently odd shift can be understood if denial is seen in the first instance as limited to protecting his right to drink. Later he needed to defend against physical and psychological pain and danger. While he was protected by his daughter, he was willing to acknowledge that he had alcoholism. But without her to protect and cover for him, knowing the risks he ran every day, aware that his life was in ruins, he now needed a much more global and rigid kind of denial, and of two kinds.

This patient's life, like most alcoholics', was full of deprivation, danger, and suffering. He did not complain of these things, or of the losses, resulting from his alcoholism, of all the activities and undertakings which are foundations of self-respect. In this he was not unusual. Complaints of pain and demands for relief are sparse in the clinical picture of alcoholism.

Perhaps this patient was "settling for less," as A.A. puts it. Believing he has brought his pain upon himself and deserves to be punished, the alcoholic acquiesces in his deprivation. Denial, then, does not extend to cover his sense of guilt.

There may be something comparable in Goldstein's (1952) observations of advanced deterioration in brain-damaged patients. Faced with a task they cannot fulfill, they become dazed, agitated, fumbling, unfriendly, evasive, or aggressive—in Goldstein's interpretation, this is a response to inner experience, not a fear of outside danger. To get rid of their anxiety, such patients withdraw to diminish exposure to threatening situations, and stay alone, liking the familiar, obsessively orderly, upset by any change (just as this patient lived unobtrusively with his daughter).

Deterioration produces more excessive emotional compensatory devices. Goldstein mentioned frequent paranoia and megalomania. These "total" compensations bring to mind the total denial of another patient.

Enoch T., a middle-aged man who had been unable to complete first grade, was brought by the police to the detoxification center. He said they had picked him up after he had drunk "one or two beers," and that they picked on him because he was a "retard." He told us he worked regularly in a sheltered workshop, and showed us how he carefully carried out the trash and lined up the chairs in the cafeteria. He liked to put them all in a row; when he took too long, they yelled at him. A lot of people picked on him. He occasionally drank one or two beers but "never hard stuff. It makes you crazy like them in there [pointing to the ward]. They say they drink and can't stop."

Perhaps because "them in there" were tremulous, sick, and helpless and we were reluctant to place this earnest innocent among them, and surely because of our own wish to believe that he had only one tragic problem instead of two, we made a diagnosis of intellectual retardation and failed to make one of alcoholism. He sat quietly in a corner, knees pressed together, leafing through a picture magazine, until we could reach his family. They informed us that he had been a chronic unemployed street alcoholic for thirty years, in addition to being retarded, and that when he drank he often fought with policemen. When we asked him about this, he grinned slyly and said he guessed his family might be wrong.

This patient's total disavowal of his miserable circumstances need not be attributed to his retardation. I have seen blanket denial of equal extent among addicted alcoholics of average and above-average intelligence. It is understandable as a response to alcoholism as a catastrophic experience—terrible losses, deprivations, the sense of being at hazard, shame and the certainty one can never atone, the ruin of self-esteem, the utter loss of hope. The alcoholic's circumstances are now wholly traumatic, and he must make a desperate effort to create a psychology for emotional survival. Denial under these conditions is a primitive defense invoked to stave off psychological collapse.

Whatever the patient's original psychopathology, most alcoholics use these psychological mechanisms. If the disease progresses, patients with diverse character styles become more and more alike. Most advanced alcoholics come to resemble each other, and demonstrate what is called "the alcoholic personality."

Treatment

Because denial protects against unbearable pain, no one using it will give it up without a struggle, and without being offered something to take its place. Expecting it to disappear on request is like expecting a psychotic to stop hearing voices when one informs him that they are not real.

If a person is to be expected to relinquish his denial, or some of it, and become accessible to treatment, several things must happen.

Denial will give way when the pain increases so massively that the defense breaks down and pain and depression rush in. It is not coincidental that so many alcoholics get sober at a time of despair, losing a spouse or a job for example. This is called ''hitting bottom.'' The internal shift that takes place when denial gives way is called in A.A. a spiritual awakening.

Alternatively a person may give denial up if the pain against which it protects decreases, or he can find another way to cope with and tolerate the pain. Something must be offered to decrease the pain, such as hope. The crucial transactions which launch an alcoholic toward sobriety include an intervention in, and revision of, the denial system and an attack on despair, which allows the alcoholic to begin to relinquish some of his denial.

The therapeutic approach in all these cases emphasizes the modification of the denial system, by two techniques. It is most effective to empathize with the pain that generated the defense, and to relieve the pain by acknowledging it, offering help, instilling hope, and contradicting despair. When the pain decreases, the defense mechanism can be abandoned. In addition, denial of the dangers of drinking must be confronted, and the patient's need for safety stressed.

Getting sober means facing the full impact of one's pain while renouncing the central means to cope one has learned to use. One interrupts, moreover, a whole way of life, a complete set of well-learned habits that include a way of perceiving, thinking, and feeling. One frustrates intense craving and rejects what may have been the prime mover of one's existence.

Some alcoholics will go hungry and expose themselves to extreme danger in order to drink. To stop is, for them, a loss comparable to never eating again, and a violation of the only form of self-preservation they know. Such alcoholics are unable to imagine what life would be like without alcohol, profoundly dependent on the knowledge that alcohol is accessible, and terrified of its loss.

Treatment of alcoholism hurts. One can only applaud the courage of those alcoholics who recover on their own, untreated, and of those who come voluntarily for help—and then use it. Most alcoholics who come to treatment facilities are coerced there, or at least persuaded, and most come with a negative attitude. Addicted drinkers cannot comprehend the idea that by taking systematic steps it is straightforwardly possible to get free of the problem. Many have experienced their failure at controlled drinking as inexplicable, perhaps as punishment for fundamental badness. Their repeated failures, along with neurological impairment, have made them feel helpless, engendering regression and giving up. No longer grasping the possibility of recovery, they cannot see that alcoholism is an understandable, treatable disease resulting from a complex pathological process.

Once detoxification is past, the mood of the newly sober alcoholic will depend on many factors. He may be elated by the relief from the chemical and reactive depression, by recovery of self-esteem from being able to stop, and by relief from the climate of terror which resulted from his repeated experience of loss of control. But he may also have a major depression in reaction to the loss of the alcohol, just as some obese people become depressed when beginning a diet, or in reaction to confronting the reality of the consequences of his drinking, staring back into the ruin of his life, sometimes for the first time. No one could be expected easily to face the difficulties left by many years of drinking, so he will still need defenses such as denial to help him with the pain at least until such time as he has built a more mature structure of sheltering defenses in his new life. He will relinquish his defenses slowly as he works through and integrates his losses and reestablishes self-esteem. He may continue to need denial to help him with stigma, shame, and humiliation from his new conscious acknowledgment of his alcohol problem. He is very likely to continue to deny his alcoholism publicly as a protection against stigma from peers and employers, often real though sometimes exaggerated.

A.A. wisely permits this, expecting the recovering alcoholic to be able to "admit" his alcohol problem only after some work against denial, and only much later to "accept" it, that is, to have dealt with the pain entailed, to have worked through and undone enough to diminish pain, fear, and shame, and to be able to face and tolerate the feelings directly.

Relapse

The use of denial in relation to the relapse is an intriguing phenomenon. When the person has been sober but is moving toward a relapse, he is faced with a difficult psychological problem. From whatever sources, possibly biological, possibly social, possibly from reasons described by learning and conditioning theory, or as a symptom, the impulse to drink is upon him (Bandura, 1969). It drives and pressures him. Perhaps he has maintained his sobriety out of a fantasy that good behavior would bring some special rewards, which he now recognizes, with disappointment and anger, are not forthcoming. Perhaps he is depressed or in other distress of the same nature as generated his early symptomatic use of alcohol. Perhaps he is longing and wishing to be a normal person, who is allowed the pleasures of moderate drinking, while he hates the idea that he is an outsider, excluded. Perhaps he is disappointed and angry with the people who have been helping him with his controls. He is so sensitive, and they are, after all, only human. When his feelings are hurt, he turns away from them and yearns to drink. Most often, movement toward relapse is unconsciously motivated, and the reasons the person gives are rationalizations.

The difficulty that faces him is that the impulse that besets him is forbidden. He knows he must not drink. Old-fashioned conflict theory may help us understand what happens.

He visualizes the idea of drinking in his mind. It is deeply seductive, for he knows that it will relieve his sickness, and, at the same time, it is forbidden. He experiences a choice between deprivation, which is equated with behaving well, and relief, or gratification, which is equated with being bad, or doing the forbidden. As in neurotic conflict the impulse, because it is forbidden, is to some extent kept out of awareness by repression and denial, while the prohibitions are more often conscious. He begins a struggle with his superego, ego ideal, ego, inner controls, self-respect, and self-preservation, all of which oppose his drinking, on the one hand, and the drive to drink, on the other. One must remember that he is regressed, mildly confused, and in despair, so these personality agencies are not functioning very well. This is where the denial system is called into operation. He will not be able to obey the drive to drink until he can quell the forces of mature personality functioning. So he must erect a whole castle of protections and supports around the idea of drinking. This is an example of denial as an agent of wish fulfillment.

Usually the first line of defense in this dilemma is to repress and deny the impulse, intensify reaction formation, and invoke added controls such as increased attendance at A.A. meetings. If these efforts are successful, the impulse will remain in check and the person will remain sober. Every recovering alcoholic has variations on this struggle thousands of times in his establishment of sobriety. If he loses one struggle once, he is likely to relapse.

Although the impulse is under cover and in check, it may continue to press for release and expression in action. The energy driving toward the expression of the impulse will align itself with every element of the personality or psychology which comes to hand to use as a weapon against the controls and prohibitions that block it. What happens is that the denial system used before to protect drinking is resuscitated to permit it again. In order for drinking to be permitted, the ego and superego forces against it must be met and mastered. In order to permit drinking, which is dangerous, the signal anxiety alerting the ego must be put aside. Superego prohibitions must be silenced, and the danger of failure to meet the ego ideal, with resulting loss of self-esteem and depression, must be prevented. All these ends are achieved by regeneration of the denial system. If the person denies that he is alcoholic, that there is a disorder in his ability to use alcohol moderately, the ego alert system saying that drinking is dangerous will be baffled by the negation "I can drink safely," the superego will be silenced, since social drinking is permitted and only alcoholics are prohibited from drinking, and self-esteem will be safe, since the ego ideal allows social drinking. The final technique permitting the alcoholic to pick up a drink is disavowal of the impulse by projecting blame for it around himself, onto what A.A. lumps together as "people, places, and things."

In A.A. this phenomenon, called "budding" (building up to a drink) or "stinking thinking," is well known, and there are clear safeguards against it, usually in the form of increased controls, including association with people who will recognize the purpose of the perversion of the defense system to allow drinking and who will confront the denial and rationalizations and empathize with the feelings.

Once the denial system has permitted the discharge of the impulse into action, a relapse usually occurs. Then denial will need to be retained as a facilitator of drinking while the alcoholism reestablishes itself, then as a protector of the drinking, and again to protect against all the kinds of pain produced by the alcoholism, as a defense against despair, shame, fear, pain, and loss.

When the person gets sober again, denial ebbs away, as it did when sobriety was first established, possibly faster because of learning from previous sobriety, because it is no longer needed. (See case on p. 84.)

To help the alcoholic out of such a complicated impasse, we have to grasp the relentlessness of the impulse to drink. It may be a long time before the recovering alcoholic can concentrate on anything else. Whatever its sources—and it helps to remember how various they can be—the drive does not rest. Like hunger or thirst it may abate, but eventually reasserts itself. No one, probably, can understand it who has not felt it. This is one great strength of A.A., that all its members have been there too. The craving for alcohol is comparable in intensity and intractability with an instinct. We can only measure it by its results.

No one claims that all recovered alcoholics can be restored to full functioning. The knowledge of time wasted must alone be a source of depression. Reparative, and then later restorative, efforts can be made at undoing the damage done, as in A.A.'s twelfth step, in which the recovered alcoholic actively helps to retrieve and reeducate other sufferers.

Whether or not the original personality predisposed him to drinking, the recovered alcoholic is not the person he was. He may be a better one, but in any case his experiences have affected him. He may need help with staying sober, and he will need help with integrating his experience.

Clinicians may choose not to work intensively with people with alcoholism, but must encounter alcoholics in their work. They should be able to make the diagnosis, confront the alcoholic, and refer the patient for treatment with some comfort, tact, and respect. The alcoholic's experience is so alien to the ordinary person that people often belittle it, not realizing that it is overwhelming to the sufferer.

The development of physiological dependence is imperceptible to the alcoholic, and often to the clinician; both of them are likely to see the excessive drinking as psychologically driven. Both physical and psychological pressures to drink may be present at once. When the person drinks heavily but not alcoholically, he may need clarification, controls, and sanctions, or treatment for the underlying psychological or social problem. When he is alcoholic, he needs an external intervention, medical treatment, often structure, support, and help with controls, and then reeducation, help with reintegrating his life and relearning, and psychological work to repair the damage done by the alcoholism.

When the phase of alcoholism is not correctly identified, the temporary balance between physical and psychological factors is easily misassessed, and the constantly metamorphosing denial system may be approached from the wrong side. Different modes of treatment have more to offer at different phases. While the clinician's first object is to get the patient sober and keep him that way until the chemical is no longer active in his system, the patient may need still further support before he is able to transcend and master his problem.

It is not enough to breach the denial system. Unless its workings and its time course are understood, intervention may be futile. This time course is contrapuntal to the phases of alcoholism and recovery. One cannot overstate the value of the denial system to the alcoholic, or the protean and yet tenacious obstacle it presents to the clinician. It provokes the frustration and contempt of many caregivers; it does much to explain the confusion and ambivalence of political bodies asked to support alcoholism treatment programs. Worst of all, it invites the despairing collusion of too many families, employers, and therapists.

Unless the denial system is successfully breached, and the physical impact of alcoholism understood, efforts to intervene with the alcoholic will repeatedly founder. In addition, work with alcoholics will be unpleasant and bewildering, dominated by magical thinking and hunches and wishes. Helpers will resort to scare tactics, coercion, indulgence, beseeching, and avoidance. It will be impossible to devise a clear program for the patient's recovery, and the result will be needless relapses and pain, frustration, inefficiency, and almost inevitable treatment failure.

Alcoholics are commonly thought to be the most unrewarding of all patients. I have not found them so. Increasing awareness that alcoholics can recover has been an encouragement. Despair blocks recovery, but recovery is possible, with hope and skill.

Conclusion

The goal of this chapter has been to describe the subjective world of the alcoholic in tandem with his clinical presentation and the psychological functions of denial during progression, recovery, and relapse. Perhaps such concepts will make it easier to develop treatment approaches elegantly fitted to the needs of the individual alcoholic, his stage of development, the nature of his restitutive denial, and its modifications by previous treatment.

Alcohol Addiction: Toward a More Comprehensive Definition*

Norman E. Zinberg

The use of alcohol in the United States is more significant and wide-spread than most Americans admit. The excessive use of alcohol, or alcoholism, is one of the most prevalent and difficult problems facing our society and our clinicians. Various groups of professionals in the field— physicians, psychiatrists, psychologists, epidemiologists, social workers, lawyers—see this problem from their own perspective and base their treatment strategies on that perspective. So far the experts have neither achieved a common definition of alcoholism nor constructed a comprehensive model that describes in a unified way the etiology (causes), motivation, and operation of problem drinking. Each of these professional groups takes only a partial view of this phenomenon, and all of them overlook the role which the social setting—the drinker's family, peer group, and society—plays in the development and perpetuation of his problem. Although no cure for alcoholism has been discovered, the most successful treatment is provided by Alcoholics Anonymous, which requires complete abstinence. That the drinker's social setting is an essen-

*Kathleen M. Fraser's research for this chapter requires acknowledgment beyond what is usual, for without her assistance the work could not have been done.

tial factor is shown by A.A.'s insistence that the alcoholic join its community and obey its social sanctions and rituals.

This chapter, which focuses on the etiology and treatment of problem drinking, will present a comprehensive or multivariate interpretation of alcoholism based on a combination of the three major current models and including the alcoholic's social setting. Case studies will illustrate the clinician's need for this comprehensive approach in order to understand and treat effectively each individual who wants to work on the problem.

Importance of Alcohol in the American Culture

In psychological circles Freud's famous comment that the two most important investments of human energy are "to love and to work" remains unchallenged. Our preoccupation with these two activities, sex and the capacity to gain self-esteem and economic viability through work, is obvious. Of the three other major human concerns not mentioned by Freud—food, intoxicants, and religion—only religion is consciously accepted as a vital concern on a par with love and work; but in our increasingly secularized culture, religion consumes far less psychic energy than either eating or drinking. Yet for some obscure moral reason dating back to our Puritan or Victorian or temperance-movement ancestors, our preoccupation with eating and drinking is minimized by society and suppressed by the individual.

A preoccupation with food is of course justifiable as necessary for survival. Sometimes this preoccupation may even develop into an art. But the extent to which we think about, plan, anticipate, or dread eating is rarely discussed openly. And in this culture the extent of interest in intoxicants, principally alcohol, is acknowledged even less than the interest in food. We play down the prevalent daily interest in alcohol by narrowly focusing attention on the alcoholic, the problem drinker, the alcohol addict—in other words, the person in trouble because of alcohol. By concentrating thus on the troubled alcohol user, most Americans suppress their constant need to make socially important decisions about whether to drink, when to drink, with whom to drink, and how much to drink.

Nevertheless, the issue of alcohol use affects us all. Demography suggests that only a fraction of drinkers are alcoholics, but to conclude from population statistics that the American culture is comfortable with alcohol is to ignore the substantial role that this drug plays in the lives of both social drinkers and abstainers.

Most of us drink. Even those of us who do not use what the colonists called "God's gifte to Man" (Kobler, 1973; Krout, 1925) and what the temperance movement dubbed "Demon Rum" are forced to give frequent if not daily consideration to the issue of alcohol consumption. Although both nondrinkers and cocktail-party habitués would protest if it were suggested that abstinence or social drinking gives them difficulty, the use or nonuse of the "neutral spirit" (Roueché, 1960) involves more than an initial postadolescent decision to drink or not to drink.

The "drink or abstain" decision is made not once but thousands of times in a lifetime. It is in fact a continuum of decisions complicated by the ubiquity of alcohol in this culture and the ambiguous mores surrounding its use. Even for the abstainer, who has presumably made a "once and for all" decision about alcohol, life presents numerous social and business occasions on which he is required to defy what amounts to a social convention, on which it would be easier to accept a drink, and on which nondrinkers and ex-drinkers alike must explain why alcohol is an issue in their lives. For the drinker, the questions of when, how much, and with whom to drink constantly present themselves and require energy-consuming decisions. For instance, while the drinker knows that a six-pack of beer is acceptable at a noontime football game in October, he is less certain how many beers are permissible at a company picnic on a July morning, or at a cocktail party on the boss's boat, or with a client at lunchtime.

Like sex, work, religion, and food, the daily behavioral issue of alcohol consumption is a matter of personal decision influenced by the individual's constitution and history and by the dictates of the immediate social context. Coping with it is a task made difficult not only by the appeal of the drink at hand but by the ambiguities of the social setting. Maddox has suggested that "Americans drink with a certain sadness" (1970), a sadness probably rooted in their culturally derived ambivalence toward the social and individual character of drinking. This cultural ambivalence has been forged and reforged during each historical period, each social and economic upheaval, and each era of immigrant assimilation (Sinclair, 1962). The resulting negation of alcohol use has led to a curious worship of abstinence, which is little practiced and, when practiced, little respected. Hellman (1975) discusses this lack of respect for actual abstinent behavior which, when combined with the worship of abstinence, results in the laws regulating alcohol consumption forming a crazy-quilt pattern that would not be tolerated in any other area of jurisprudence. These laws are accepted because of the unspoken moral dictum that we really should not be using alcohol at all. Hellman goes on to demonstrate conclusively that this would not be tolerated in any other area of jurisprudence. This abstinence orientation has made it difficult to acknowledge the advantages inherent in the use of intoxicants and has mistakenly set up the abstainer as a model of moral strength. This attitude has affected our treatment strategies, spread confusion about what we want to prevent, and led to unfortunate theoretical oversimplifications concerning the causes of drinking.

Definitions of Alcoholism

The refusal to recognize the widespread interest in alcohol in the United States may be a key factor in the frequent failure of clinicians to distinguish between two basically different types of alcohol users: the heavy drinker who will never become an alcoholic and the problem drinker who is actually in an early phase of alcoholism. Clinicians must have a clear understanding of what alcoholism is in order to tell the difference between these two types of drinkers.

Because the professional community has not been able to reach agreement on such a definition, clinicians are faced, as Mark Keller points out in a concise and brilliant article (1962), with at least five definitions proposed by experts from as many different fields: medicine; pharmacology; the behavioral sciences; medicine, psychiatry, and psychology combined; and learning theory. Each definition expresses only the view of the field from which it originates.

Whereas the old-fashioned medical view defines alcoholism as "a disease caused by chronic excessive drinking" (Keller, 1973), pharmacology classifies it as a drug addiction marked by the need to increase doses to produce the desired effect and by a withdrawal syndrome if alcohol is not available.

The behavioral definition describes alcoholism as a disease of unknown cause without recognizable anatomical signs, manifested by addiction or dependence on alcohol. The combined psychological, psychiatric, and medical definition states that alcoholism may be a disease in its own right or the symptom of another underlying, possibly psychological disease; in the first case it is in itself a chronic and usually progressive illness, while in the second case it is symptomatic of an underlying psychological or physical disorder characterized by (1) dependence on alcohol for the relief of psychological or physical distress or for the gratification resulting from intoxication, and (2) the consumption of alcoholic beverages in sufficient quantities and with sufficient consistency to cause physical, mental, social, or economic disability. Finally, the definition based on learning theory describes alcoholism as a learned (or conditioned) dependence upon (or addiction to) alcohol that irresistibly activates drinking behavior whenever a critical or internal or environmental stimulus (or cue) presents itself (Keller, 1973).

As Mark Keller makes clear, each of these five definitions has its limitations as well as its merits. Reflecting the view of its field of origin, each fails to satisfy the needs of all the other experts concerned with alcohol problems, such as the epidemiologist, the sociologist, and the lawyer. Epidemiologists, who need to identify whole populations that are not available for individual examination, must rely on quantity-frequency measures and on statistical reports of other injurious conditions known to be alcohol-related. Sociologists need to identify drinkers whose behavior deviates sufficiently from the customary social or dietary use of alcohol in the drinker's community to be considered a problem. Thus they are interested in the drinker's arrest rate, hospitalization, and clinical diagnosis, in whether he has defined himself as a deviant by joining A.A., and in how he is viewed by the community. Lawyers have still other needs: to judge whether an individual under the influence of alcohol is a threat to the public welfare and to decide whether he is a danger to the health, welfare, and competence of himself and others.

Because it deals with the causes and treatment of alcoholism, this chapter is more concerned with the needs of the clinician than with those of the other professionals in the field. From the clinician's point of view, these five rather superficial definitions leave much to be desired. For one thing, they do not distinguish between genuine alcoholism on the one hand and heavy drinking on the other, for they fail to take into account the duration and extent of drinking. That omission becomes particularly significant in relation to drinkers who have severe but time-limited bouts with alcohol. While such bouts, accompanied by job loss and auto accidents, certainly are indications of a serious disturbance, it is doubtful whether they can be classified as alcoholism if they are indeed time-limited and nonrecurrent. This same ambiguity poses a problem even for those who do not regard alcoholism as a disease in its own right, but rather as the symptom of an underlying psychological disorder.

The five definitions have still other limitations for the clinician. The medical view, which simply regards alcoholism as a disease that results from drinking, does not attempt to spell out precursors, factors of causal significance, or degree. Similarly, the pharmacological definition fails to account for the many drinkers who either never show withdrawal symptoms or do so inconsistently, sometimes severely and sometimes not at all. (It must be remembered that tolerance to alcohol does not continue to develop until it approaches the lethal dose, as in the case of the opiates; at various stages of drinking there may in fact be an actual decrease in tolerance.) The strict behavioral view of alcoholism as an addiction or dependency suffers from the existence of individual differences in the signs and symptoms that follow large intakes of alcohol. The more comprehensive medical-psychological definition gives disablement of some kind as evidence of alcoholism, but some extremely heavy drinkers do not show any of the classical disabilities. Moreover, by not referring to a genetic component, this definition excludes the possibility of genetic or genetotrophic causal factors. Learning theorists have not been able to prove that drinking is actually triggered by specific stimuli or cues because often the drinking is either continuous or too erratic to contribute validity to the idea that a specific stimulus operates in a specific situation. In addition, the tendency to rely on the drinker's own assessment of the extent of his problem is far from helpful: some genuine alcoholics deny that they are alcoholics and prefer to be seen as neurotics, while some neurotics prefer to attribute their responses to what is essentially a nondestructive intake of alcohol.

In our society, where the importance of alcohol use is underestimated and there is no agreement on a common definition of alcoholism, it is not surprising that each professional group continues to cling to the definition that suits its particular purpose. But something beyond a series of disparate definitions is needed to illuminate the causes of alcoholism and enable clinicians to treat it successfully. During the past thirty years or so valuable insights have come from three views or models of alcoholism: the modern medical and biomedical, the genetic or genetotrophic, and the psychosocial. These models go beyond simple definitions, beyond what alcoholism "is," and provide comprehensive views that include also the causes or motivational factors (etiology), the process through which the phenomenon operates, and the types of treatment that are likely to be most effective in coping with it.

Three Models of Alcoholism

Medical and biomedical.   The medical model is made up of three components: an infectious or toxic agent, a host, and a specific degenerative response resulting from the interaction of agent and host. This model has a long history, beginning with the medical definition of alcoholism already discussed. Since about 1800, prolonged drunkenness has been recognized as an "odious disease," to use Benjamin Rush's term (Kobler, 1973). From then until 1950, the physician's view was made up of rough generalizations expressing his medical and moral distaste for alcoholism. E. M. Jellinek, acting at the behest of the World Health Organization, took these generalizations and defined alcoholism as a specific medical entity (Jellinek, 1960; Kobler, 1973). His early formulations envisaged three phases of development: (1) "symptomatic drinking," which preceded the development of the disease; (2) "addictive drinking," in which some irreversible change took place which might have a physical basis, possibly of a constitutional nature, and which marked the onset of the disease; and (3) the "organic complications" phase. The elusive semantic problems inherent in Jellinek's formulation have plagued the field ever since, raising the unanswerable question "Is the disease the result of drinking or its cause?"

If it were possible to define alcoholism as the exclusive result of the interaction between a toxic agent (alcohol) and a human host, there would be no problem. But such a simplistic view of interaction ignores both the genetic and psychosocial aspects of the disease. It does not make clear that defects of a constitutional and a psychological nature—a preexisting disability, a virtual allergy, or a preexisting personality disturbance—are diseases in their own right rather than only part of the "disease" of alcoholism. Nor does it take account of the fact that changes in the social setting—the mores, values, and attitudes of the larger culture or of smaller social groups—crucially affect the extent of alcoholism as well as its development in particular individuals.

In the 1960s the advent of Antabuse (disulfiram) buttressed the validity of the medical model. Here was a genuine treatment, a way to neutralize the toxic agent. Now a drug could be prescribed, just as penicillin could be prescribed for conditions caused by the pneumonia bacteria, although obviously the mechanisms were vastly different.

In some cases the prescribing of Antabuse was done in the same strict medical sense. Generally, however, motivating the host (the drinker) to take medicine to neutralize the agent (alcohol) responsible for his "disease" proved a formidable task, whereas pneumonia patients rarely refused the use of penicillin as an antidote to their disease. Thus, while Antabuse could be a useful adjunct to the treatment of an alcoholic personally committed to recovery, it could not usually be the key treatment factor. Persuading the alcoholic to take a stand against his wishes to drink remained the crucial aspect of any treatment and did not easily fit the strict medical model.

The search for a valid medical-disease model has gradually taken a new direction, shifting to the biomedical study of physiology in the hope that some defect in the body's way of handling alcohol can be shown to be the cause of alcoholism. Here, too, however, the same question must be asked: "Is the disease the result of drinking or its cause?" Because most biomedical studies have been done on animals or humans who have ingested excessive quantities of alcohol, it is not clear whether the findings are innate or acquired.

The physiological mechanisms that might result in the development of alcohol dependency have been widely studied. Joseph Cochin (1966) of Boston University, for one, has posited four possible mechanisms: (1) altered metabolic disposal of the drug (alcohol); (2) blockade of the drug from its usual active site; (3) occupation and saturation of the site by the drug; (4) cellular adaptation to the drug resulting from biochemical transformation of the metabolic activity of the cell. All these mechanisms refer to an alteration in cellular or site activity which results in functional impairment when the drug is not used. Goldstein and Goldstein (1961), to take another example, have formulated an extremely complex hypothesis regarding the possibility of the enzyme system which regulates in inverse ratio its product. The drug inhibits the enzyme system so that less product is formed, thus permitting the formation of greater amounts of the enzyme whose activity is balanced by the inhibitory effect of the alcohol. If alcohol is removed, the enzyme effect is unchecked and a withdrawal syndrome results. Unfortunately, not Cochin's or the Goldsteins' or any other attempt to account for the acknowledged physical dependency on alcohol specifies whether what happens to the body is exclusively the result of alcohol intake or whether it expresses preexisting potentialities. The same conundrum is inherent in the other well-known biochemical effects of alcohol, such as those occurring on the release of catecholamine or indoleamine.

The difficulty in constructing a biomedical model for the development of alcoholism is partly due to the existence of great individual differences in both the body's handling of alcohol and the effect of long-term excessive intake. It also stems from the inherent toxicity of alcohol, as indicated by the limited development of alcohol tolerance, which is likely to cause severe physiological changes.

So far the medical-disease concept has been most useful to Alcoholics Anonymous. A.A. bypasses the semantic problems of the medical definition and uses the disease concept of alcoholism as the cornerstone of its program, thereby alleviating the dreadful guilt of the alcoholic. By calling attention to his helplessness in the face of this disease, A.A. modifies his guilt and justifies the need to call on a higher power for help in the struggle for sobriety. Even this loose symbolic notion of disease has aroused controversy, however. Keller (1973) points out that calling alcoholism a disease gives the alcoholic an excuse for his drunkenness, reinforces his dependence, and shifts responsibility to the medical profession, which is usually unable to deal with the condition.

A.A. pays little attention to the question of whether the "disease" precedes alcoholism or, as Jellinek suggests (1960), results from the excessive drinking. The A.A. disease concept is purely heuristic, intended to exemplify the helplessness over drinking experienced by the alcoholic and to separate attempts to work with the uncontrolled alcoholic as he is—lost, alone, in poor health—from attempts to work with him by trying to reconstruct those issues—medical, psychological, or social— that may be instrumental in his being as he is. According to the A.A. credo, the alcoholic must be worked with as he is. While there is some evidence that this is clinically effective when working with the long-term deteriorated drinker, the A.A. concept of disease should not be confused with the more specific strict medical models described by Cochin (1966) or by Goldstein and Goldstein (1961). An important emphasis in this chapter is to point out that the effectiveness of A.A. for its members may vary according to how the condition of alcoholism is defined. Elsewhere we (Zinberg & Fraser, 1979) have considered whether the psychological factors that enable A.A. to be successful with hard-core alcoholics may be detrimental to efforts toward prevention of alcoholism or to work with drinkers who are in early stages of difficulty.

Genetic and genetotrophic.   The genetic model, which bases the development of alcoholism on some specific birth defect, is closely related to the medical or physiological model. It simply shifts the "disease" or the defect in functioning that prepared the way for alcoholism back to an earlier time in the development of the individual. In 1974 E. M. Pattison suggested that ideological factors (such as racial discrimination) rather than scientific concerns accounted for the continued focus on physiological theories, particularly on the notion of the possible genetic factors. This emphasis on being inherently defective is congruent with the alcoholic's own preoccupation that his inability to drink successfully represents some sort of inherent defect. In positing an underlying biological defect as the cause of alcoholism, these theories are consistent with the disease model, justifying medical intervention, providing an effective defense rationale for those who suffer from the condition (e.g., "I have an illness"), and, most important of all, holding out the promise of a discoverable medical cure.

One of the first genetic theorists was R. J. Williams, who in 1947 approached the possibility of an inherent metabolic defect by considering individuals whose metabolic makeup dictated the consumption of certain nutrients in amounts far in excess of the quantities present in a "normal" diet. Assuming that the consumption of alcohol alleviated symptoms of deficiency but did not provide needed nutrients, he hypothesized the existence of an alcoholic "vicious cycle" resulting from the afflicted individual's attempt to relieve unpleasant symptoms with increasing amounts of alcohol, which in turn led to alcohol addiction without relieving the original deficiency. Williams's theory of alcoholism, as well as similar theories about the nutritional use of alcohol by individuals with aberrant metabolism (Williams, 1959), has been refuted empirically by a number of experimenters (Lester, 1960; Mardones, 1951; Popham, 1947; Randolph, 1956).

Another area which for a time offered hope of finding a genetic root for alcoholism was endocrine dysfunction. Hypoglycemia, for example, was cited as a symptom from which alcohol could offer temporary relief by raising the level of blood sugar. Long-term dependence upon alcohol was also seen as overmedication by the individual who ingested progressively larger amounts to cope with the (reverse) effects of alcohol itself. There is a famous Orson Welles movie (*Touch of Evil*, 1958) in which he, large as a mountain, continuously munches on candy bars. When Marlene Dietrich, who remembers him in his younger, more handsome days, says, "You better lay off the candy bars," Welles replies, "Better than the hooch." Although that passage could be interpreted by proponents of psychological theories as an indication of the need for oral gratification, it underscores how strong in the popular imagination is the notion that some form of nutriment, alcohol or a replacement, may be needed to quell powerful inborn fires. Similar reasoning led C. P. Richter in 1956 to report an association between alcoholism and congenital hypothyroidism. Little empirical evidence has emerged, however, to support the endocrine dysfunction point of view.

Until recently, in spite of the appeal of the genetic model to some students of alcoholism, its validity, as Pattison pointed out, seemed to rest on an ideological rather than a scientific basis. In fact, the effort to attribute the frequency of alcoholism among American Indians to a genetic rather than a psychosocial component was attacked as frank racism: just one more way of characterizing that minority group as inherently defective. In 1973, however, as a result of the tenacity of investigators and superb record keeping by the Danish government, evidence emerged which indicates that there is indeed a propensity for alcoholism in some individuals and some families that cannot be explained on a psychosocial basis (Goodwin & Guze, 1974; Goodwin et al., 1973; Schuckit et al., 1972).

The basic study, begun in the 1940s, was made of Danish twins, one of whom was adopted and the other raised by the birth family. This and other carefully controlled studies that followed show that children of alcoholic heritage are more likely to exhibit alcoholism than are children whose adoptive parents are alcoholic. That is, children whose birth families show alcoholism will develop alcoholism more readily when placed with families that have no alcoholism than will children whose birth families do not show alcoholism. And conversely, children whose birth families do not show alcoholism are less likely to develop alcoholism when adopted into alcoholic families than are children who are both born and raised in alcoholic families.

In addition, there are other studies which, taken separately, do not provide conclusive evidence for a genetic link in certain cases of alcoholism, but which, in combination, do provide considerable support for it. McLearn and Rodgers (1959) and Rodgers (1966) found and explored an inherited preference for alcohol in certain strains of mice. Wolff (1972) discovered that the "flushing" response to alcohol in certain human racial strains probably indicates an inborn response. Cruz-Coke (1964) and Camps and Dodd (1967) documented the association between alcoholism and assumed inherited characteristics ("genetic markers"), while Winokur et al. (1970) were able to provide clear documentation of alcoholism in certain families.

Although the Danish twin studies and the other studies just mentioned indicate strongly that a genetic factor exists in certain cases of alcoholism, the available statistical correlations have been developed from a very small fraction of the total number of alcoholics. Thus they do not show that all cases or even most cases of alcoholism have a genetic component. Moreover, little or no evidence exists concerning the mechanisms of the inheritance of susceptibility to alcohol addiction. In 1945 E. M. Jellinek characterized the problem of the role of genetics as a question of the interplay of social and cultural factors with an inherited "breeding ground" for alcoholic behaviors and illnesses. But researchers since that time have been able to add only limited empirical data to his theoretical suggestion.

Psychosocial.   Most of the work done on the etiology and treatment of alcoholism during the past thirty years or so has centered on the psychosocial model. This is an enormous area, including all the psychological, social, and economic causes and components of problem drinking. It is the field studied not only by the psychologist and psychiatrist but by the social historian, anthropologist, sociologist, and economist. It includes such topics as (1) the vulnerability of particular personality types and the influence of child-rearing patterns; the differing attitudes and customs surrounding alcohol use (2) in America at different historical periods, (3) in primitive cultures, and (4) in different ethnic groups; and (5) the impact of widely varying economic circumstances.

First, the psychological theory that difficulty in handling alcohol is rooted in the personality of the individual and based on conflicts and deprivations experienced in his early relationships with his parents or significant others began to take hold very shortly after Sigmund Freud developed the theory of psychoanalysis. Alcoholism was, after all, a profound and obvious behavioral disorder which brought great pain to the sufferer, to those around him, and even to his society. Any theory purporting to understand the aberrations of the human psyche could hardly ignore it. And the ability of this powerful and comprehensive theory to explain so many things that had formerly been seen as vices, curses, or physiological disturbances caused by long-buried, unbearable affects within the individual himself led to high hopes that psychoanalysis would illuminate the mysteries of alcoholism.

At first sight, the problem of alcoholism seemed transparent to the psychoanalytic theorist. The drunk's attachment to a fluid container, his inability or unwillingness to care for himself, and his unending self-castigation when sober seemed the very epitome of unresolved oral wishes. To conceptualize those symptoms in terms of an early unresolved attachment to the mother and her breast, to see the unwillingness to care for oneself as the expression of a wish to return to infancy, and to interpret the ensuing depression as a sense of inner emptiness and a guilt about the greedy wish to fill it fitted neatly into the early discovery of the "id" with its unconscious wishes and concerns.

People with such unresolved oral wishes do indeed exist, and some of them become alcoholics. And there are accounts of the successful treatment of such people by psychoanalysis or by the various allied dynamic psychotherapeutic techniques. As the studies of alcohol use progressed, however, it became increasingly clear that in certain individuals the phenomenon was far too complex to be explained solely through early conflicts. Also, the direct psychiatric treatment of alcoholics was not successful enough to generate much confidence in that approach. But most sophisticated psychologists continued to believe that certain early child-rearing experiences, relationships to key figures, or early deprivations might become a "breeding ground," or area of potential vulnerability, in an individual if other alcoholism-inducing social and psychological circumstances were also present.

Second, as for the social and cultural aspects of the psychosocial model, we described in an earlier paper (Zinberg & Fraser, 1979) the differing social attitudes toward alcohol use that characterized five main periods of American history: the colonial period, the Revolutionary and post-Revolutionary era, the nineteenth century, the prohibition era, and the period after repeal.

The American colonists, who firmly believed in the medical and spiritual benefits of regular drinking, virtually soaked themselves in alcohol. However, because they had powerful rules concerning quantity of consumption and acceptable deportment, they were able to control the use of alcohol and contain drunkenness.

During the Revolutionary War, when the government used liquor to encourage men to fight, a basic change seems to have occurred in the social view of alcohol. After the war its use and manufacture rapidly became commercialized: men began to drink large quantities of manufactured hard liquor in taverns owned by businessmen who were more concerned with profits than deportment.

Early in the nineteenth century the advent of the Industrial Revolution, which split families, opened frontiers, and created quite different social standards from those of the pre-Revolutionary colonists, introduced an era of excessive alcohol use. During this time drunkenness abounded, the rate of alcoholism grow, and alcohol consumption tended to lead to violence. By the end of the nineteenth century, however, markedly greater control over alcohol again began to be the norm. Saloons became family gathering places rather than hangouts for lonely and angry men and for prostitutes, and their provision of a free lunch reintroduced the idea that drinking should be associated with eating.

Ironically, the prohibition movement, whose origins earlier in the nineteenth century had been based on firm figures concerning the terrible consequences of uncontrolled alcohol use, became more shrill, more moralistic, and much more politically successful at the very time when the ways in which alcohol was being used had begun to improve. By the time the federal Volstead Act was passed, twenty-one states were already dry. In effect prohibition ushered in another era of excess, centered in the speakeasies. Speakeasies were not family places; they were associated with illegality and violence and rarely served food. While *The Untouchables,* the popular television series about revenue agents, was a tremendous exaggeration, its success symbolized the extent to which alcohol use was linked to gangsterism, immorality, and corruption. Also and perhaps most important, prohibition once again changed drinking patterns. The casual drinker did not go to the risk and trouble of seeking out a speakeasy just to buy a glass of beer. All too often the people who went to speakeasies went there to get drunk.

The repeal of prohibition was greeted with a degree of rejoicing that made the customary New Year's Eve celebration seem like a damp firecracker. The period after repeal was very wet indeed. Alcohol use increased every year until 1965. From then until 1978, the year for which the latest firm figures are available, there was some fluctuation in use, though the rate of use has remained relatively stable since 1974 or 1975. There are five conditions that cross-cultural researchers have found to be correlated in most societies with nonabusive drinking practices and low rates of alcoholism. The slow progress made through the 1970s in attaining a relatively high degree of social control over alcohol use seems to be based on the increased acceptance of these five conditions:

1. Group drinking is clearly differentiated from drunkenness and associated with ritualistic or religious celebrations. Historically, one way of strengthening this stricture has been the group's participation in the preparation of the alcoholic beverage consumed.
2. Drinking is associated with eating, preferably ritualistic feasting.
3. Both sexes and several generations are included in the drinking situation, whether all drink or not.
4. Drinking is divorced from the indivudal's effort to escape personal anxiety or difficult (intolerable) social situations, and alcohol is not considered medically valuable.
5. Inappropriate behavior when drinking (aggression, violence, overt sexuality) is absolutely disapproved, and protection against such behavior is offered by the "sober" or the less intoxicated. This general acceptance of a concept of restraint usually indicates that drinking is only one of many activities, that it carries a relatively low level of emotionalism, and that it is not associated with a male or female "rite of passage" or sense of superiority.

Third, many of the anthropologists who have observed the behavior of distant primitive groups have discovered high correlations between most of these five conditions and low rates of alcoholism and drunkenness. For example, in 1943, D. Horton, who studied alcohol consumption in fifty-six primitive groups, reported the existence of consistent correlations between controlled drinking patterns and the maintenance of steady, ritualized tribal customs, as well as the breakdown of such moderate patterns at the interface between the primitive culture and more developed cultures.

Anthropologists have found that the advent of mechanization has brought a drastic change in the beliefs, behaviors, and rituals associated with alcohol use. Primitive cultures, rather like the American colonial culture, prepare their own alcoholic beverages and consume them in family, cross-sex, and cross-generational groups on ritual occasions with food and with a strong proscription against violence. But after machines are introduced, the men often go out to work, buy and consume commercially produced alcohol, and drink only with other men or with prostitutes in an atmosphere that encourages unruly behavior if not violence. Under these changed circumstances drinking habits that have been moderate quickly change and become uncontrollable.

The three factors which R. Freed Bales proposed in 1944 and 1945 as contributing to the incidence of alcohol use in a given society may also be applied to the changing situation in these primitive cultures. According to Bales, the three crucial factors are the amount of inner stress and anxiety, the degree to which the culture provides alternatives, and the group's continuing attitudes toward alcohol. These anthropological studies of primitive cultures undergoing mechanization reveal all three of Bales's factors. Other anthropological studies show that those cultures which continue to associate alcohol use with a male "coming of age" ritual, especially when the amount consumed by youths is viewed as a measure of manhood or power, are negatively correlated with "successful" or controlled drinking practices.

Fourth, in addition to the anthropological examinations of relatively underdeveloped societies, sociological studies of European and Americanized groups provide direct evidence of the influence of ethnic attitudes and socialization practices upon rates of alcoholism. The Jews have been closely studied because of their legendary low rates of alcoholism. And indeed Jewish alcohol socialization practices virtually duplicate the five conditions that are correlated cross-culturally with nonabusive drinking patterns and low rates of alcoholism. Alcohol use is introduced early in life but is closely related to ritual feasting. Its use is consistently cross-generational and cross-sexual, and untoward or violent behavior is absolutely proscribed.

Sociologists frequently contrast the Jews with the Irish, who in America have the highest rates of both alcoholism and abstinence, indicating an initial lack of interest in moderation. Irish men frequently prefer to drink together, excluding women. They put little emphasis on eating while drinking, sometimes equate quantity of consumption with strength or manliness, and their troubled political history exemplifies the association of alcohol with violence.

The abundance of well-correlated predictions of alcohol rates based on ethnic variations in socialization evidently supports a sociocultural view of alcoholism and challenges all-out adherence to the biomedical and genetic theories. But selecting the best model of alcoholism is not so simple. A few long-range studies and many retrospective studies of family patterns of alcoholism suggest the existence of what could be called either social learning or early identification. For example, J. R. MacKay (1961) in a study of alcoholism among youth found that the largest portion of his sample had alcoholic fathers and that the sons' drinking patterns closely imitated their fathers' patterns even down to specific details. Other studies have supported these findings of "familial tendencies" toward alcoholism that cut across ethnic groupings and are not explicable by either sociocultural or genetic theories alone.

Fifth, the efforts of economists to draw usable correlations between poverty and unemployment and the prevalence of problem drinking and alcoholism should not be minimized. Pearlin and Radabaugh (1976) specifically found an "interlocking set of economic, social and psychological conditions that both contribute to the arousal of anxiety and channel behavior to drinking as a means of coping with it." The St. Louis studies by Robins et al. (1962) of the drinking behavior of low-skilled, working-class youths, particularly black males, who had been consistently unemployed from eighteen to twenty-five indicate in a frightening way an unmistakable link between poverty, the inability to find work, and incipient alcoholism.

All of these psychosocial factors can operate at some time or other, with one individual or another, as significant precipitants for destructive drinking behavior. By contrast, factors that operate to prevent such declines are more difficult to specify. Just how our culture translates into specific social sanctions and rituals the five precepts that effectively modify potentially destructive use of alcohol has been discussed in a paper by Zinberg and Fraser (1979).

Since the repeal of prohibition, such precepts as "Know your limit," "It is unseemly to be drunk," and "It's O.K. to have a few beers on the way home from work or in front of the TV but don't drink on the job" seem to have had an effect. The consumption of hard liquor has been reduced by about 15 percent as purchases have shifted from 100-proof whiskey to 80- or 86-proof vodka, scotch, and blends. Also, and perhaps more significant, the consumption of beer and wine has increased enormously. A great deal of it is drunk while eating and in groups mixed in both sex and age. The acceptance of moderating social sanctions has led also to a fading out of the belief that high alcohol consumption indicates strength and to a decline in the acceptance of alcohol rowdiness as mere playfulness.

These changes toward moderation carry with them the necessity to condone drinking when the precepts are followed. In the often heard invitation "Let's have a drink," the use of the singular "a drink" encourages conviviality but specifies a limit. It is a far cry from "Let's go out and get drunk." At the same time, the view that social controls over alcohol use in the United States are actively promoting moderation should not be accepted overoptimistically. While it is likely that fewer people are drinking hard liquor, it is also likely that drinking starts at an earlier age and that the use of alcohol in combination with a wide variety of other drugs, such as marijuana and cocaine, is far more frequent. Nevertheless, the increasing interest in the psychosocial model of alcoholism, including the development of controlling sanctions and rituals, shows a marked advance beyond the mentality that led to prohibition, which Richard Hofstadter, in the preface to *Prohibition: The Era of Excess* (Sinclair, 1962), describes as "the incredibly naive effort to fix a ban on drinking into the Constitution itself as a final assertion of the rural Protestant mind against the urban and polyglot culture that had emerged at the end of the nineteenth and the beginning of the twentieth centuries."

Case Studies

All three models of alcoholism—medical, genetic, and psychosocial—have validity and usefulness. They help the clinician distinguish between heavy drinkers and alcoholics, and they offer him or her a choice of perspectives from which to view each alcoholic's problem, determine its causes, and evaluate the treatment strategies that are available. I believe, however, that the value of each of these models is enhanced by considering it in conjunction with the other two. Clinicans need the insights provided by all the models in order to deal effectively with the great variety of problem drinkers who are seeking aid. And further, we have found that this combined or multivariate model must be viewed against the background of the drinker's immediate social setting: the attitudes and behavior patterns of his family, group, and culture.

The three case studies that follow illustrate some of the possible behavior patterns of alcoholics, some of the causal factors underlying alcoholism, and some of the methods of treating it. They also show that it is not always easy to distinguish between alcoholism on the one hand and heavy drinking on the other.

CASE 1

Robert W. is a thirty-two-year-old, white, Irish Catholic male who has been an avid A.A. member for almost five years and works as an alcohol counselor. He stands 6 feet 4 inches, weighs 210 pounds, and is the picture of health. After even a brief conversation Robert (or Bob) makes it clear that he was not always in such good shape and readily goes into his alcohol history.

Both his father and his father's younger brother were alcoholics. The screaming fights between his father and mother, an abstemious woman, over drinking are among Bob's earliest consistent memories. Interestingly enough, his only sibling is a sister two years younger than he who drinks very moderately and has little recall of this struggle, which Bob sees as dominating his childhood. From his early childhood his mother implored him never to drink, and he did not until he was almost fifteen, one or two years later than most of his peers. The very first time he gave in to his friends' teasing and shared a case of beer with them at the beach, he loved it. That night, he was told later, he drank almost the whole case, became argumentative and almost violent, proclaimed what a good time he was having, and awoke the next day remembering almost nothing about the evening before.

The experience frightened him. He swore never to drink again and thanked God that his mother had not seen him drunk. This resolution lasted almost two months, after which he indulged in a virtual repeat of the first episode. For the next two years or so he drank about once a week, always getting blind drunk and never remembering much of what happened. During this period he continued to do well at school and was the star of the basketball team. His relationship with his mother had turned sour, however; she complained about his drinking constantly, and he bitterly resented these recriminations, claiming he was only having "a little fun."

By his senior year in high school his drinking had increased so much that his basketball coach spoke to him about showing up for practice with alcohol on his breath and eventually benched him. This public humiliation made him even more bitter, and his expressions of those feelings resulted in the withdrawal of an offer of a basketball scholarship at a good college. (For years Bob claimed that he himself had decided against continuing his education beyond high school.)

He managed to graduate from high school despite the deterioration of his acedemic record. By this time he and his mother did little but scream at each other, and he was determined to move out as soon as possible. One of the most astonishing things about that whole period was that his father never mentioned

Bob's drinking. Bob got a job with an insurance company which he rather liked and moved into a small apartment. There was a company basketball team, and he again starred. He began to date a young woman who worked for the same company. During this period of relative tranquility his drinking subsided to approximately one bout a week, and he convinced himself that he was in control of his life and his drinking. In fact, he recalls telling his girlfriend and others how worried he had been about his drinking, although he does not recall actually being worried, only angry when the drinking was at its height.

Every once in a while his drinking escalated, but he responded to his girlfriend's criticisms by curbing the intensity of his bouts. A year and a half went by in this way. When both were twenty-one, his girlfriend wanted to get married, but Bob wanted to hold off and save some money. He had reestablished relationships with his family; his girlfriend had become particularly friendly with his sister, and to his great surprise his father had "gone on the wagon." When he was twenty-two, his girlfriend broke with him. She claimed that she had warned him repeatedly about his drinking bouts, which he saw as minimal, and she said that because of his preoccupation with basketball and drinking she had gradually stopped loving him.

This disappointment, which came as a great shock, sent him into a frenzy. He pleaded with her, threatened, and promised everything. She told him to give up drink and get back in touch with her after a year. He swore to do so and indeed abstained for six months before he heard that she had become engaged to another man. By then he was over the worst of his disappointment. He began drinking again, but moderately, and resolved to prove to that girl what a great mistake she had made. Within six months he was drinking as heavily as he had in high school. Within a year he was fired, and in the following year he lost three more jobs.

By that time he was drinking more than a quart of hard liquor a day, rarely eating, and living on the street. It was a rapid fall from grace. The occasional day-labor jobs he got only enabled him to buy cheap wine. In the ensuing three years he was detoxified some ten to fifteen times—he doesn't remember how often or where—but he was thrown out of a dozen halfway houses for drinking and was known as an unpleasant disrupter of many A.A. meetings because of his size and strength. He also was arrested several times for drunkenness, assault, and petty thievery. Brief periods in the hospital or in jail were his only times of sobriety.

It was during one of those periods of detoxification when he was attending a compulsory A.A. meeting that he "got the message." Something clicked, he says, and he hasn't touched alcohol since. His devotion to A.A. is enormous. After five years he still attends several meetings a week beyond those required by his counseling job.

He is doing well at work and is respected by his colleagues despite a strong argumentative streak which may cause him to change jobs shortly, but his life otherwise is not a bed of roses. Four years ago he married a black woman, also

A.A., three years his junior. They have a two-year-old child and a small house in a suburb. The marriage is in serious trouble, and Bob is currently living in a room near his job. His wife objects to his temper and his lack of interest in anything but A.A. After a period of reconciliation, he is again fighting with his parental family, particularly his sister and her husband, over a blighted business deal.

Bob is proud of the fact that he has not drunk during these five troubled years, but he refuses to become complacent and quotes the A.A. line that one can never be sure that "the Demon" is licked. His degree of insight into his own rage and stubborn passivity is mixed with considerable denial of his part in his troubles, and his tendency to blame the woman (mother, sister, former girlfriend, wife) still remains uppermost in many of his conversations.

CASE 2

Jonathan C. is a thirty-five-year-old, Jewish associate professor of sociology at a prominent university, with a pregnant wife and a son of three. As the middle child of a busy physician father and an antique-dealer mother, Jonathan always did well at school and was generally seen as a quiet but tenacious child who kept to himself and was not close to either his older sister or his younger brother.

Until his third year at college Jonathan was distinguished only by his studiousness and his steadfast avoidance of frequent dating or drinking parties. At that time he moved off campus into an apartment with three classmates who were considerably more active socially. During that year he began to date more and drink more at parties. However, on only two occasions did he get very drunk. Each time he threw up for hours and felt awful the next day. During his senior year and his first year in graduate school, he continued to "party" now and then but did not have another episode of drunkenness.

After two years of graduate school Jonathan found himself racked with indecision about his dissertation subject. Acting on the advice of his father, he found a job at a small, isolated, private secondary school teaching social studies and history. At first he liked the job very much, but by the winter he began to feel confined, restless, and resentful of his often unmotivated students. He became increasingly friendly with two other teachers who, he discovered with surprise, were homosexuals. They had other friends in the area, also homosexual, with whom Jonathan began to spend most of his time listening to music, talking, and doing amateur theatricals.

This group drank heavily and Jonathan drank with them, at first only on weekends but eventually on a daily basis. In the spring, on his way home after having had a great deal to drink, Jonathan smashed his car into a telephone pole. Although he himself was only badly shaken up, his car was virtually demolished.

Until this time no one in the group had ever made a pass at him. But after the accident, when he spent a day in the infirmary being examined for possible injuries, one man with whom he had spent a lot of time came to see him and in a teasing way made an overt sexual advance. Jonathan was nonplussed and did not know how to handle the situation. He did not want to hurt the man's feelings, but he also did not want any homosexual involvement. Because there was a nurse nearby, this initial pass could be parried, but Jonathan began to worry about what would happen next.

When he left the infirmary, he avoided the group for a few weeks despite numerous phone calls, using as excuses his lack of a car and the need to prepare his students for year-end exams. During this period he felt terribly lonely and became quite depressed. The only way he could get to sleep was to have several drinks. His liquor consumption remained at over a pint of hard stuff a day, but of even more concern, now he was drinking by himself. He invariably had a headache each morning, and his work suffered.

He began to regret his decision to return to the school the following year, but as he still had no idea what he wanted to do, he felt he had no alternative. The headmaster commented in his year-end evaluation on the slackening of Jonathan's enthusiasm after a good start and indicated his hope that the next year would be better. Jonathan spent the summer at the family beach house trying to develop a project for his thesis. He dated some, felt unsuccessful with women, and continued to be extremely depressed. Despite great difficulty in sleeping, however, he drank much less.

Shortly after his return to his teaching post, he again began to feel restless and resentful and took up with the same group. He tried to avoid the man who had accosted him sexually and as a result no longer felt comfortable in the group. His drinking increased sharply both when with them and when alone, until he was drinking a fifth a day. Just before the Christmas holiday he skidded on an icy road when drunk and smashed up another car. This time he broke his dominant right arm and several ribs, and was badly bruised. He was also sharply taken to task by the headmaster.

Upon his return from Christmas holiday, he continued to drink and the headmaster told him not to return for the second term. At this point, for the first time, his parents became aware of his difficulties. Jonathan told them that he was an alcoholic. They previously had accepted his explanation of bad luck about the accidents. Although his father was extremely antagonistic to psychiatry, he now urged Jonathan to consult a psychiatrist. Jonathan agreed with great relief.

The consultation revealed long-standing conflicts about his sexual preference, conflicts that he had tried to deal with by avoidance. The same ambivalence had crept into his work and kept him from being able to decide about almost anything. Jonathan began an intensive psychiatric treatment subsidized by his father. The course was stormy with long periods of depression and many fights with his father, who for a long time saw too few results for too much money. Jonathan did return to graduate school, however, and after a protracted struggle finished his thesis. At no point during these difficult years and up to the present has Jonathan engaged in anything more than moderate social drinking.

CASE 3

Mark N. is a forty-seven-year-old Protestant accountant, the only child of a doting, domineering, and wealthy mother and an ineffectual, passive father, both of whom were abstemious. Spurred on by an early determination to be different from his father, Mark always did well at school and worked exceedingly hard in business. Although he appeared lively and gregarious, he had few if any really close friends. A year after becoming a certified public accountant, he married a young woman from another city whom he had known only on weekends. She came from what appeared to be a conventional well-to-do family, but shortly after the marriage it became clear that her father, whom Mark liked enormously, led a separate life with a succession of mistresses. Mark couldn't stand her mother and brother, with whom she was close. This considerable area of conflict about her family did not prevent them from having three children in the first six years of marriage. The children are now seventeen, fifteen, and fourteen.

Until the early years of his marriage, Mark had been a moderate drinker, close to the mold of his parents. After five years of marriage he was having a drink or two every evening with his wife upon returning home from work, and he drank regularly at social events. This was a distinctly different pattern from his parents', but it was quite typical of his social group. For the next six years his life's course remained relatively stable. Periods of intense, almost overwhelming work alternated with periods of only average labor. Mark was successful and began to collect some of his fees by participating as a partner in the businesses he serviced. His marriage was acrimonious but more or less stable, though his sexual relationship with his wife began to decline chiefly because, as he claimed, overwork left him too exhausted. They became friendly with two other couples, who took the lead in actively planning outings and joint vacations, and whose marriages were similarly socially proper but personally unsatisfactory.

Just when things began to change is hard to specify. One couple got divorced. A few months later, almost exactly on Mark's fortieth birthday, the husband of the other couple, who was a few years older than Mark, had a massive coronary and died suddenly. In retrospect Mark feels that those two events were significant if not crucial factors in his personal deterioration. He was deprived of two male friends who may have been the closest he ever had, and the divorce stimulated his wife to more open expression of her dissatisfaction with him and their marriage. Mark no longer felt part of a stable social group upon whose leadership and mores he could depend.

As the fights with his wife escalated in frequency and bitterness, Mark began to stay downtown for dinner more and more often. The companions available to him there tended to be hard-drinking, usually divorced, and were business associates or competitors. These evenings were tense and full of discussion about deals which involved larger and larger sums of money. The alcohol Mark drank reduced his anxiety, and he thought at that time that he was thinking and planning more clearly than he ever had in his life.

His drinking escalated sharply, so that soon he was drinking heavily not only downtown but at home when faced with his wife and children. Several times at social events he got so drunk that he passed out in public, to the intense humiliation of his wife. His work pattern shifted to accommodate his drinking. He got up early, went to his office, and attended to the most pressing and urgent matters. Lunch, which was almost entirely liquid (alcohol), marked the start of drinking for the day. There would be further occasional nips during the afternoon with heavy continuous drinking after nightfall. Remarkably, during this period Mark managed to get enough work done to keep his business flourishing, but he could not take care of anything else. He completely neglected himself, making but not keeping dental and medical appointments. He rarely bought clothing, so that he began to look seedy. He abandoned even the minimum of social commitments: missing outings and rituals with his children, forgetting to send bills for services, and finally neglecting to file his federal and state income tax returns. Somewhere within the alcoholic fog that covered his day, he knew what was happening and each day planned to take care of these pressing matters. But time had the funny habit of vanishing; he had all he could do to take care of his most urgent business matters.

Mark had numerous automobile accidents, most of a minor variety, such as sideswiping a parked car on a narrow street leading to his house, but several more serious. Twice his license was suspended for drunken driving, but on each occasion, with the aid of political acquaintances, he had the suspension reduced and got his license back in a short time. All sexual relationships with his wife ceased, and in fact the two had little to do with each other after he once became violently vituperative toward her mother when he was drunk.

Three months ago everything in Mark's world collapsed. He was indicted for failure to file U.S. and state income tax returns for the previous five years, his license as a certified public accountant was suspended, and his wife forced him out of the house and sued for a divorce. Upon the advice of his lawyer he went to a hospital to be detoxified and stayed two additional weeks for further drying out. Since then he has not returned to drinking but looks unfit physically and is extremely depressed. Perhaps of even more concern is his attitude. Several attempts to get him to attend A.A. meetings have aroused nothing but intense opposition. He sees himself as different from those "drunks" largely because he has been able to work and make money throughout his period of drinking. (This, ironically, was one of the chief points used by the prosecutor in the income tax case against Mark's plea that the alcoholism prevented him from filing.) In fact, at times, Mark can now convince himself that his wife was responsible for his drinking and that without her he could handle alcohol. He will admit that he is extremely neurotic in his relationships with women and is willing to see a psychiatrist. And, finally, after a short period in which he attempted to form a social group around two or three people whom he had met while being detoxified (who were involved in A.A.), he has returned to depending socially on his hard-drinking business acquaintances, who tease him about his enormous consumption of soda water.

Discussion of the Cases

In order to analyze effectively the cases of Robert W., Jonathan C., and Mark N., the clinician must keep in mind all three of the current models of alcoholism—the medical or biomedical, the genetic, and the psychosocial. Of course, this use of etiological models to devise treatment strategies is not new. For many decades, as H. C. Solomon pointed out in 1962, professionals in the field have been weighing the current assertions concerning the etiology of alcoholism and attempting to develop these assertions into treatment programs. Late in the nineteenth century they developed the asylum movement, while in the early twentieth century they based their strategies on neurophysiology, biochemistry, and protein metabolism. In the mid-twentieth century their modes of treatment rested on dynamic psychoanalytic theories, and now in the latter part of the century they have turned to straight behavioral models.

I, on the other hand, propose the adoption of a comprehensive or multivariate model similar to Keller's (1973):

> This comprehensive conception takes into account not only the possible genetic, pharmacological, psychological, and social factors but also the sociocultural context. It recognizes that the society defines and labels the phenomenon of alcoholism, that the culture contributes to its development or inhibition, and that behavior that in one culture matches an adequate rational definition of alcoholism may not constitute alcoholism in another. Thus, periodic intoxication causing sickness for several days and necessitating absence from work may define alcoholism in a modern industrial community but, in a rural Andean society, periodic drunkenness at appointed communal fiestas, resulting in sickness and suspension of work for several days, is normal behavior. An essential aspect of the difference is that drunkenness at fiestas is not individually deviant behavior.

Our model, though, is broader than Keller's, and it gives the social factors more prominence. It includes all the applicable biomedical factors, all the possible genetic factors suggested by the Danish twin studies, and all the psychosocial factors—individual, family, group, and cultural—that lay the foundation for alcoholism. Many psychosocial conditions may pave the way for vulnerability to alcohol: lack of parental care and affection, overindulgence, or inconsistency in child-rearing practices during infancy and early childhood; certain family and ethnic responses to alcohol; and the lack of consistent, coherent social sanctions and rituals that condone moderate alcohol use and prevent alcohol abuse.

It is clear that under certain conditions, both psychological and social, a vulnerable individual may learn to react to difficulties by resorting to intoxication. Whether psychological or social, this vulnerability is a matter of degree. A more vulnerable person may find prominent rewards in alcohol regardless of social strictures, while a less vulnerable person may succumb only in a social milieu that permits or encourages heavy drinking and intoxication.

While we believe that the comprehensive model provides the best understanding of all the factors involved in the development and operation of alcoholism, we also recognize that its very inclusiveness forces the clinician to choose among many different treatment strategies instead of simply, for example, recommending abstinence, the treatment prescribed by the genetic model, or drugs, which would be prescribed by a strict medical model. The cases of Robert W., Jonathan C., and Mark N. illustrate this difficulty.

Robert W. is the classic alcoholic. He has a strong family history of alcoholism and a personal history of drinking alcoholically—that is, in order to get drunk—with all the blackouts, unruly behavior, and denial of the import of drinking that alcoholism includes. He believes, and few experienced observers would disagree with him, that he can never drink again. A single drink would be the beginning of a binge despite his years of sobriety and his pride in what he has accomplished since becoming sober.

Growing up with an alcoholic father and a mother preoccupied with her terror of alcoholism certainly could be seen as early developmental factors that might lead to psychological conflict. And Bob's situation at present indicates that although the curse of drinking has been lifted and he has a steady job that he likes and is good at, he still has a number of serious interpersonal conflicts that cause trouble. It is hard, however, to make any direct links between these psychological difficulties and his drinking or, indeed, his abstinence.

It is true that his early drinking education outside the family as well as in his ethnic background neglected many of the principles that lead to the social sanctions which support controlled drinking. His peer group did not clearly differentiate group drinking from drunkenness; they purposely drank as a unigenerational group of males even though it caused them some embarrassment to exclude women and other generations. Their drinking was not associated with any sort of ritual feasting and generally not with eating. They drank to "have a good time," which for them included escaping from the rigors of unsatisfactory work, difficult interpersonal relationships, and demanding women. Finally, both the extent of their alcohol consumption and their aggressive and belligerent behavior were aggrandized and accepted as measures of manliness.

Only quite late in Bob's drinking career, when he was already a serious alcoholic, did his peer group register disapproval of his drinking by suggesting that he cut it down. In retrospect Bob realizes that he was acquainted with the usual cultural sanctions about drinking—"Don't drink on the job"; "Drink to be sociable and not to get drunk"; "Don't drink alone"; "Falling down drunk looks awful"—but he insists that at no time were such sanctions really meaningful to him. Although he experienced considerable shame and guilt about what his drinking was doing to him and especially to others, the conventional stereotypes about controlled drinking meant little to him because drinking was too precious to be qualified or moderated. He loved it and now he is willing (just barely, he says) to lose it, but he could not bear "playing games" with it, which is his way of looking at control mechanisms.

The case of Jonathan C. is vastly different. Here it is a question of whether alcoholism is indeed the issue. Although he went through a period of extremely heavy drinking that resulted in automobile accidents and job loss, damaging his capacity to function effectively, to get along with people, and to maintain his health, it is doubtful that such a sharply encapsulated drinking period can properly be called alcoholism. At the same time, the criteria for alcoholism proposed by such an authority as Cahalan (Cahalan et al., 1969; Cahalan and Room, 1974) can be met by Jonathan, and, interestingly enough, he thought of himself as an alcoholic.

But there is nothing in his history that would indicate alcoholism. There are no known hereditary, familial, or ethnic vulnerabilities. And in his case the knowledge and acceptance of social sanctions concerning drinking were conscious and well integrated. The fear that his friends (other than his drinking group) or his family would see him drunk was strong, and the accompanying guilt about his behavior was sharp and painful. Generally speaking, Jonathan believed in drinking as relaxation but not to get drunk, preferred to drink in mixed company, did not believe it manly to drink a lot, and did not become aggressive under the influence of alcohol.

Nevertheless, it became clear after Jonathan's year of heavy drinking when he was a secondary school teacher that he had deep-rooted and serious unconscious conflicts around his sexual identity. Not only did he attach himself to a social group that was less concerned than he with the principles sanctioning moderate drinking, but he chose a group that triggered his most painful and unacceptable wishes. It would not be going too far to describe Jonathan as being in a homosexual panic at that time. He could neither accept his homosexual wishes and interests nor detach himself from the stimulating interactions of that particular social situation.

The combination of severe internal conflict and lack of controlling social sanctions and rituals allowed alcohol, with its potential for amnesia and its tranquilizing qualities, to become Jonathan's escape route. He could not of himself decide to seek out a psychiatrist because that came too close to acknowledging the unthinkable—his forbidden homosexual wishes. But once an outside agent, his father, had virtually made the decision, he could gratefully accept it, just as he had when the headmaster by firing him had separated him from the social group that he secretly wanted to leave.

It is very questionable whether Jonathan could be classified as an alcoholic, but even if he were so classified, his alcoholism would be quite different from Bob's. In Jonathan's case the psychological strains leading to drinking were clear-cut, and once these were made conscious, the pressure to drink receded. Jonathan reverted to his usual acceptance of social sanctions against excessive drinking and returned to social groups that supported and reinforced those sanctions.

Mark N. provides still another perspective on alcoholism. Here, as with Jonathan, there are no obvious genetic, ethnic, or family vulnerabilities to alcoholism, but there are indications of lifelong psychological difficulties. A doting, controlling mother and a father who is seen as a failure; a longing for male friends but little talent for making such friends; and a hostile, dependent relationship with women (the case history does not include his twelve-year relationship with his secretary, which in most details was a recapitulation of his relationship with his wife)—all these factors coalesce to form the classical neurotic picture.

Such a picture indicates potential vulnerability to almost any serious psychological symptom. But did it lead directly to Mark's drinking, as was suspected in the case of Jonathan? That point seems far less clear. The loss by divorce and death of his two closest men friends seems to have forced Mark further into the intolerable relationship with his wife. After the disappearance of his old friends, he chose a new social group that offered him an escape and at the same time shared his business interests, thus serving both his self-esteem and his wish for isolating mechanisms. Was it simply fortuity that his new companions were hard drinkers, or did

Mark seek them out for that reason? It is difficult to know. Nevertheless, it is unlikely that he himself would have led others into heavy drinking, and for a long period, at least, he was not a lone drinker.

In Mark's family background there had been little opportunity to learn and integrate social sanctions that condoned controlled drinking. His parents, his mother in particular, regarded intoxication and excessive social drinking as morally wrong and somehow vulgar. Throughout his youth he had accepted those precepts and avoided situations that would conflict with them. It was only after marriage and exposure to his wife's family that he took social risks for which he was unprepared.

There is little doubt that Mark is an alcoholic. Just as Jonathan has tried to deny his painful, destructive sexual conflict by seeing himself as an alcoholic, so Mark tries to deny his alcoholism by seeing himself as a neurotic. Neither can bear the idea that he is unable to deal with certain social functions that most other people can handle. In Jonathan's case it has been important to accept the drinking as merely a symptom and attempt to get around his denial of underlying sexual anxieties. In Mark's case, however, to treat the alcoholism only as a symptom of his obvious psychological problems might cause him to continue his self-destructive drinking while "waiting" for the resolution of underlying conflicts to do away with his wish to drink. This type of treatment would obviously be nonsense: few therapists would go on treating psychologically an alcoholic patient who was continuing to drink. But many would see the drinking as a symptom that interfered with the treatment instead of as a well-developed "disease" entity, whatever the original etiology. In such a case some therapists might find abstinence essential during treatment, but they might also expect that after treatment had succeeded, the patient would be able to return to controlled drinking.

This attitude raises an extremely delicate problem that is related to the essential issue of discriminating between the alcoholic and the heavy drinker. Our reviews of the etiological models of alcoholism as well as our case studies indicate that a different etiology or combination of etiologies is at work in each specific case. Yet despite this variety of cases and causes, A.A., which offers by far the most successful mode of therapy, always prescribes the same method of treatment. A.A., in fact, goes so far as to develop a tautology: any "alcoholic" who successfully returns to controlled drinking was not an alcoholic in the first place. This outlook lumps the long-term alcoholic—one, for example, whose service career was interrupted thirty years ago because of alcoholic excess and whose life now revolves around a quart of cheap muscatel—with the young executive who has resorted to a $30 weekly scotch expenditure since his promotion into a hard-driving office circle. Such an outlook leaves A.A. successful in treating the first type of case but may interfere with its capacity to intervene early and act preventively in the second.

The prescription of abstinence would most certainly apply in Bob's case, where early and powerful psychosocial determinants (cultural and family) pointed specifically to alcoholism. Even the possible existence of a genetic determinant of alcoholism could not be ruled out in his case. The genetic model, which roughly equates drinkers who have a constitution vulnerable to alcohol with those who are allergic to penicillin, rightly includes the prescription for abstinence.

Another group of individuals unlikely to be able to drink again includes those who have been attached to the bottle for many years and have lost their capacity to function socially, psychologically, and even physically. It matters little whether their years of alcoholism have brought about a metabolic or other physiological change, whether psychological deterioration and sensitization to the alcohol experience have occurred, whether the learned behavior precipitated by alcohol use has led to drunkenness, or whether the ability to use social sanctions and rituals for purposes of control has been totally and irrevocably lost. The profound experience of long-term alcoholic deterioration seems to rule out further contact with alcohol.

But certain other cases are less clear-cut. Had Jonathan, by some definitions an alcoholic, been seen by some clinicians during the fall of his second teaching year, they might have prescribed lifelong abstinence, which in retrospect would have been a mistake. The jury is still out on Mark N. on several counts. The attempt of Mark's psychological treatment to work through his problems with women may be of lesser importance in the long run than his return to a hard-drinking social group. An experienced observer cannot help sensing that Mark is not yet through his run with alcohol. So far it is impossible to tell to what extent his drinking stemmed from psychological vulnerability and to what extent it resulted from the breakdown of social groups on whom he depended for the moderating social sanctions and rituals that were missing in his home.

It is our contention that consideration of the social context in which the drinker lives must go beyond attempting to separate out etiological factors in order to determine whether the prescription is abstinence or a return to controlled drinking. Indeed, we are cnvinced that in many cases the social context of drinking itself may provide the critical etiological variable. It is obvious, for example, that when the developed social sanctions and rituals break down, loss of control results; and if that breakdown can be established as the essential factor leading to alcoholism, it must be specifically taken into account when deciding upon a treatment regimen, especially if some treatment other than abstinence is being considered.

But whether the clinician considers the breakdown of the social context to be of direct causal significance, or believes that early psychological problems are crucial, or finds the impact of family or genetic predilections to drinking uppermost, or sees the difficulty as a learned disability, all drinking occurs in a social context. And as American social history shows, the capacity of the existing social sanctions and rituals to control alcohol use varies from one period to another. Because these social factors set the boundaries within which people drink, they affect how people drink and the extent to which they drink. Even those who must remain abstinent live in a social context that either helps or hinders their efforts to abstain. It is paradoxical that the same set of social controls (sanctions and rituals) that is crucial to the promotion of controlled drinking and thus the prevention of abuse, or alcoholism, is not effective in the prevention of use, or abstinence. In American society, which condones drinking and has gradually developed sanctions and rituals that encourage moderate use of alcohol, the kinds of sanctions and rituals necessary to prevent all alcohol use can only be maintained by a small, cohesive, and, in the case of A.A., desperate community willing to erect specific social barriers to separate itself from the larger society. In this modern, heterogeneous, pluralistic nation the attempt to impose abstinence through legislation has proved a miserable failure.

Our comprehensive or multivariate model of alcoholism encompasses a series of interlinked etiological factors, one or more of which are predominant in specific cases but all of which exist within either a limiting or an expanding social setting. So far, clinicians have tended to develop treatment strategies and overall ways of looking at the patient's problems and attitudes by focusing on the predominant etiological factors. They have seen the social context, including both the larger society's attitude toward intoxicants and the patient's social group situation, as ancillary, almost as a necessary nuisance, rather than as a critical determinant of the patient's situation regardless of the more specific etiology.

Depending on the way in which they have interpreted their patients' histories, therapists have usually suggested that patients try psychotherapy or drugs or self-help groups. Because few histories have specified the relationship of the patient to his social context, few therapists have taken that relationship into account. True, this narrower approach has often worked out. Bob's referral to A.A. was correct and so was Jonathan's referral to a psychiatrist. But it should be pointed out that these referrals did not in fact exclude the social setting. In Bob's case, A.A. automatically prescribed a particular social context as paramount in the treatment. As it happened, Jonathan had changed his social setting just before beginning psychotherapy. It is probable that the social aspect of his case would have needed more careful attention if he had begun psychiatric treatment while still teaching at the secondary school. As for Mark, his social situation is still a problem that may require the most careful consideration if he is to remain sober. The outcome of his therapy will depend primarily on the decisions he makes in regard to his social setting: whether he changes his mind and joins A.A. or continues to socialize with his hard-drinking friends.

Alcoholism, A.A., and the Governance of the Self*

John E. Mack

It is idle to say that men are not responsible for their misfortunes. What is responsibility? Surely to be responsible means to be liable to have to give an answer should it be demanded, and all things which live are responsible for their lives and actions should society see fit to question them through the mouth of its authorized agent. [Samuel Butler, *Erewhon*, p. 113]

There has been a relative lack of psychoanalytic attention to alcoholism in recent years (see the chapter by Margaret Bean for a review of the current literature). This is the result not only of therapeutic discouragement, for psychoanalysts have often written persuasively about clinical conditions for which no suitable therapeutic application of analytic formulations had yet been developed. The lack also seems to reflect the failure to discover an appropriate theoretical framework within which to consider the disorder.

The popularity of the "disease concept of alcoholism" (the term, though not the idea, derives from Jellinek's [1960] book by that title) seems to have discouraged efforts to explore the psychological aspects of alcoholism. Jellinek's emphasis upon alcoholism as a disease (he re-

*In his article, "The Cybernetics of 'Self': A Theory of Alcoholism," Gregory Bateson, employing different language and another theoretical model, anticipated some of the concepts I have introduced here.

garded "illness" as a "more felicitous" term [p. 11]) appears to have been motivated by a desire to secure legitimacy for alcoholism within the medical profession, and to help bring about changes in social attitudes and policies that would permit better care for alcoholic patients and lead to the support of clinical and research activities. The disease concept was, in the words of Robin Room (1972), "a means," in some ways unsuccessful, "of getting a better deal for the 'alcoholic' " and not "a logical consequence of scholarly work and scientific discoveries" (p. 1056).

Although he felt that research in alcoholism should focus upon the pharmacological process of addiction (p. 154), in considering alcoholism as a disease Jellinek did not intend to exclude psychological factors. He accepted the definition of disease offered by the *Journal of the American Medical Association* in 1957 as "any deviation from a state of health; an illness or sickness" (quoted in Jellinek, 1960, p. 11), which does not specify whether psychosocial or organic factors predominate. After reviewing the relevant literature before 1960, Jellinek pointed to the unsatisfactory nature of existing psychological formulations in explaining any of the phases of alcoholism but seemed to encourage investigations of the psychological aspect. Jellinek's target was not psychology or psychiatry, but traditional views which thought of alcoholism primarily as the consequence of sin, vice, or weakness or character and the alcoholic as a person to be punished rather than understood or treated.

The disease concept has clearly been useful in bringing greater acceptance of the idea that the alcoholic is a person in need of help, or as a treatment strategy for relieving guilt. Its unwarranted but perhaps inevitable extension has also, however, given rise to a good deal of mischief, as Pattison, Sobell and Sobell point out in their book *Emerging Concepts of Alcohol Dependence* (1977). The narrowly organic connotation of "disease" has led to the espousal of over simplified physiological models and a territorial smugness within the medical profession which disregards the need for careful psychological study, discourages appropriate psychotherapy, and precludes a sophisticated psychodynamic understanding of the problems of the individual alcoholic (see also Robinson, 1972). Finally, the disease concept has produced potential confusion and contradiction about the idea of responsibility, a problem which the inherent sophistication of the A.A. approach has found a way around through holding the individual alcoholic responsible for initiating the steps toward sobriety while relieving him of responsibility for the drinking or the illness. The models of sin and disease do not exhaust the possibilities. "It is time," as Peter Dews wrote, "to move to new attacks" (p. 1047).

As Jellinek pointed out himself, there is a crucial distinction between the mechanisms that lead the gamma alcoholic (his term for the alcoholic who has lost control of his drinking, constituting more than 80 percent of his sample of two thousand A.A. members) to begin a *new* bout of drinking and those that drive him to continue to drink once the bout has begun. The issue of responsibility is quite different depending upon whether one is considering the initiation of a new bout of drinking or the ability to bring the drinking under control once an episode is underway. This is consistent with Jellinek's (1960) view that "psychological formulations" were "more satisfactory" than physiopathological ones "as far as the initiating stage of alcohol addiction goes" but that this "does not extend to the later developments" (p. 80).

When psychoanalytic concepts or terms derived from psychoanalysis are employed, they may be used merely as straw men to be blown away in a puff of ridicule. Generally it is a conflict theory, with stress upon the alleged role of unconscious guilt, that is marked for demolition. Or sweeping statements are offered which presume knowledge that we do not yet possess, or seem to equate psychodynamic elements with conscious control. Vaillant, for example, in his chapter in this volume, asserts that "the etiology of alcoholism is uncontrolled drinking" and "uncontrolled drinking is not symptomatic of some underlying disorder," and that "for most alcoholics return to controlled drinking lies outside an appeal to reason or to a dynamic unconscious. Like the hypertensive or the diabetic, the alcoholic cannot usually cure himself by will power or insight alone" (page 37).

Certainly formulations which regard uncontrolled drinking as if it were no more than a psychoneurotic symptom, manifesting itself within a psychic organization that is, by and large, intact and functioning smoothly, will fail to shed much light upon acute and chronic alcoholism in either its symptomatic or its addiction phase. But there does exist now within psychoanalysis an emerging body of theory relating to drive organization and regulation, personality structure, narcissistic vulnerability, the formation and maintenance of a cohesive self, and a set of ego functions concerned with self-preservation, self-care, and what I call self-governance (see below) that may have relevance for the understanding of addiction in general and alcoholism in particular.

The success of Alcoholics Anonymous in the treatment of alcoholism may not be equaled by any other known therapeutic approach. Traditional forms of insight-oriented psychoanalytic therapy, however valuable in helping the alcoholic to understand various aspects of himself, have not generally been successful in giving him power over his drinking, in enabling him to master the problem (Bales, 1944b, pp. 273–274; Zinberg, 1977, p. 100). The history, organization, and procedures of A.A. have been well described (Alcoholics Anonymous, 1976; Bales, 1944b; Bean, 1975; Leach, 1973; Leach et al., 1969; Stewart, 1955; Tiebout, 1943–1944, 1961; Trice, 1957; Alcoholics Anonymous, 1977; Zinberg, 1977), but A.A. as a psychosocial modality of treatment offers in addition a rich arena of observation that has been underutilized for learning about the psychological aspects of alcoholism. In this chapter I will examine in psychodynamic terms the role of A.A. in the treatment of alcoholism, drawing especially upon the reported experiences of alcoholics who have attended A.A. meetings. From these observations and other relevant clinical data I will suggest tentative formulations and directions in which further clinical investigation could proceed if a more complete in-depth understanding of the psychology and psychopathology of alcoholism is to be obtained. My comments and observations will have particular relevance to the following aspects of the problem of acute and chronic alcoholism:

1. The initiation of a new bout of drinking in an alcoholic who is sober
2. The ending of a bout of drinking outside of an institution
3. The maintenance of sobriety
4. The vulnerability of the individual to becoming an alcoholic

There will be less discussion offered on the mechanisms which underlie the continued drinking of an addicted alcoholic during an actual bout, as physiological and biochemical factors appear to play a larger role in this phase of the illness. It should be pointed out, however, that many alcoholics in the middle of a drinking episode have been able to muster sufficient control to bring themselves to A.A. and to initiate thereby the chain of events leading toward sobriety.

A.A. and Self-Governance

The psychoanalyst Ernst Simmel (1948), writing a decade after A.A. was formed, asked, "Does our theory, derived from psychoanalytic research, provide any possibility of application to the therapy of groups of patients to meet the universal danger which alcoholism signifies for the mental health of the country?" He answered his own question in the affirmative: "It has already been applied intuitively and successfully in a mass psychological experiment—Alcoholics Anonymous" (p. 28). Simmel went on to point out that the therapeutic principles employed by A.A. corresponded "basically to psychoanalytic findings." He stressed the recognition by A.A. of the overpowering nature of latent drives in the alcoholic and the need for a countervailing power upon which he can rely, a higher power which is embodied in the phrasing of A.A.'s step 3, "God as we understand Him" (Alcoholics Anonymous, 1977, pp. 5, 35). Simmel's paper was published posthumously and was incomplete at the time of his death. Notes written in longhand on the last page of the manuscript indicate that he was thinking about the interrelation of ego psychological, group dynamic, community, and religious dimensions of the understanding of alcoholism that was implicit in A.A. (see also Zinberg & Fraser, 1979, p. 379). The notes concluded with this hope: "possibilities for Alcoholics Anonymous from the collaboration of psychoanalysts" (Simmel, 1948, p. 31). But such collaborations have been quite limited. This chapter may be regarded as one effort to carry forth the hope which Simmel expressed.

In 1978 A.A. estimated that its membership was greater than 1 million in more than thirty thousand groups worldwide (Alcoholics Anonymous, 1976, 1978 printing, p. xxii). The therapeutic success of A.A. is difficult to evaluate, in part because of the self-selected population. But the available data suggest that although A.A. may only reach 5 to 10 percent of alcoholics, for those who attend meetings on a regular basis it is the most effective means of maintaining sobriety currently known (Leach, 1973). This suggests that whatever the forces are which drive the alcoholic to drink, they can be successfully counteracted by a form of treatment that relies entirely on a human mode of intervention. In my opinion this salient fact must dampen the hope that biochemical explanations or forms of treatment alone will be of much help in the preaddiction phases of alcoholism. What I am interested in pursuing are the psychological mechanisms relevant to A.A.'s success and the implications of the fact that any form of group treatment could have such an extraordinary impact upon a disorder which is so difficult to control.

Before proceeding further in this discussion, I wish to introduce a concept that I have found useful in trying to understand alcoholism and other disorders in which a problem of impulse control is involved. I am referring to the notion of self-governance. Self-governance has to do with that aspect of the ego or self which is, in actuality or potentiality, in charge of the personality. Self-governance is a supraordinate function, or group of functions, in the ego system. It is concerned with choosing or deciding, with directing and controlling. The functions of self-governance are similar to what Hendrick (1943), in relation to the capacity to work, and more recently Bean (1975, p. 25), in discussing the paralysis of the alcoholic's problem-solving capacities by magical thinking, have called ego executant functions. But "executant functioning" connotes a solitary operation of the ego, while "self-governance" is a psycho-social term, intended to leave room for the participation of others in the governance of the individual. Self-governance as a theoretical concept is intended, unlike ego executant functioning, to allow for the sharing of control or responsibility with other individuals or groups. It acknowledges the essential interdependence of the self and others. Psychotherapy always has among its goals extension of the areas over which the individual has sovereignty, his domain of self-governance.

There are many situations in which self-governance is impaired—manic and schizophrenic psychoses and aggressive impulse disorders are obvious examples. The disorders of substance abuse in general and alcoholism in particular, offer other striking examples of such impairment. The powerlessness which the alcoholic experiences in relation to alcohol reflects an impairment of self-governance with respect to the management of this substance. It has not been ascertained whether this powerlessness is specific to the drive to drink or is experienced by alcoholics in relation to certain other strong impulses as well. In the A.A. approach acknowledgment and acceptance of this powerlessness are the *first step* in the path to recovery ("We admitted we were powerless over alcohol—that our lives had become unmanageable").

Self-governance—the sense of being and the power to be in charge of oneself—is one of the most highly valued of human functions. The admission that one cannot manage an aspect of oneself which is expected ordinarily to be under one's own control is experienced as an important failure, a major personal blow. One has only to note how vigorously a friend or colleague who has had a few drinks too many will resist letting someone else drive him home from a party, will cling to the belief that his judgment remains intact and that he is still responsibly in charge of himself. One frequently hears from alcoholics statements like "I can't bear to admit I can't control my drinking." Even though the loss of voluntary control is perhaps never absolute (Pattison et al., 1977, p. 98), it is a far more useful step *therapeutically* for the alcoholic to acknowledge his powerlessness than to have it demonstrated that he still retains an element of control. For even in this early stage in the development of his drinking problem he may not be able to exercise control in any useful or practical way. Therefore any emphasis at this time upon the dimension of control which remains will only give more cause to feel guilt and deepen the sense of failure.

One reason, I believe, why alcoholism is so difficult to treat derives from the general acceptance of drinking in our culture. This acceptance is accompanied by a high level of expectation that controlled drinking is both possible and desirable together with a deep, though often unconscious, opprobrium attached to the idea that one is unable to manage one's drinking. The profound reluctance of most family members, and even medical and mental health professionals, to confront the problem drinker with the fact, by then usually obvious, that he cannot control his drinking derives, I believe, from the widely internalized belief that it is a shameful and embarrassing failure to admit that this function is no longer within the governing capabilities of the self (DiCicco et al., 1978).

A.A. in its graduated twelve-step program seeks to enlarge progressively the capacity of the chronic drinker to govern *the impulse to drink* in the absence of alcohol. The seemingly single-minded emphasis in A.A. upon sobriety derives from the experience that for the alcoholic this is the essential first step without which nothing else can be achieved. In other words, the management of the impulse to drink when drinking—"controlled drinking"—whether for psychological or physiological reasons, is outside of his capability. The question of nonabstinence as a treatment goal for alcoholics is a highly complex and controversial subject which will not be considered here (see, for example, Pattison, 1976). Perhaps it is sufficient to say only that "alcoholism" embraces a spectrum or continuum, and that many alcohol-abusing individuals may reasonably strive to achieve controlled drinking (Vaillant, 1979).

The success of A.A. is due to its intuitive and subtle grasp of the complex psychosocial and biological nature of self-governance, not only for the control of problem drinking but in a far more general sense. For A.A. recognizes that the self never functions as a solitary entity. It is always participating with others—other persons, the family, neighborhood, social, ethnic, religious, or national groups—in its realization and fulfillment.* The psychic representations within the self are not static structures. They are constantly resonating or interacting with the ongoing communications or representations of other individual selves or groups which are continuously being taken in and exerting a strong guiding or moderating impact on the self. A.A. has perceived that certain forms of group activity, expecially if placed in the context of religious experience and values, can have a more powerful influence upon the capacity of the individual to govern himself than can any form of individual psychotherapy. Bales (1944b) was referring to this aspect of A.A., I believe, when he wrote, "There is a certain type of control within the individual personality which can have its source only 'outside of the

*Bateson regards the "self" as "a false reification of an improperly delimited part of this much larger field of interlocking processes" (1972, p. 331).

self'—for practical purposes, in the moral principles advocated by a closely knit solidary group—and can only be internalized and made effective against self-centered, satisfaction-directed impulses by an involuntary feeling of belongingness and allegiance to such a group, i.e., a 'moral community' " (p. 276).

Many visitors to A.A. meetings who are not alcoholics have an experience which they describe in such comments as "I could use this myself," or "This isn't just for alcoholics. There is something here which could be valuable for everybody." What is being referred to is, I believe, the aspect of belonging to which Bales refers, the unembarrassed acknowledgment of the need for participation in a caring community without ulterior motives, one which accepts the individual totally for what he is. At a more theoretical level what is being perceived is the fact that the self cannot exist as a solitary structure, that its survival, governance, and value require participation in a social structure or community.

Alcoholics continue to attend A.A. meetings after they have achieved sobriety and reordered their lives. Some continue to attend even after the group is no longer essential for controlling the impulse to drink. These individuals recognize, I believe, the personal importance of the A.A. community in ways which may have very little to do with their drinking problem. From the standpoint of A.A. itself the policy of a perpetual open door contains an implicit recognition that A.A.'s values, philosophy, and program offer a community of purpose which has a significance beyond the explicit goal of maintaining sobriety or controlling the impulse to drink in chronic alcoholics, a purpose that could have clinical and theoretical relevance for understanding aspects of the self-psychology of nonalcoholics as well.

A.A. and the Psychology of Narcissism

Professional and paraprofessionals who work in the alcohol field are most reluctant to use such terms as "character problem" or "ego defect" in talking about individuals who suffer from chronic alcoholism lest they impose thereby an additional onus upon the patient and reinforce negative attitudes among caregivers. Once again, what began as a well-meaning and useful therapeutic strategy has discouraged systematic exploration of the developmental problems of alcoholics and stands in the way of achieving psychological understanding of the disorder.

A.A. itself has not been as concerned with this sort of protection and does not hesitate to stress the character problems of alcoholic members. Step 6 is the readiness ''to have God remove all these defects of character'' and step 7 asks ''Him to remove our shortcomings.'' But beyond this the authors of *Twelve Steps and Twelve Traditions* (Alcoholics Anonymous, 1977) observe ''that character defects based upon shortsighted or unworthy desires are the obstacles that block our path toward the achievement of A.A.'s objectives'' (p. 77) and how reluctantly alcoholics ''come to grips with those character flaws that made problem drinkers of us in the first place, flaws which must be dealt with to prevent a retreat into alcoholism once again'' (p. 74). Perhaps it is the connotation of moral condemnation and inferiority that is attached to the word ''character'' in its *popular* usage that has led alcohol workers to avoid the term. But it needs to be emphasized that in psychoanalysis the word has usages which carry no more of a value connotation than do ''personality,'' ''ego,'' or ''self.''

Although nontechnical, everyday terms are used, A.A. leaves no doubt that it is in the sector of narcissism and narcissistic development of the personality that important clues may be found to the understanding and treatment of alcoholism. Narcissim is defined psychoanalytically as ''the libidinal investment of the self.'' We may consider it here more simply as the realm of self-love and self-regard. As Heinz Kohut and others have noted, there is with narcissism, as with character, ''an understandable tendency to look at it with a negatively toned evaluation as soon as the field of theory is left'' (Kohut, 1966, p. 243).

Kohut and his followers (Kohut, 1971, 1977b; Kohut & Wolf, 1978; Goldberg et al., 1978) have attempted to separate narcissism, or self-love, from object relations, and have studied its normal and pathological manifestations as separate lines of development. Healthy narcissism is a fundamental aspect of general emotional health and includes a feeling of well-being, a confident sense of one's worth and potential, and a balanced perspective about one's importance in relation to other persons and groups and in the cosmos (see Vann Spruiell [1975] for his discussion of the ''three strands'' of narcissistic development). This kind of health is a prerequisite for satisfying relationships with others and for gratifying and successful work and recreational experiences. Manifestations of pathological narcissism include exaggerated preoccupation with oneself and one's own needs and desires, a diminished sense of one's value or an exaggerated belief in one's worth or importance, described in its extreme expressions as grandiosity. Severe disturbances of narcissism are associated with fragmentation and disorganization of the self as seen in acute schizophrenic psychoses or in the regressive clinical picture sometimes brought about as the result of acute drunkenness or prolonged drinking (one reason why alcoholics are so often misdiagnosed as schizophrenic). Ego disorganization can take place as a result of physiological or psychological causes, or a combination of both, which is one of the reasons why it has been so difficult to determine the basis of many of the states of ego regression that are found in association with alcoholism in its various phases.

We have already seen how one sort of narcissistic disturbance stands in the way of the alcoholic's obtaining help—his inability to acknowledge that his drinking is out of control. This reluctance is the result not only of resistance to giving up the drinking itself, but derives from the degree of investment which, for the alcoholic and for all of us, is attached to the belief that one is in charge of oneself, i.e., has the capacity for autonomous governance of impulses in general and the drive to drink in particular.

A.A.'s literature is filled with descriptions and insights into aspects of healthy and pathological narcissism. A.A.'s founder, Bill W., wrote in his "story" that the achievement of sobriety "meant destruction of self-centeredness" (Alcoholics Anonymous, 1976, p. 14). Though "just underneath there is deadly earnestness," he also found a "vast amount of fun" in the whole recovery process, recognizing the healthy dimension of humor (an aspect of A.A. which has, in my opinion, received insufficient attention) (p. 16). *Twelve Steps and Twelve Traditions* contains many discussions of self-centeredness, of egoism and the need for "ego-puncturing," and of the consequences of injured self-regard.

Harry Tiebout (1943–1944, 1961) was the first to recognize that A.A.'s approach to the treatment of alcoholism was directed primarily at the narcissistic dimension of the disorder. In A.A., Tiebout wrote, the alcoholic came to realize he had always "put himself first" and that effective treatment depended upon recognizing that "he was but a small fraction of a universe peopled by many other individuals" (1943–1944, p. 471). In order for the A.A. experience to work effectively, the alcoholic must "lose the narcissistic element permanently" (p. 472) and replace the "big ego" of infantile narcissism with a more humble self (1961, p. 59). What seems not to be found in Tiebout, in subsequent writings about narcissism and alcoholism or, for that matter in A.A.'s own publications, is a differentiation of the manifestations of pathological narcissistic expression and vulnerability that are contained in the prealcoholic character of the individual from those which are the regressive consequences of the chronic or addictive drinking itself. Until this is clarified, it is presumptuous to write of the "narcissistic core" of the disorder or of a "fundamental wound of the addict's ego" (Simmel,

1948, p. 27). For the experience of chronic drunkenness contains so many inevitable hurts, so many catastrophic injuries to the self that are a *consequence* of the alcoholic's drinking, that one must be very careful not to conclude without better indications that the narcissistic aspects of the clinical picture antedated the excessive drinking.

It is its recognition of the dangerous egocentric pitfalls of leadership that accounts for the absence of perpetuating offices or positions of directing authority in A.A. (Unterberger, 1978). "Tradition Two" of A.A. (Alcoholics Anonymous, 1977) states that "for our group purpose there is but one ultimate authority—a loving God as he may express Himself in our group conscience. Our leaders are but trusted servants; they do not govern" (p. 136). The authors of *Twelve Steps and Twelve Traditions* describe clearly the temptation to grandiosity that may, for example, attach to the experience of having founded a successful A.A. group. "Being on the human side," they observe, "the founder and his friends may bask a little in glory" (p. 137). But if these individuals should try to "run this group forever," they are likely to find themselves "summarily beached" by "the rising tide of democracy" at the election to A.A.'s rotating committee (p. 138). This committee does necessary chores for the A.A. group, but it does *not* govern or direct the group and is sharply limited in its authority. A defeat of this sort, in which, for example, a founder's status is sharply reduced, can cause a severe sense of injury, a fall in self-esteem. A.A. calls such individuals "bleeding deacons," and some "hemorrhage so badly" that they get drunk. "At times," it is observed, "the A.A. landscape seems to be littered with bleeding forms" (p. 139). But most, A.A. observes, survive their disappointment and become "elder statesmen," valued members of the group who have grown in *wisdom,* one of the cardinal dimensions included by Kohut among his examples of healthy narcissism. These elder statesmen become the "real and permanent leadership of A.A." to whom the group turns for advice. They lead by example and "become the voice of the group conscience" (p. 140). Thus, although A.A. has its heroes, there are no leadership positions.

There is in this aspect of A.A.'s tradition a profound recognition of the artifical inflation of self-regard and the stimulation of archaic grandiose structures in the self that can occur through holding positions of leadership and authority. Furthermore, from the standpoint of the group, the idealization and investment of limited narcissistic resources in a leader can deplete the sense of self-worth of individual members and increase the risk of further drinking. Inevitable disappointment in a leader on the part of the members would lead to personal criticism of him with the inevitable risks of damage to self-regard for member and leader alike.

It seems that A.A.'s eschewing of authority positions within the organization is based on more than the need for democratic structure that is characteristic of most voluntary self-help groups. This policy may reflect, in addition, the recognition of narcissistic vulnerability as an aspect of alcoholism, and the realization of the likely injuries to self-regard ("hemorrhaging") that would be incurred for member and leader alike if authority positions were to be created.

The monologues of drinking experience, the often humorous "drunkalogues," which are such an important and appreciated part of the program at A.A. meetings, seem at times just a public self-excoriation, an exhibitionistic and self-centered confession. But they are more than this. They are, in addition, a serious effort on the part of individual alcoholics to reinforce the new self-respect they have achieved since becoming sober, the healthy shifts in the economy of their narcissism that have been accomplished since becoming A.A. members. The speaker offers an experience with which the group members can identify in their efforts to consolidate their own personal growth. The group recognizes the familiar elements in the various stories and offers legitimate approval and appreciation of what the speaker has to say. There is an exhibitionistic aspect, but it is in the service of the healthy development of the individual and the group. It is to this group aspect of A.A. that I now wish to turn.

A.A. and the Collective Dimension of Self-Governance

Freud's (1921, 1930) writings about groups related mainly to mass organizations and to institutions, such as an army or a church. He was interested particularly in the psychological importance of the leader and the effect of large groups upon superego and ego ideal structures in the individual. A.A.'s reference to the "group conscience" (see above) is interesting in this connection. More recent studies of group psychology have included a consideration of the need-fulfilling and ego-sustaining aspect of small and large groups (Calder, 1979; Kernberg, 1977; Scheidlinger, 1964, 1974); the regressive and destructive potential of mass organizations (Mitscherlich, 1971); the distinction between mature (work) groups and regressive (basic assumption) groups (Shapiro, 1977);

and the relationship of group and organizational structures to the stability of the self (Zaleznik, 1977). Erik Erikson (1959, 1968) has made important contributions to our understanding of the importance of social structures, of groups and institutions, in the formation of ego identity. It remains for others to describe more specifically the ways in which specific groups function in maintaining the structure and stability of the self. A comprehensive theory of group psychology will have to include the part played by family, community, and other group formations in the development, structure, and continuing stability of the self.

AA recognizes the importance of the powerlessness of the individual in relation to alcohol and the drive to drink. Anyone who has worked with alcoholics will appreciate their helplessness in the face of this drive no matter how vigorously and sincerely they may protest that it is now under control. A.A. does not interpret the psychological or biological *basis* or *reason* for this powerlessness within the individual. It does not need to. A.A. simply takes it into account and provides a powerful counterforce to make up for its absence and a series of steps whereby the individual can gain for himself *in part* the power to manage the impulse to drink.

I have noted earlier the essential part played by family, group, and institutional representations in the formation of a cohesive self. I have focused especially upon the executive functioning of the individual, what I have called self-governance. It is my contention that A.A.'s approach *can* be helpfully understood in terms of the functions of self-governance. The association's effectiveness derives from its recognition of the fact that the self is a *social organization* and that self-governance for all individuals is never entirely a solitary activity. It is, rather, a function or set of functions which depend upon the individual's participation in social structures and institutions. A.A. succeeds in enabling the individual with a drinking problem to become sober through providing a network of reliable individual and group relationships that operate powerfully in the governance of the need to drink.

It might be useful at this point to note how little we know about how individuals who do *not* have drinking problems govern their desire to drink. Clearly in addition to internalized ego controls there are powerful social attitudes, pressures, institutions, and structures which operate subtly within the self-system to enable persons who might otherwise become problem drinkers to control their drinking. Zinberg and Fraser (1979) have shown, for example, how much more of a problem alcoholism was in the nineteenth century than in the colonial period in the United States. They hypothesize that this was due to the breakdown of family social structures which had restricted drinking to ritualized and ceremonial occasions, and to the increased availability of taverns and barrooms to which men, who were already experiencing social dislocation as a result of industrialization and urbanization, flocked in large numbers. In societies such as France, where there is an institutionalized tolerance of large daily amounts of alcohol intake, paradoxes arise with regard to alcoholism. There seems to be rather widespread addiction and low-level impairment of functioning due to the presence of alcohol in the tissues. But at the same time the socialization patterns seem to prevent the occurrence of as much uncontrolled drunkenness as is found in societies, such as the United States, which have a relatively low level of acceptance of large daily amounts of alcohol. (See Jellinek, 1960, pp. 25–32, for a more detailed discussion of the relationship of drinking patterns to cultural attitudes.) The increase in alcoholism among some American Indian tribes and in certain African countries needs also to be studied in terms of the impact upon the individual of the destruction of tribal structures which have served essential functions in the ongoing governance of the self.

A comprehensive consideration of why some individuals lose the capacity to govern their drinking cannot be limited to an examination of the development or breakdown of drive and ego structures within the individual. We need also to consider losses or shifts in the role of essential social and community structures that have heretofore helped individuals who are biologically and psychologically vulnerable to alcoholism, to govern their drinking. Personal loss, which frequently precedes the onset of excessive drinking, is generally looked at from the affective standpoint. In terms of my argument, we must also consider a meaningful loss or losses as the removal of an important presence, or of a stabilizing force or social structure, which has aided in governing the impulse to drink. Many individuals who become problem drinkers seem recently to have lost family members or other sources of social stability that have been part of their self-governing system.

Whatever theory may be espoused, workers in this field seem for the most part to agree that alcoholics need to substitute people for alcohol. For those who choose it, A.A. does this in abundance but without the evident risks which often seem to attend the intense relationships of individual psychotherapy. As Vaillant points out in his chapter in this volume (page 53), some alcoholics have suffered from early maternal neglect which may impair their capacity to care for themselves. This neglect, or other troubling developmental experiences, may have left the alcoholic acutely vulnerable to further hurt or humiliation. Certainly once alcoholism has developed, the individual will suffer many personal wounds and failures and become vulnerable to further injury. Such disappointment can occur in the course of individual psychotherapy. The time may come when the patient will call his therapist drunk, perhaps on a Sunday or other inconvenient time, and the therapist will have insufficient time or patience to meet his needs or to make the arrangements for hospitalization. Hurt and disappointment with the therapist, to whom exalted expectations may have become attached, can follow with the result that the sense of injury in the self can be deepened.

A.A. groups offer many individuals who care, who have similar stories and do not tire of hearing new ones. Because of this caring and support, AA members individually and in group meetings may be able to do a good deal more confronting of the alcoholic with his maladaptive defenses of denial, rationalization, and magical thinking (see Bean, 1975, and in this volume) without inflicting new wounds upon the self. The alcohol-controlling capacity of these other individuals is gradually internalized and becomes a part of the self-governing structure of the individual. The A.A. group itself, as a caring object, also may be internalized. A twenty-six-year-old young man, sober for several months, when asked what it was in the A.A. experience which enabled him to get on top of his drinking, replied, "It's the fellowship. It's the companionship. It's the love within our program. That's why it's more successful than any other program with alcoholics.... I got to know many fine people and it still continues. My circle continues to grow. Very good people, who were loving, caring and understood, and *still do understand* [my italics]. That's probably one of the greatest reasons why it works so well—because it's a fellowship.'' There is in this statement the recognition of the need-filling aspect of the A.A. group and also of the importance of its ongoing nature.* A.A. remains an important part of this man's self-governing structure. The twelve-step program of A.A. is another way in which the association provides order, a system, even ritual, which can be utilized by the alcoholic in the development of internalized self-governing structures, although complete autonomy of the self with respect to alcoholism is not an explicit or reasonable goal for A.A.

A.A., Narcissism, and the Religious Dimension

It has frequently been noted that A.A. functions more like a religious organization than a medical one. Many alcoholics, including A.A.'s

---

*H. Grunebaum and L. F. Solomon (1980) are developing a peer theory of group psychotherapy which may have particular relevance for understanding the effectiveness of a fellowship such as A.A.

founder, Bill W., achieved sobriety through conversion-like spiritual experiences (Simmel, 1948; Tiebout, 1961). Rituals analogous to confession, penance, and absolution are found in A.A. (Bean, 1975). The language of salvation is often heard at A.A. meetings and the war against alcoholism sometimes takes on the shape of a holy crusade against an evil demon, embodied by alcohol itself. Bill W. wrote, "If there was a Devil, he seemed the Boss Universal, and he certainly had me" (Alcoholics Anonymous, 1976, p. 11). Harry Tiebout, who wrote astutely of the religious aspect of A.A., observed that A.A. achieves its result through a spiritual awakening. A.A.'s "Big Book," *Alcoholics Anonymous,* states bluntly, "The great fact is just this, and nothing less: that we have had deep and effective spiritual experiences which have revolutionized our whole attitude toward life, toward our fellows and toward God's universe" (Alcoholics Anonymous, 1976, p. 25). It has been noted that a "parallel to the A.A. experience occurs within Fundamentalist Protestant experience" (Bean, 1975, p. 54), although the sacramental elements are more typical of Catholicism. I have also heard aspects of A.A. likened to Eastern religions, and the religious conversion of A.A.'s cofounder has been compared to the Buddha's experience of Satori (Shimano, Douglas, 1975).

Much of this is, I believe, misleading. The phrase "God as we understand Him" in A.A.'s step 3 has provided a flexibility that allows for a vast range of spiritual concepts and attitudes. A.A. states explicitly that not all spiritual experience that leads to change in A.A. is the result of sudden or spectacular conversion. Personal development that A.A. calls spiritual may occur gradually over a period of many months or years. Most A.A. members find "that they have tapped an unsuspected inner resource which they presently identify with their own conception of a power greater than themselves" (Alcoholics Anonymous, 1976, Appendix II, pp. 569–570). The concept of a greater power may have little or no necessary relationship to any of the ideas of God that occur in the world's formal religions. Many alcoholics resist attending A.A. meetings on the grounds of their inability to accept the religious aspect. Yet A.A. includes among its members many people who consider themselves agnostic or even atheist (Stewart, 1955, p. 255). A number of A.A. members interpret the idea of a greater power in humanistic terms, expressed as the belief in something of value larger than themselves. The central point is that for an alcoholic to recover in A.A. a significant psychological shift in what seems universally to be called a spiritual dimension must take place within the self.

There is a paradox with respect to the psychology of narcissism inherent in Judeo-Christian religious attitudes. On the one hand certain religious ideas and emotions are profoundly egocentric and childish. As Freud pointed out in *The Future of an Illusion* (1972), the only one of his books concerned primarily with the psychology of religion, man attributes caretaking functions and omnipotence to a superior being whose activity replaces the parents that formerly protected him in his childish weakness and helplessness (p. 24). Death need not be an ending, "a return to inorganic lifelessness." There is a superior and judging being in the universe who, far from being indifferent to our fate, has a special interest in us and reviews our conduct like a conscientious parent. Our sufferings and terrors are not in vain, but will be compensated in a hereafter, and our good and evil deeds will be rewarded or punished as they deserve. Freud thought that men should admit the "full extent of their helplessness and their insignificance in the machinery of the universe." He urged the abandonment of egocentric illusions, remarking that "men cannot remain children forever; they must in the end go out into 'hostile life' " (p. 49).

But the paradox is this. Throughout the history of civilization human beings have had great difficulty managing their childish desires, their self-oriented drives and grandiose wishes, their *narcissism,* without reference to a greater power in the universe, someone or something they call God. One may argue that the cultural development of the ego, or the universal internalization of humanistic values, may ultimately lead us to triumph over our aggressive narcissistic aims. But from a historical perspective, no reference to moral values, even if incorporated in a shared group ego ideal, that is not *perceived* as deriving from a force in the universe greater than man himself has generally proved powerful enough to prevail in the face of man's egoistic desires. One reason men have formed religions has been to bring order out of the chaos of the primitive rapaciousness which they exhibit when left to their own moral devices.

There is a state of mind which might be called a primary religious attitude, an experience of awe in the face of the universe and its wonder, which is not at root narcissistic in an infantile sense. It is an attitude of humility in the face of existence and an awareness of vastness and of unlimited forces in the cosmos, of eternity. This perspective may in itself help to subvert an egoistic orientation. Heinz Loewald (1978) has written of the ways in which we may grasp eternity through a kind of fundamental awareness, closer to primary- than to secondary-process thinking. If it makes any sense at all to discuss these attitudes of awe and humility in terms of narcissism, they would have to come under the category of "mature" narcissism. As Leowald wrote, "Freud did not recognize (or refused to recognize) that religious life, as anything else in human life, is capable of evolving more mature forms of functioning and expression, no less than human love, for example'' (pp. 71–72). (See also Meissner, 1978, for discussion of mature aspects of narcissism in relation to religious faith.)

There is nothing inherently childish in acknowledging a powerful authority, a power greater than ourselves. To ask an alcoholic to surrender his will and his life to a greater power is to acknowledge a fundamental truth, that when it comes to his drive to drink he has no authority *within* his body or personality capable of managing. The idea of God, or of a greater power, becomes a powerful governing force within the self, a force as strong and fulfilling as the powers attributed to alcohol. Just how a problem drinker is enabled to gain mastery of his drive to drink through this surrender and through the experience of a holding, caring group is a subject that deserves much further study. What seems clear from the ''mass psychological experiment'' (Simmel, 1948, p. 28) of A.A. is that the experience of relating to a power greater than oneself can start an alcoholic on the road away from the self-ministration of drinking and begin to move him in the direction of object love. Vann Spruiell (1975) has identified three strands of narcissism in childhood and adult development: self-love, omnipotence, and self-esteem. The second strand, omnipotence, has to do with feelings of power or weakness, and begins in the second year with the toddler's sense that he can make things happen. Spruiell relates the beginnings of the psychology of power (or, I expect, also of its converse, powerlessness) to this period of childhood. The idea of God, of a power greater than oneself, may represent one of the steps in the transformation of infantile omnipotence. The small child's recognition of the limits of his power may also represent an intermediate stage in the establishment of object relations. The love of God may thus be a transitional step (as in A.A.) between infantile narcissistic omnipotence and object love.* The fulsome and mechanical quality which often attaches to talk of love in religious groups may have to do with the failure to achieve this transition in a genuine sense.

It is in this area of ''mature narcissism,'' or more accurately through its work in the maturing of narcissism, that much of A.A.'s success in the treatment of alcoholism may lie. If I am correct in this thought, our understanding of the religious aspect of A.A. may have importance for the mental health field beyond the treatment of alcoholism. A.A. strikes

---

*I am indebted to Dr. Ana-Maria Rizzuto and Sister Nancy Kehoe for helping me to think about the possible relationships to God in terms of the psychoanalytic theory of object relations.

at the heart of the infantile egoistic aspect of chronic drinking and provides an antidote to it. It confronts directly the denial, rationalization, and make-believe which would perpetuate the addictive and destructive use of alcohol. To the self-serving activity of chronic drinking, and the wallowing self-pity that is its regressive by-product, A.A. apposes directly an attitude of religious humility, a narcissistically demoting perspective of self-in-the-universe.

The admission of powerlessness and the surrender of self to a greater power which are in A.A.'s early steps—the steps are offered as suggestions only—have been misunderstood as an abnegation of responsibility. They represent, on the contrary, a breaching of the narcissistic defensive structure which maintained twin illusions: on the one hand the illusion that the drinking could be controlled and on the other hand the illusion of self-autonomy or self-sufficiency. The admission of powerlessness over alcohol represents the first defeat of infantile egoism, a first step in the assumption of responsibility (Kaiser, 1955). At the same time, acknowledgment of a basic dependence upon others, and upon some power greater than oneself, begins the abandonment of a grandiose posture. The child's idea of God, based as it is on omnipotent and idealized fantasy structures, is a logical first step in the transition from narcissism to object love. God may be loved on the model of a dependent, anaclitic relationship, but it is a relationship which replicates archaic, grandiose self-structures. God is all-loving, omniscient, all-powerful. He accepts and may forgive all. In Kohut's terminology He might be thought of as the perfect mirroring parent. But He, like a good parent or psychoanalyst, is not just a projection of infantile narcissism. He is—again using Kohut's (1971) terminology—a self-object, an intermediate figure between self-love and object love, a being who can provide or represent much needed authority and structure within the self.

For individuals who conceive of a greater power in more personal terms God can, of course, be experienced as a literal being or presence. It is sometimes possible to see in such instances the way in which the relationship to God may seem to fulfill the same functions that the individuals were seeking to provide themselves with alcohol. A forty-six year-old woman (Rizzuto, 1976), who was hospitalized for gastritis and fatty liver complicating chronic alcoholism, had been drinking from her late teens. For fifteen years alcohol had severely complicated her life. When she attended A.A. regularly, she was able to stay sober. She was clear about the fact that whether in A.A. or outside of it she felt no need to drink when she felt God's intoxicating presence. This presence she described as like a bright light of hallucinatory intensity, with her and within her. For this patient God was experienced as an omnipresent, all-powerful person who was always there and who gratified her craving for affection, peace, understanding, and comfort. God, she said, knew just what her needs were and could take care of all of them, already knowing what they were without her having to tell him. He also accepted her totally and uncritically. God for this woman also served a self-regulatory function, guiding her and, together with the church, providing structure and direction. For her, Christ, ministers, and A.A. seemed to serve as mediators or intermediaries between herself and her idea of God. The childish roots of this patient's image of God are obvious, yet her religious experience allowed her to give up her drinking, to achieve some satisfaction of intense emotional hunger and self-esteem, and to govern her life on a daily basis in a less self-destructive manner.

The relationship with God can have its own ups and downs. These vicissitudes can be approached in object-relations terms and may have a direct bearing on the drinking problem. A fifty-year-old Catholic woman, hospitalized in a state institution because of her alcoholism, was clearly struggling with her relationship with God. Feeling overstressed in her life, she began to feel annoyed with God for giving her a ''burden'' larger than her ''back could carry.'' ''Foolishly,'' she said, ''I questioned His wisdom, that He thought perhaps I was stronger than I really am.'' As the patient felt more distant from God, she felt less able to use His help to control her drinking. Part of the job of the mental health professionals responsible for her care was to help her repair her relationship with God so that she could resume her participation in A.A. and her steps toward achieving sobriety.

Each of A.A.'s suggested steps after step 3 represents further potential movement away from narcissistic postures and toward caring for others. I am anticipating here the objection that narcissism, at least in the writings of analysts who follow Kohut, should be considered as a separate line of development rather than be set in opposition to object love. I would reply that this may be true if one is focusing upon the development of capacities such as humor and creativity which represent healthy expressions of narcissism. But the antagonism recognized by Freud and other psychoanalysts between immature narcissism and the capacity for unselfish love of others still remains valid. Mature object love cannot occur without an abandonment of a large amount of infantile egoism.

The later steps of A.A.—self-examination, making amends to others, continued ''personal inventory,'' and carrying A.A.'s ''message'' to other alcoholics—may all be conceived of as movement in the direction of greater concern and love for others. Step 12 is essentially a prescription for full human maturity, for "love that has no price tag on it" (Alcoholics Anonymous, 1977, p. 109) and "devoted service to family, friends, business or community" (p. 128). It means giving up the childish, overly sensitive and grandiose aspects of personality (p. 127), enjoying the ordinary "give and take" of relationships (p. 119), accepting the limitations of ambition (pp. 126–127), and settling for the "permanent and legitimate satisfactions" of a useful life (p. 129). If it could be shown through careful research that A.A.'s methods achieve permanent structural change in the narcissistic sector of the personality, this would be a finding of considerable theoretical significance.

Implications of A.A.'s Approach

In most of the remaining pages of this chapter I will discuss what I believe are some of the theoretical implications of A.A.'s approach and effectiveness. No effort will be made to provide a complete psychodynamic formulation of alcoholism. Rather, I will suggest what seem to me to be some of the directions in which clinicians and theoreticians who are interested in applying psychoanalytic concepts and approaches might proceed, the areas to look at, in their efforts to understand and help patients with drinking problems.

ALCOHOLISM AS A TOTAL SOLUTION AND THE PRINCIPLE OF MULTIPLE FUNCTION

I know of no patterns of behavior that better illustrate Robert Waelder's (1936) principle of multiple function than those associated with alcoholism. Waelder, it will be recalled, noted that every psychic act is overdetermined, serving simultaneously instinctual gratification, the tendencies of the ego—including its own inclination to repeat—the superego, and the requirements of the outside world. Every act is, in this sense, an attempt to solve a problem or "a *group* of problems" (p. 48). Thus behavior, or a pattern of behavior, which may seem to be maladaptive, or even relentlessly self-destructive, may at the same time be solving other problems which, from the standpoint of the "central steering" of the organism or executant functioning of the ego, have a higher priority. Such a priority might include the eradication of overwhelming anxiety, fulfillment of grandiose fantasies, or the avoidance of an intolerable reality. But, as Waelder points out, each attempted solution creates "a new piece of reality." Through the attempted solution itself "everything is changed, so that now new problems approach the ego and the attempted solution fundamentally is such no more'' (p. 60).

This describes very well the situation of many alcoholics. They may tell us that they began to drink as an attempt to satisfy a craving, to comfort themselves, to feel more complete, to deal with depression, or to ease anxiety experienced with other people. One tends too hastily to label these explanations entirely as ''rationalizations.'' These they may be in part, but in addition, these observations can be true though incomplete accounts. If one looks further, it turns out that drinking was used as a total solution, a multidetermined form of adaptation (including the satisfaction of a physiological craving), serving all of the functions which Waelder described. As one patient put it, ''for me alcohol was a total personality orientation.''*

A forty-one-year-old man, for example, described how drinking was an antidote for loneliness, gave a feeling of warmth, substituted for people, and ''washed out'' all painful as well as all pleasurable affects. It also brought him in contact in fantasy with his dead father and other family members who had also been alcoholic. A forty-year-old separated mother of five children, whose life had been destroyed by her drinking, still found it difficult to give up alcohol. When this was explored with her, she said that when she was drinking, she had the feeling that all problems, all painful realities, even the shattered dream that her husband would return, were obliterated. When drinking she felt more at ease and less guilty, and had the sense of being totally taken care of and at peace. In the face of her utter inability to manage her life, and her troubling affects, the self-destructive pattern seemed to her of little weight. A thirty-five-year-old married woman who knew that drinking ''in the long run makes it all worse'' was quite candid about the fact that alcohol simultaneously took away painful feelings and memories, substituted for the closeness she missed with others, and punished her for her sins through its inevitable consequences.

It may be argued that any or all of these statements occurred after the fact and may, therefore, rationalize a more fundamental reality—that for these individuals drinking is out of control. It will require prospective and longitudinal studies, attention to the stage of the illness, careful observations made in advance of a bout of drinking, and detailed examination of the context in which drinking occurs to sort out the relative role of biological and psychosocial factors in chronic alcoholism. Part of A.A.'s effectiveness surely derives from its comprehensiveness. Its approach

---

*Bateson wrote ''the total personality of the alcoholic is an alcoholic personality which cannot conceivably fight alcoholism'' (1972, p. 312).

considers human beings in their totality. As Zinberg and Fraser (1979) have recently pointed out, A.A.'s "prescription" for recovery includes "every aspect of human functioning: spiritual, mental, emotional-communal and physical" (p. 27).

SELF-PSYCHOLOGY

I have indicated the ways in which A.A. explicitly addresses infantile regressive attitudes among alcoholics and have suggested that its effectiveness may derive in part from its success in helping the alcoholic to abandon certain maladaptive defensive positions for more object-related orientations. We have also seen how the caring and supportive A.A. community and the relationships to a "greater power" (mediated through the structure provided by the group) help to overcome the powerlessness that the alcoholic feels in relation to his drinking. A.A. helps an alcoholic to reverse this state of powerlessness, initially by acknowledging that it exists in relation to his drinking, implicitly recognizes the shared or psychosocial nature of self-governance, and enables the problem drinker to govern his drive to drink through the nonjudgmental interdependent experience of the group.

There is a growing literature, inspired especially by the work of Heinz Kohut (1971, 1977b), which seeks to understand the development of a cohesive sense of self through the study of archaic narcissistic structures that are regarded as precursors of the mature self. These include especially what Kohut calls the grandiose self and the transitional idealized "self-object" or parental imago. Kohut suggests that in persons who may become addicts early disappointments, especially in relation to the mother, act as traumatic experiences which interfere with the normal development of these precursor mental structures. In treatment the early structural defects are repaired, according to Kohut, by means of an empathic "mirroring" transference in which the analyst mirrors, i.e., accepts fully, the patient's exhibitionistic display. Kohut writes, "Traumatic disappointments suffered during these archaic stages of the development of the idealized self-object deprive the child of the gradual internalization of early experiences of being optimally soothed, or of being aided in going to sleep. Such individuals remain thus fixated on aspects of archaic objects and they find them, for example, in the form of drugs. The drug, however, serves not as a substitute for loved or loving objects, or for a relationship with them, but as a replacement for a defect in the psychological structure" (1971, p. 46).

James Gustafson (1976) has applied Kohut's theory and approach (and also Michael Balint's views on "benign regression") in the psychoanalytic psychotherapy of an alcoholic with a "narcissistic personality disorder." It is clear in the report that Gustafson's mirroring, caring approach helped his patient to reduce bodily tensions and to give up the need for alcohol. But at the end of treatment unanalyzed aspects of the man's narcissistic transference persisted and continued to be acted out in self-destructive "mirror transference relationships" (p. 83). Although Gustafson has used Kohut's formulation, there is no specific mention of alcoholism by Kohut. In fact, the hypothesis seems to apply more accurately to certain drug addicts than to alcoholics, among whom a vulnerability to ego regression, especially under the influence of the substance itself, seems better to describe the more frequent pathology than a structural defect in the self. Similarly, Leon Wurmser (1978) has observed that "alcoholics are in general far more socialized, have much better inner structures (controls, capabilities to adapt) than most compulsive drug users" (p. 221).

Although many alcoholics seem to have narcissistic problems and conflicts—many occurring as a *result* of their drinking—I do not believe that most would be correctly diagnosed as "narcissistic personality disorders" in Kohut's sense, especially prior to the onset of the drinking problem (see also Wurmser, 1978, p. 221). What seems to me useful in this theoretical approach is the emphasis it places upon the cohesive self and its vulnerabilities. In order to search for areas of vulnerability in the development of the self, it is not necessary to assume basic defects in early infantile psychic structures. We are concerned here with elements in the developing personality which might make the individual *susceptible* to alcohol addiction. These vulnerabilities are most likely both biologically and psychologically rooted and may have to do with difficulties in quite specific areas of drive regulation, body tension, or affect management—inadequate functions which alcohol is later expected to serve.

If these formulations are correct, in alcoholism we are more concerned with poorly developed functions (precursors of what I have called self-governance), i.e., *specific susceptibilities to regression,* than with a pervasive structural defect in the development of a cohesive self such as Kohut postulates is the basic pathology in the immature individuals whom he calls narcissistic personality disorders. These susceptibilities could well be present in spite of a history of early accomplishments, retrospectively good childhood relationships in the manifest sense, and even a successful prealcoholic adult adjustment. In fact, many alcoholics seem to have had a relatively good earlier capacity for object relationships, and are sometimes able to undo the harm they have caused others and "make amends" (A.A. steps 8 and 9) quite readily once they are able to become and remain sober. A.A., when it is effective, seems more to supply certain *functions* for the self, or to offer a gratifying and supportive set of object relationships, than to repair structural vulnerabilities within the ego organization. A.A. members, and others who work clinically with alcoholics, recognize that professional help is needed in addition to A.A. for patients with severe "self pathology"—some character problems, such as are found among poly-drug abusers (Vaillant, 1979) for example, and borderline or schizophrenic alcoholics.

PROBLEMS IN SELF-CARE AND SELF-PRESERVATION

Because the effects of chronic drinking can be so disorganizing, it is difficult at times to appreciate the global extent to which alcoholics may depend on alcohol to manage their lives. Destructive as alcohol may be in reality, many patients leave little doubt that they use it, nevertheless, to help them survive, that drinking is employed by the ego for problem-solving purposes. Such expressions as "I drink to get a grip on myself" or "It helps me to keep hanging together" are frequently heard. In many cases patients successfully escape from decisions, even trivial ones, by getting drunk.

Until the end of his life Freud discussed the functions related to taking care of oneself, of self-preservation (or what he called the ego instincts), largely in terms of the vicissitudes of libido. Freud (1913, p. 182; 1915, pp. 124–126; 1916–1917, p. 430; 1925, pp. 56–57) saw self-preservation as the activity of narcissistic libido, a reflection of the instinct to preserve the life of the individual in contrast to object libido, which served to perpetuate the species. Only in one of his last works (1940) did he place self-preservation explicitly among the functions of the ego when he wrote, "The ego has set itself the task of self-preservation, which the id appears to neglect" (p. 199). Freud thus left it to later investigators to explore how the ego develops the capacity to accomplish this task.

Part of learning to take care of oneself has to do with the ability to plan and to anticipate the consequences of any given action, to foresee danger to the self. Freud's concept of signal anxiety bears directly on this point. Small amounts of anxiety are experienced by the ego as a signal to mobilize psychic defenses and to forestall the occurrence of a more serious danger. "The individual will have made an important advance in his capacity for self-preservation," Freud (1926) wrote, "if he can foresee and expect a traumatic situation of this kind which entails helplessness, instead of simply waiting for it to happen" (p. 166).

Alcoholic patients often will, as we know, tell us with seeming conviction that they do not intend to drink again, that the experience of their last hospitalization has persuaded them it would be folly to do so. I have heard such assertions frequently enough myself to be convinced that the patients are often quite sincere in these statements, and may not be aware of the denial and rationalizations involved. Naturally, once they are released from the hospital, it is often not long before they are drinking again. What is striking in such situations is the absence of any anticipatory or signal anxiety which can mobilize effective defenses against the impulse or desire to drink. The anticipation of danger is merely intellectual, without real conviction, and the trauma of drunkenness recurs. One professional man, for example, who had been sober for several months, knew that if he drank again, it could severely jeopardize his marriage and his entire carreer. He became drunk, nevertheless, with disastrous consequences. When asked how he understood the fact that he had gotten drunk once more, he replied candidly, "I missed having a drink at the bar with the guys on the way home." This man remained unable to anticipate that if he were to drink at all, he would surely become drunk.

There is a problem in the functioning of the ego with respect to self-care or self-preservation in cases such as this, a difficulty made worse perhaps by biological factors as yet unknown. What is not understood, and is a problem for future research, is whether self-preservative or self-care functions have failed to develop adequately in childhood or have been obliterated by the alcoholic disorder. The above patient favored the latter view, commenting that "the strength of the urge to drink enables one to rather gently set aside a rational evaluation of consequences." But this too may be a rationalization to explain the impairment of an ego function which never developed adequately.

DRIVE AND AFFECT MODULATION AND REGULATION

Drive theory is somewhat out of fashion nowadays in psychoanalysis, and reference, for example, to the "orality" of alcoholics or to their oral eroticism is considered in poor taste. Yet if we follow Schur (1966) in considering drives or instincts in the psychoanalytic sense as energies having their source ultimately in the soma but exerting pressure upon the executive apparatus of the ego, any comprehensive theory of alcoholism will need to give some consideration to the drive or motivational aspect of normal and problem drinking. In discussions of alcoholism this drive is usually referred to as a craving or "compulsion" to drink.

Experimental studies have shown that the sense of powerlessness which alcoholics experience in relation to their problem cannot be attributed simply to the strength of the craving they feel for alcohol per se (see Gottheil et al., 1973; Pattison et al., 1977, Chapter 4; and Mathew et al., 1979). Ludwig (1972), for example, showed that among 176 patients who resumed drinking during an eighteen-month follow-up period only 1 percent attributed their resumption of drinking to subjective feelings of craving or the "need to drink." Instead, most attributed their resumption of drinking to some form of psychological distress, family problems, or a variety of other reasons and rationalizations (which may or may not have been actual determining factors). There is experimental evidence which suggests that even among alcoholics who have resumed drinking, situational variables—drinking, for example, associated with pleasant expectations and behaviors recalled from previous drinking episodes or activity—interact with the effect of the alcohol itself in determining further alcohol intake. The craving is by no means absolute or constant. Psychoanalysts might be able to contribute further to the understanding of the psychological and contextual elements which affect the intensity of the craving, to a clearer appreciation of the drive's subjective quality, and to further appreciation of the factors which determine the capacity to control or modify it.

As Pattison et al. (1977) and others have demonstrated, and has been discussed earlier in relation to the effectiveness of A.A., the "loss of control" (defined by Jellinek [1960] as loss of the ability to control the quantity of alcohol ingested once one has started to drink) which alcoholics experience is also far from absolute. Mello and Mendelson (1972), for example, have shown that alcoholics placed in a situation with unrestricted access to alcohol do not drink all the alcohol available to them. That A.A. can enable an alcoholic to interrupt a drinking episode is itself evidence of the less than absolute nature of the loss of control. One of the purposes of this chapter has been to provide a framework in which the psychological, social, situational, and even biological factors which affect the ability to control the drive to drink may be studied and understood. Control is always a relative concept. The ego always participates in the *decision* to drink or not to drink.

The psychologist Silvan Tomkins (1962) has noted that drives have a rigid and unmodifiable character, and that even if they activate the affect system, it is primarily feelings or affects which we experience and which determine actual behavior.* Affects have a flexibility which drives do not possess. "It is affects, not the drives, which are transformable," he notes (p. 143). Tomkins has demonstrated that "most of the characteristics which Freud attributed to the unconscious and to the Id are in fact salient aspects of the affect system" (p. 130). I have found this point of view valuable in trying to understand the way in which alcoholics handle affects.

Anyone who has worked with alcoholics has frequently been told that a given episode of drinking started when the patient felt sad, anxious, or even joyous, that a bout began after a painful failure or an unexpected success, etc. These remarks tend to be treated as rationalizations, as excuses par excellence. They may indeed be used in this way, but they also indicate, I believe, a deeper truth. For alcoholics seem, at least once they are in an active period of the disorder, unable to deal with intense feelings, to modify or transform them. It is precisely the flexibility to which Tomkins refers that they seem to lack, and this deficiency may antedate the onset of problem drinking. Many alcoholics will say how helpless they feel when experiencing disturbing or intense feelings in the face of the most ordinary life situation. The alcohol may be sought to make more manageable guilt, sadness, ordinary anguish or pain, even joy.

Vaillant, in his chapter in this volume (page 40), seeks to refute the argument that the alcoholic drinks to relieve emotional distress on the grounds that if this were so, "it should raise self-esteem, alleviate depression, reduce social isolation, and abolish anxiety." He cites a study by Tamerin and Mendelson (1969) which he states "suggests that despite what alcoholics say, objective observation of drinking reveals that chronic use of alcohol makes alcoholics more withdrawn, less self-confident, more depressed, and often more anxious" (page 40). This is true but somewhat misleading. Alcoholics are generally ready to acknowledge that the drinking ultimately made them feel worse. What they make clear, however, is that at times they drank to obtain *immediate relief* of emotional pain and that to a degree the alcohol achieved this result on a temporary basis. They were not anticipating the long-term destructive effects, or, if they could, were willing to risk them for the short-term result. But that is a different problem. What Tamerin and Mendelson (1969) found among the male alcoholics in their study of experimental alcohol administration was that for all four of their subjects

*For reviews of psychoanalytic conceptions of affect see Green (1977) and Brenner (1974).

"the initial effect was uniformly experienced as pleasurable. Subjects felt more relaxed, less inhibited, and generally elated." After this initial phase, however, "the subsequent experience was frequently painful as drinking persisted over a period of days and weeks" (p. 889). These findings are consistent with the observations made in a case reported in detail by Wurmser (1978). "All forms of pain: physical and emotional, including anxiety, guilt and shame, are at first mitigated, but subsequently deepened by alcohol, *her* drug" (p. 227).

The relationship of chronic alcoholism to fundamental disturbances in the psychology of affects constitutes, in my opinion, a particularly fertile field for psychoanalytic investigation. One alcoholic man in psychotherapy made clear that without alcohol he felt himself to be utterly without inner resources with which to deal with emotional pain. Although in many ways he was a competent man, when he experienced ordinary sad feelings and tearfulness in his therapist's office, he said it seemed like he was "coming apart." In the light of such vulnerability it is quite understandable that A.A. would discourage the experience of strong or troubling emotions, such as resentment, or that psychotherapy which elicits in alcoholic patients disturbing affects before new ego resources are developed to manage them could be of more harm than help (Vaillant, this volume). Once again, what is not known, and will require careful prospective studies to establish, is whether these ego capacities were never present or were lost as a result of the regression associated with alcoholism.

For many alcoholics their psychopathology in the affective realm seems to be more complex than simply the problem of bearing or dealing with painful emotions. It has to do with varying degrees of impairment in a sequence of functions which begin early in a child's development with the differentiation or recognition of specific affects. Other elements in the sequence include learning to name feelings, to bear them oneself (Zetzel, 1949, 1965), to communicate or share the experience of them with others (Basch, 1976), to transform or modify them, and ultimately to take responsibility for the full experience of the feelings themselves. One alcoholic woman of thirty-five told her psychiatrist that she had great difficulty even identifying within herself painful feelings such as loneliness. She would turn to alcohol for relief of distresses that she could only vaguely apprehend. Once she was sober and the damage caused by her drinking was reversed, an essential first step in learning to manage her drinking problem was helping her become aware of the quality of specific feelings, to find words by which to name and recognize them, and a means thereby to talk to others about them before they became overwhelming. Only then did words such as "taking responsibility for managing one's own feelings" take on any real meaning. Again, the extent to which these ego functions have never developed in certain alcoholic patients, or, instead, are lost by regression as a result of the illness, is a problem requiring much further research.

EGO DEFENSE AND STRUCTURE

A complete discussion of the ego defense system of alcoholic patients is beyond the scope of this chapter. I wish to stress two points only, the significance of rationalization and of certain identification processes. The great importance of denial in maintaining symptomatic and addictive drinking is discussed by Dr. Bean in her chapter. Equally important in my opinion is the use of rationalization by alcoholics, a defense so extensively employed as to seem almost pathognomonic for this disorder. Again, it will be important to investigate the degree to which the powerful presence of this defense mechanism or personality style is the result of childhood ego fixations as opposed to regressive processes resulting from drinking itself which bring these defensive modes into prominence.

We have seen in numerous clinical instances how powerfully rationalization operates in alcoholics to explain to others, and probably to themselves as well, a psychophysiological process in whose grip they experience helplessness and whose cause they really are unable to identify. Rationalization operates to defend the alcoholic patient against the painful blow to his self-regard that full acknowledgment of his bewilderment and helplessness would present. Like denial, rationalization prevents the acknowledgment of alcoholism. It precludes true understanding of the motives for drinking and thus works in the service of perpetuating the addictive process.

Incorporation and identification are fundamental processes in the development of ego defensive and adaptive mechanisms. The anamnesis of many alcoholics reveals that family members have been alcoholics over several generations. This fact has an importance over and above whatever evidence of genetic loading or of the role of "environmental influences" it may provide. A number of alcoholics have powerful memories of family closeness achieved *only* when they were drinking together with their fathers or mothers. The classic Chaplin film *City Lights* shows the little tramp befriended and accepted by the millionaire only when the latter is drunk. When sober, his benefactor rejects him abruptly. Alcohol may facilitate certain kinds of object ties. It is a vehicle through which the chronic drinker seeks to recapture in adult life, sometimes in social drinking before symptomatic and addictive phases occur, the memories and associations of a lost past. The use of alcohol in this way by individuals may be more likely to occur in ethnic groups for which alcohol is a culturally sanctioned vehicle for the facilitation of closeness within the family or community.

Also of importance may be the incorporation of, and identification with what might be described as an alcoholic style of dealing with conflict and the outside world. One man in his mid-forties had been unable to manage his drinking for over a decade, with ensuing destruction of family life and deterioration of his professional situation. His history revealed that from early childhood his father had drunk heavily. The father seemed to be able to manage, nevertheless, and the mother never treated her husband's drinking as a problem. The patient became aware in psychotherapy of how deeply he had internalized his father's style, his pattern of using alcohol to manage feelings and to deal with human relations. But forty years later the father was still drinking and had not gotten into serious physical difficulty, nor had he developed the severe psychosocial problems which afflicted his son. It would be valuable for us to know what factors determine whether an individual can employ alcohol as a successful form of defense or adaptation, or cause him to be at risk for pathological regression and addiction as a result of psychological and/or biological vulnerabilities.

THE SOCIOCULTURAL DIMENSION AND SELF-GOVERNANCE

Norman Zinberg has provided in his chapter a comprehensive examination of the sociocultural dimensions of alcoholic and nonalcoholic drinking, an aspect of the problem which has received insufficient attention by psychiatrists. I will not review here his data or arguments. I wish, rather, to point out that if we accept the importance of social factors in determining either the *ability* or the *failure* to drink in a controlled manner, there remains the problem of determining the psychological mechanisms whereby social or cultural elements are incorporated and put into effect within the individual.

I have used the term "self-governance," which implies that the decision-making functions of the individual are themselves shared or socially interdependent, in order to develop a model that may enable us to understand how social and cultural factors operate within the self. A.A. represents a new social context for the problem drinker, one which has a powerful impact in enabling him to become and remain sober. It thus provides a valuable natural experimental context for studying how a particular social institution or group may affect specific aspects of choosing with respect to alcohol, beginning with the initial decision to go to A.A. The early parts of this chapter are concerned with this question. I would hope that the concept of self-governance might prove of value in trying to understand how a variety of other social contexts—families, groups of friends, neighborhoods, ethnic groups—and *changes* within social structures affect the ability of an individual to manage his or her desire to drink. I wish, finally, to point out that even the choice of what social context to *be in,* as, for example, the decision to go to A.A., may be one in which the individual himself participates, although with varying degrees of freedom. Again, the various determinants of this "freedom," and the factors which increase or limit it, relate to what I have in mind in the idea of self-governance.

Implications for Treatment

What implications for the treatment of chronic alcoholism are contained in these thoughts? To begin with, it is clear that one must pay attention to the stage of the illness, whether the individual is drinking symptomatically, is alcoholic but not physiologically dependent, or is physiologically dependent. For even if we may agree that the "loss of control" is never absolute, the power the drinker experiences in relation to his problem will depend a great deal upon the phase of his alcoholism. The idea of "responsibility" should not be used inappropriately, i.e., to expect of the individual management capabilities in relation to his drinking which are not consistent with the stage of his problem, or to burden the patient uselessly with its moral implications. In asking the alcoholic to take responsibility *initially* only for acknowledging his powerlessness in relation to alcohol, A.A. is gauging the ability to be in control during the early period of treatment.

The point of view described here does not argue against the value of appropriate individual or group psychoanalytically informed psychotherapy. Rather, my emphasis upon the decision-making functions in the self implies that the model or theory of psychotherapy to be applied cannot be based on the transference neuroses. As indicated by Vaillant in his chapter, an approach which mobilizes in the therapeutic relationship powerful needs and expectations which cannot be fulfilled in the transference (or anywhere else in the patient's life) may lead to intolerable frustration and aggravation of the drinking problem.

The therapeutic approach should, therefore, be consistent with the felt limitations of the patient in bearing strong or painful affects in the context of his intrapsychic and external resources. Continuing drinking undermines obviously the patient's ego integrative and self-governing capacities, alienates others, and painfully erodes self-regard. Sobriety must, of necessity, be the only initial goal. The psychotherapist during this stage of the illness functions as an agent of change, confronting skillfully the denial, rationalization, and other defenses which protect the patient from the narcissistic injury of recognizing his powerlessness in the face of alcohol. The therapist should recognize early the probable limits of his own power to help the alcoholic become sober and act to get the patient to go to a detoxification center, to A.A., or to whatever institution or group may be needed to provide the self-governing function which may not be within the patient's own capacities, even with the enabling efforts of the therapist.

The further stages of psychotherapy must be conducted with these same principles in mind. The very great limitations of autonomous self-governance in individuals susceptible to alcoholism must continue to be appreciated. The adjunctive power of A.A. or its equivalent (''adjunctive'' refers here to our vantage point—I am focusing in these paragraphs on psychotherapy—not to relative value, as A.A. may remain the more important modality of treatment) in providing essential enabling or self-governing capability for the individual may constitute an essential part of the treatment for many years. A collaborative, noncompetitive approach between the psychotherapist and A.A. can be helpful. A.A. provides an altered social context and directly addresses the egoistic defenses and the burdens and vulnerabilities in the self, meeting directly through its group supportive and spiritual approach the functional deficiencies in self-governance from which the patient suffers in relation to alcohol. A.A. furnishes a series of graded tasks which provide initial relief of pain, trauma and conflict, followed by the expectation of continuing shift away from pathological self-love in the direction of object love and altruism.

Psychotherapy needs to incorporate the insight implicit in A.A.'s approach. The therapist needs to recognize the burden of failure and pain which the alcoholic carries within him (deepened greatly by the humiliations of his problem and his inability to manage it), the use of alcohol as a form of self-ministration and self-caring, the evident limited capability of the alcoholic to deal with many if not all strong or painful affects, and the importance of the reality or social context in the vicissitudes of the drinking problem. The therapist needs to recognize the complexly overdetermined meaning of alcohol and its physiological, psychological, and social functions in the patient's total self-management, meanings in which ego-syntonic and ego-alien elements are intertwined. The therapist should realize that in some cases, because of the peculiar susceptibility of his patient to the addictive use of alcohol, the internalization of new self-governing capabilities in relation to the drive to drink may be of limited power. The therapist's own vanity should not be injured or challenged by having to acknowledge that some patients may always need the help of A.A., or of an equivalent collective power, in the management of alcoholism. Perhaps the therapist's self-regard will be less affected if he can realize that self-governance is never entirely an individual matter, is to a degree for everyone always a shared or collective responsibility.

Summary

For an alcoholic, as for a person who does not have a drinking problem, the determination to take a drink, especially an initial drink when sober, involves a kind of decision, however difficult it may be for the individual to choose otherwise. What Ernst Simmel (1948) called the "mass psychological experiment" that is A.A. has demonstrated that if the social circumstances are altered in specific ways, the balance for many individuals can be shifted so that they are able more consistently to choose *no*. By introducing the psychosocial concept of self-governance, I am trying to develop a theoretical framework within which it may be possible to consider all of the factors—biological, psychological, and sociocultural—which affect this decision.

The examination of A.A.'s approach to the treatment of alcoholism reveals that this institution or association (what we call it depends upon which of its multiple functions is being considered) embodies most if not all of the elements—psychological, biological, social, and spiritual—which go into successful self-governance not just for alcoholics but for all human beings. In the later parts of this chapter I have considered certain implications which I believe A.A.'s approach contains for the psychoanalytic understanding of alcoholism. In particular, I have considered how the psychoanalytic psychology of narcissism and the self, aspects of drive and affect theory, self-care and self-preservation, ego defenses and identification, if considered from the psychosocial perspective which I am suggesting, may be found to shed more light on the problem

of alcoholism than they have heretofore. I have pointed to areas which
might be explored if we are to understand more fully how the decision to
drink is governed and what accounts for this failure of self-governance in
certain individuals.

Some Treatment Implications of the Ego and Self Disturbances in Alcoholism

E. J. Khantzian

Effective treatment of alcoholism must address the core problems of the alcoholic, namely, the enormous difficulties that such people have had in controlling and regulating their behavior, feelings, and self-esteem. Although psychoanalysis is rarely the treatment of choice for alcoholics, it does offer a special understanding of many of the alcoholic's problems and a rationale for the treatment choices and decisions that must be made to help the alcoholic.

Although in its early application to alcoholism* psychoanalysis stressed the instinctual and regressive-pleasurable aspects of alcohol use (Freud, 1905; Abraham, 1908; Rado, 1933; Knight, 1937a; Simmel, 1948), many investigators also appreciated other contributing factors such as mood disturbance, particularly depression, diminished self-esteem, faulty ego ideal formation, and other forms of narcissistic disturbance. Blum (1966), Blum and Blum (1967), Rosenfeld (1965), and Yorke (1970) have published excellent reviews and critiques of these trends in the literature. In this chapter I shall elaborate on more recent psychoanaly-

---

*For the purposes of this presentation, "alcoholism" refers to a frequency and amount of alcohol consumption sufficient to result in significant physical-psychological, social, legal, or employment difficulties for the individual.

tic explanations which have attempted to identify more precisely impairments and disturbances in the ego and self, especially involving problems in self-care, affect management, and self-other relationships and related problems in coping. I shall then review through case examples some important implications for treatment of these ego and self disturbances in alcoholics.

Some of the distinctions made in this presentation between "ego" and "self" are arbitrary and artificial. Although structure and function are stressed in relation to the ego, and subjective attitudes and states in relation to the self, clearly the ego has subjective elements associated with it, and the self has structural and functional aspects. The distinctions are made for heuristic purposes and to delineate more precisely the nature and qualities of the alcoholic's psychological disturbances.

Ego Functions and the Alcoholic

As already indicated, early formulations of alcoholism were heavily influenced by an instinct psychology that stressed the oral dependency and fixation of the alcoholic. More recent attempts to explain alcoholism from a psychoanalytic point of view have understandably focused on the ego to delineate better the nature of the structural impairments that cause alcohol to become such a compelling and devastating influence in an individual's life. The nature of the ego disturbances and impairments in the alcoholic are varied and manifold. I shall selectively focus on and explore some of those that seem to me most germane in understanding a person's problems with alcohol.

In the broadest terms, it seems to me that the alcoholic has been most vulnerable and impaired in two areas of ego functioning. One area involves functions of self-care; whether sober or drunk, the alcoholic demonstrates a repeated tendency to revert to or persist in drinking behavior despite all the apparent indications that such behavior is self-damaging and dangerous. The second area of obvious difficulty has been in the alcoholic's inability to regulate his/her feelings. When sober, he/she often denies or is unable to identify or verbalize feelings. At other times he/she experiences nameless fears and suffers with depression that might be vaguely perceived or experienced as overwhelming and unbearable, even leading to suicide.

THE EGO AND SELF-CARE

The defense mechanism of denial is frequently invoked to explain why or how alcoholics persist in their self-defeating behavior. In such instances the presence of conscious and unconscious destructive impulses, intentions, and behavior is assumed; presumably there is awareness of real or potential danger, but the individual resorts to an active process or defense against such awareness. Although there is probably a reasonable basis for these assumptions, such explanations are excessively influenced by early instinct theory that stressed pleasure seeking and life-death instincts to the exclusion of other considerations. In contradistinction to such a formulation, I am of the opinion that the self-damaging aspects of alcoholism can be better accounted for by considering a deficiency or impairment in development of an ego function we have designated as "self-care."*

The self-destructiveness apparent in alcoholism is not willed or unconsciously motivated by suicidal wishes (i.e., the model of the nemoses) as often as it is the result of impairments and deficiencies in ego functions whereby an individual fails to be aware, cautious, worried, or frightened enough to avoid or desist in behavior that has damaging consequences. This function originates in the early child-mother relationship when the caring and protective functions of the mother are gradually internalized so that the individual can eventually take care of and adequately protect himself/herself from harm and dangerous situations (Khantzian et al., 1974; Khantzian, 1978). Extremes of parental deprivation or indulgence may have devastating subsequent effects, and it is not surprising that both patterns are frequently identified in the background of alcoholics (Knight, 1937a; Simmel, 1948; Blum, 1966).

Self-care is a generic or global function and is related to ego functions such as signal anxiety, reality testing, judgment, and synthesis. When self-care is impaired, certain other ego mechanisms of defense are prominent or exaggerated. In fact I suspect such mechanisms might be related to and perhaps even secondary to impairments in self-care. That is, in working with individuals who have self care problems I have been impressed by how they are vaguely aware of their susceptibility to mishaps and danger and they sense in themselves the lack of a self-protective or

*I am indebted to Dr. John E. Mack for the germinal idea of self-care as an ego function. We are currently collaborating on a project to further explore and understand self-care functions.

self-caring ability and thus need and depend on others to protect them and to help in making judgments about dangerous situations. The ill-defined fears of vulnerability and feelings of helplessness associated with such states compel those who are so affected to counteract these feelings and to externalize their problem by resorting to such mechanisms as justification, projection, and phobic and counterphobic avoidance. In the absence of self-care, such defenses are prominent in alcoholics.

I believe that self-care is deficient, impaired, or absent in many if not most alcoholics and that this accounts for much of the disastrous and destructive behavior in their lives, in addition to the malignant involvement with alcohol. In studying over fifty alcoholics, I have observed the problem of self-care in their histories of poor attendance to preventable medical and dental problems, patterns of delinquent, accidental, and violent behavior, and other forms of impulsivity that predate their alcoholism. It is most obvious in their apparent disregard for the consequences of drinking; there is little evidence of fear, anxiety, or realistic evaluation of the deterioration and danger when they revert to or persist in drinking. Although much of this is secondary to the regression and deterioration in judgment as a function of continued drinking, I have been impressed by the presence and persistence of these tendencies in such individuals both prior to their becoming alcoholic and subsequent to detoxification and stabilization (Khantzian, 1978, 1979b).

THE EGO AND REGULATION OF FEELINGS

Whereas self-care serves to warn and protect against external dangers and the consequences of careless behavior, the ego functions involved in regulation of feelings serve as signals and guides in managing and protecting against instability and chaos in our internal emotional life. Many of the same processes which establish self-care functions and originate from the nurturing and protective role of the mother in infancy are involved in the development of ego functions that serve to regulate feelings. It is not surprising, then, that alcoholics also suffer from a range of ego impairments that affect their capacity to regulate their feeling life. These impairments take such forms as an inability to identify and verbalize feelings, an incapacity to tolerate painful feelings such as anxiety and depression, an inability to modulate feelings, problems in activation and initiative, and a tendency to exhibit extreme manifestations of feelings including hypomania, phobic-anxious states, panic attacks, and labile emotional outbursts.

As has been suggested for other mental processes and functions, affects develop along certain lines and are subject to fixation, distortions, and regression. Krystal and Raskin (1970) have helpfully traced and formulated how the affects of anxiety and depression develop out of a common undifferentiated matrix. At the outset feelings are undifferentiated, somatized, and not verbalized. Normally, the tendency is for feelings to become differentiated, desomatized, and verbalized. If this process proceeds optimally, it contributes significantly to the development of an effective stimulus barrier. As used here, "stimulus barrier" refers to aspects of ego function that maintain minimal levels of unpleasant feelings through appropriate action and mechanisms of defense when they reach high or intolerable levels (Krystal & Raskin, 1970; Khantzian, 1978). In such instances, feelings act as a guide or signal to mobilize ego mechanisms of defense in response to internal emotions and external stimuli. Either as a result of developmental arrest or because of regression caused by traumatic events later in life, alcoholics fail to differentiate successfully, with the consequence that they are unable to use feelings as signals or guides because they are unable to identify affects or their feelings are unbearable or overwhelming. Because of defects in the stimulus barrier, alcoholics use denial and/or the effects of alcohol to ward off overwhelming affects (e.g., undifferentiated anxiety-depression). That is, in lieu of an affective stimulus barrier "drugs or alcohol are used to avoid impending psychic trauma in circumstances which would not be potentially traumatic to other people" (Krystal & Raskin, 1970, p. 31).

Borderline and narcissistic pathology has been implicated in alcoholism (Kernberg, 1975, p. 117; Kohut, 1971, p. 46; Klein, 1975), but there has been little systematic attempt to understand the relationship between the structural impairments of such pathology and alcoholism. Kernberg has emphasized ego weakness in borderline conditions and has singled out lack of anxiety tolerance and impulse control, primitive defensive operations including rigid walling off of good and bad introjects, and splitting and denial in the service of preventing anxiety related to aggression (pp. 25–45). Kernberg fails to make it clear whether he believes that such borderline symptomatology is at the root of alcohol problems or that borderline conditions and alcoholism have similar processes operating that affect both conditions. Presumably, the borderline processes delineated by Kernberg are consistent with those identified by Krystal and Raskin, who have detailed more precisely how such problems in coping with feelings affect alcoholics.

Taking a somewhat more descriptive approach, Klein has similarly focused on unpleasant dysphoric affect states associated with borderline conditions and alcoholism. He discounts the role of "ego defects" in borderline conditions and instead emphasizes the importance of a descriptive approach for purposes of diagnosis and classification. Klein stresses the ubiquity of labile, anxious, and depressive states associated with so-called borderline pathology. He believes the "border" in such conditions is more with affective disorders than with neurosis, character pathology, or schizophrenia, and that it is on such a basis that certain individuals welcome the effects of alcohol. He has singled out several syndromes which alcohol and antianxiety agents are sought for relief, namely hysteroid ("rejection sensitive") dysphoria, chronic anxiety-tension states, and phobic neurosis with panic attacks. Despite his disclaimer about ego defects in such conditions, I believe his own description of these problems as an "affective or activation disorder, or a stereotyped affective overresponse" (Klein, 1975, p. 369) speaks for an impairment in the ego's capacity to regulate feelings in such individuals. This is further supported by his observation that psychoactive drugs are effective with such patients because "they modify states of dysregulation of affect and activation." Along these lines, Quitkin et al. (1972) have impressively demonstrated that a small but significant proportion of alcoholics suffer from a phobic-anxious syndrome and respond to imipramine with marked symptomatic improvement and elimination of their dependence on alcohol.

In brief, then, I believe there is convincing evidence from several convergent lines of inquiry to support the point of view that significant impairments in ego structure predispose to alcoholism. Impairments in self-care leave individuals ill equipped to properly weigh, anticipate, and assess the consequences of risky and self-damaging behavior, but particularly in relation to the consequences of their alcohol involvement. The other area of ego impairment in alcoholics involves problems in recognizing, regulating, and harnessing feeling states to the point that conditions of immobilization or being overwhelmed with affects result, and alcohol is sought to overcome or relieve such dilemmas.

The Self and the Alcoholic

Alcoholics suffer not only because of impairments in their ego. They also suffer because of impairments and injury in their sense of self. As in ego disturbances, developmental problems loom large in the self disturbances of alcoholics. Both the development of the ego and the sense of self are results of internalization processes. Optimally, the developing child acquires qualities and functions from the caring parents such that the individual can eventually take care of himself. When successful, the process of internalization establishes within the person a coherent sense of the self, an appreciation of the separate existence of others, and adequate ego functions that serve purposes of defense and adaptation (Khantzian, 1978).

In the previous sections we focused on how alcohol problems were related to impairments in ego function which resulted in a deficiency and/or inability to appreciate consequences of dangerous behavior and to regulate emotion. In this section I will emphasize and explore how alcohol problems are also the result of impairments in the sense of self whereby the individual is unable or ill equipped to value, comfort, soothe, care for, and express himself/herself. Although I have designated the impairments around self-care and affect regulation as ego disturbances, such problems are not entirely distinguishable from self disturbances. As indicated at the outset of this chapter, some of these distinctions are arbitrary. It is likely that the nature of the self disturbances I will delineate in this section significantly impact upon and interact with ego disturbances involving self-care and (affect) regulation.

DEPENDENCY AND THE SELF

Alcoholics are desperately dependent people. Formulations about the nature of this dependency have, however, been overly simplistic and reductionistic, placing undue emphasis on the symbolic, oral, regressive aspects of the alcoholic's dependency on the substance itself. Similarly, the personal relationships of the alcoholic are characterized as infantile and clinging (Khantzian, 1979b). The dependency of alcoholics is not primarily the result of oral fixations and oral cravings. The dependency has more to do with deficits and defects in psychological structure and sense of self whereby the alcoholic depends on the effects of alcohol and attaches himself to others to compensate for deficiencies in self-care, affect regulation, self-esteem, and subjective sense of well-being.

Balint (1968) has characterized the alcoholic's dependency as a "basic fault." He emphasizes that it does not have the form of an instinct or of conflict, but is "something wrong in the mind, a kind of deficiency which must be put right." According to Balint, the alcoholic seeks the effects of alcohol to establish a feeling of "harmony—a feeling that everything is now well between them and their environment—and . . . the yearning for this feeling of harmony is the most important cause of alcoholism or, for that matter, any form of addiction" (p. 56). Along these same lines, Kohut (1971) has observed that dependency of such people on substances (Kohut does not distinguish between alcohol and other substances) says less about the person's attachment to substances and/or people as loved or loving objects than about the search for "a replacement for a defect in psychological structure" (p. 46).

The "fault" or "defect" that alcoholics experience in their psychological-self structure is the result of developmental failures in ego ideal formation. The developing child and adolescent insufficiently experience admired and admiring feelings in response to parents and other adult figures. Because of this deficiency in the relationship with parents and others, such individuals fail to internalize and identify with the encouraging, valued, and idealized qualities of important adults.

Although alcoholics indeed suffer as a result of conscience or superego and seek to drown their guilt and self-condemnation in alcohol, I am impressed that they suffer more from the lack of an adequate ego ideal that would otherwise help them to evaluate themselves as worthwhile and good enough in a whole range of human involvements and activities. Because of faulty ego ideal formation, self-esteem suffers and there is an inability or failure to judge one's relationships, work, or play as sufficient or satisfactory. As a result, individuals so afflicted constantly seek external sources of reassurance, recognition, solace, and approval. Such individuals feel especially wanting from within for an approved self by an approving ego ideal, and it is in this respect that they are so desperately dependent. They seek out alcohol, people, and activities not primarily for gratification of oral, infantile drives and wishes, but more in an attempt to feel better or good about themselves, as they are almost totally unable to achieve this feeling for themselves from within.

Corollary to the disturbance in ego ideal formation are disturbances related to the capacity to comfort, soothe, and care for oneself. Alcoholics seem to adopt modes of polar extremes with regard to such needs and functions. Alcoholics' search for "external supplies," their dependency on alcohol and leaning on others, are the result of a failure to internalize adequately and to develop capacities for nurturance within the self, which causes them to turn primarily outside themselves for comfort, soothing and caring, or defensively to deny such needs or wants.

PATHOLOGICAL SELF-FORMATIONS

One of the main consequences of the ego and self disturbances in alcoholics is that such individuals have developed and display troublesome and self-defeating compensatory defenses and pathological self-structures in response to underlying conflicts around need satisfaction and dependency. In some instances the defenses that are employed serve to compensate for and counteract the sense of incompleteness such people feel as a result of deficits in affect defense and self-esteem. In other instances the more rigid and primitive defenses that are employed seem to be the result of pathological internalizations, identifications, and self-structures. The alcoholic seeks the releasing effect of alcohol to overcome rigid and overdrawn defenses and to facilitate and regulate the experiencing and expression of affectionate or aggressive feelings in the absense of ego and self structure that helps to modulate such affects and drives (Khantzian, 1979a).

Some of the recent elaborations on self-pathology are probably pertinent with regard to the facilitating and regulating influences of alcohol and help to explain why alcoholics need to depend on such effects. Kernberg (1975) has emphasized the importance of pathological self structures in borderline conditions and has also implicated them in alcoholism. He believes that rigid and primitive defenses of splitting, denial, and projection serve to cause the repression, splitting off, and dissociation of parts of the self, and that the effect of alcohol acts to "refuel" the grandiose self and to activate the "all good" self and object images and to deny the "all bad" internalized objects (p. 222). Despite the emphasis on a deficit psychology, Kohut places equal if not greater emphasis on compensatory and defensive reactions such as massive repression, self-disavowal, and denial of needs. According to Kohut, substance users resort to the effects of substances to lift these defenses in order to feel the soothing and resurgence of self-esteem they are otherwise unable to experience (Kohut 1977a). Although Kohut does not specify any particular drugs or substance, in my experience it is precisely this effect that the alcoholic seeks to achieve with the use of alcohol.

On a similar basis, Krystal and Raskin (1970) and Krystal (1977) stress the special and exaggerated defenses of denial and splitting that are adopted by individuals dependent on alcohol. These defenses serve to "wall off" and suppress aggressive and loving feelings in relation to the self and others. Krystal emphasizes the great difficulty alcoholics have with ambivalence, and how they prefer to use the short-acting effect of alcohol to experience and give vent to such feelings briefly, and therefore "safely."

Finally, on a somewhat different basis, Silber (1970, 1974) has focused on the developmental impairments of alcoholics that have been the result of pathological and destructive identifications with psychotic and/or very disturbed parents. The self-damaging and destructive aspects of alcohol involvement parallel and represent identifications with self-neglecting, self-destructive aspects of the parents.

Treatment Implications

As I have indicated, alcoholics suffer tremendously in their attempts to regulate their behavior, feelings, and relationships with other people. Effective treatment of these problems must be based on a more precise identification of the disturbances in the ego and self structures of alcoholics, and our psychotherapeutic and psychopharmacological interventions should be based on such an appreciation. In this final section, using case material, I will explore some treatment implications of the alcoholic's ego and self disturbances.

IMPLICATIONS FOR INITIAL CARE

At the outset, the most urgent and often life-threatening aspect of alcoholism must be faced, namely, the impulsive unbridled use of alcohol. Alcoholics Anonymous has been most effective in helping alcoholics gain control over their drinking; "They have become experts in sobriety" (Mack—personal communication). It is little wonder that A.A.'s success rests upon an emphasis on abstinence as the single most important goal to be achieved by the alcoholic. A.A. has often worked because it skillfully manages and compensates for the impairments in self-care. A.A. also works because it contains and partly satisfies some of the other determinants of alcoholism, namely, problems in regulating emotions and maintaining self-esteem and related dependency problems.

Unfortunately, A.A. is unacceptable for many if not a majority of alcoholics. For many alcoholics, psychiatric and psychological approaches become a logical if not necessary alternative. If such becomes the case, it remains critical that the clinician appreciate, as much as A.A. has, the urgency and dangers of the uncontrolled drinking, as the equally important determinants and causes of the alcoholism are explored and understood. Clearly, until control over the drinking is established, exploration of predisposing causes is of little value.

I have evolved an approach that has proved to be surprisingly useful and effective in dealing with uncontrolled drinking when contact is first made with the alcoholic. As indicated, it is in regard to the uncontrolled drinking that impairments in self-care are most alarmingly and dangerously apparent, and this must become the first focus of any treatment intervention. Rather than stress abstinence or sobriety, I immediately attempt to ascertain the amount and pattern of drinking and ask the patient respectfully and empathically to share with me his/her own reasons for drinking, especially what the drinking does for him/her. I also ask patients as tactfully as I can to reflect on how much danger and harm they have caused themselves as a result of their drinking. Such an approach helps a patient to ease into a treatment relationship where his or her enormous shame about and desperate dependence on alcohol are not immediately challenged or threatened, but which at the same time begins to focus early on some of the important determinants of the uncontrolled drinking.

Once satisfied that the drinking is out of control, I emphatically point this out with undisguised concern and stress that it is the single most immediate problem to be faced. Unrecognized impairments and evident rationalizations are identified as well as the unacknowledged physical and behavioral consequences of the drinking. I openly discuss how difficult it will be to stop drinking, but share with the patient my conviction about the urgency for control and an intention to keep this the main focus for both of us until it is achieved. Keeping the focus on control allows a strategy to develop that avoids premature insistence on permanent abstinence, or an equally untenable permissive acceptance of uncontrolled drinking. Alternative models and methods of control are described explicitly, such as gradual curtailment or abrupt cessation with short-term drug substitution if physiological dependence is evident. If the latter is the case, or if deterioration is evident and/or there is need for external support and control, hospitalization is recommended. In some cases I insist upon it if it seems necessary. Surprisingly, this is rarely the case, and often there is a margin and opportunity in such an approach for the therapist to share with the patient information, experiences, and knowledge about how others have gained control over their drinking. In most instances then, the emphasis in this approach is on establishing control and giving the patient a chance to make a choice.

In one case the discovery that a choice about one's drinking can be made in collaboration with the therapist evolved over several months.

CASE 1

This patient was a fifty-one-year-old tradesman who had worked successfully at his job and consumed large amounts of distilled alcohol daily dating back to his late teenage years. He was considered a leader among his peers and until four years prior to seeking treatment had functioned effectively as the elected shop steward for his union. His drinking usually began at mid-day, and he continued drinking from the end of the workday at 4:00 P.M. until supper. He drank with his co-workers in a local pub which was also a gathering place for people of his own nationality. He insisted and his wife confirmed that he never was drunk or reacted adversely to alcohol until four years before, when his shoe shop went out of business and he was unable to find employment because most of the other shoe shops in the area were also going out of business.

At the time of evaluation he indicated that over the past year and a half his drinking had been totally out of control, stating, ''I wouldn't dare count how much I was drinking a day this past year or so—all I know is I needed it to start the day and finish the day.'' He stated that during this period he was experiencing ''shakes'' every morning. I immediately shared with him my sense that his drinking was out of control and agreed with him that it probably dated back to the loss of his job. I indicated that it would be extremely important to gain control, but I avoided explaining then what this would entail. During the initial sessions he alternated between being garrulous, expansive, and bantering and being irritable and defensive, especially about his drinking. According to the patient,— again confirmed by his wife, who was reliable—he made significant but only moderately successful efforts to curtail his drinking over the first two months of weekly contacts with me. After his ninth session I felt he was more at ease with me as he was sharing both pleasant and troubling reminiscences from his childhood years, as well as his challenges and experiences as a union steward. In this context of a more relaxed treatment relationship with me I expressed my concern that he was not sufficiently controlling his drinking. I told him that I was not sure he could take one or two drinks and then leave it alone. I told him that curtailment could be one form of control but I suspected it was not working for him. I shared with him my own discovery that I could not control my use of cigarettes and that smoking one cigarette inevitably led to my resuming smoking a pack a day and how after much experimentation I had learned that abstinence from cigarettes (and the occasional substitution of a cigar) worked best for me. I reviewed with him my knowledge of A.A. and my experience with other patients for whom abstinence from alcohol seemed to work best as a form of control, but I said it remained to be seen what would work for him.

In an interview one month later he reported being discouraged in his efforts to modify his drinking and appeared dejected and depressed. In this context I told him that he seemed to be least able to control his drinking when he felt ''lousy.'' Shortly after this session he stopped drinking. In an interview another month later in which he was evidently feeling much better, he indicated he was not craving alcohol at all. After a thoughtful review on his part of how he planned to approach finding a new job, I puzzled out loud with him how he had managed to gain control over his drinking. He told me that he had thought about my comment two months previously about whether he could have one or two drinks and then stop. He said he decided to try it out and he discovered he couldn't. Again he stressed that once he had stopped drinking, he didn't crave alcohol at all. Reflecting out loud, he reminded me again how much alcohol he needed to get a ''little high,'' an amount that would make others ''go staggering.'' Not without significance and characteristic of this man, he made a playful reference to my example of substituting cigars for cigarettes and revealed some successful substitutions of his own—he said he was ''drinking lots of Moxie [a bittersweet, pungent carbonated beverage] and milk.'' He also added that he was eating well. Over two years of follow-up this man has remained totally sober and abstinent, and he has resumed working in a supervisory capacity. He has also considerably improved his relationship with his wife.

Taking an approach such as the one I have presented here, I have now had the experience of seeing several patients significantly modify and ultimately gain control over their drinking behavior. However, in the majority of the cases I have treated, the patients have *chosen* abstinence as the most reliable means of control. For some, this occurs at the outset; for others, after some tentative experimentation and attempts at continued drinking, such as those I described in Case 1. What has been most impressive has been the salutary discovery by the patient and myself that some choice can be exercised in achieving the goal of control over drinking behavior. In taking such an approach, struggles tend to be avoided, the patient feels a gradual sense of mastery over his/her own problems, and the joint effort to solve a problem fosters a healthy alliance rather than an adversary role between patient and therapist (Khantzian, 1980).

As the urgency and danger of the destructive drinking behavior recede and the patient begins to develop an alliance with the therapist, examination and treatment of the predisposing disturbances can and should be considered. Although psychotherapeutic and psychopharmacological treatment of alcoholics has often been dismissed as ineffective and possibly even dangerous, I believe growing clinical understanding and experience with alcoholics suggest that alcoholics are eminently suitable for such treatment. In the preliminary phases of treatment it is most important that decisions about treatment alternatives (psychotherapy and/or drug therapy) be based on identifying more precisely the particular qualities and extent of the ego and self disturbances and other target symptoms that are ascertained. Although I have stressed certain ego and self disturbances in this chapter, it should be apparent that a whole range of psychiatric problems may contribute to or be a part of an alcohol problem, and specific treatment modalities should be tailored to the particular psychopathology or symptoms that may be identified. Of course allowances should also be made in the early phases of treatment, especially with psychotherapy, for cognitive impairments due to toxic aftereffects of prolonged drinking (usually reversible) that make integration of information and interpretations more difficult for the patient (Krystal, 1962; Moore, 1962; Rosett, unpublished).

IMPLICATIONS FOR PSYCHOTHERAPY

Critics of psychotherapy for alcoholism have focused on the impulsive, dependent, demanding characteristics and lack of introspection of alcoholics which make them ill suited for therapy, and others have stressed the destructive and unworkable regressive transferences that develop in psychotherapeutic relationships with alcoholics (Hill & Blane, 1967; Canter, 1969; Pattison, 1972). These accounts give an unnecessarily pessimistic view of the alcoholic and do not consider how such reactions surface as a result of passivity on the part of the therapist and an outmoded model of therapy that emphsizes uncovering techniques alone. These approaches reflect once again the influences of an early instinct psychology that is based on the assumption that recovery and cure take place by making the unconscious conscious, reconstructing the past, and uncovering feelings. More recent approaches have better taken into account the alcoholic's impairments and disturbances in identifying and tolerating painful feelings, and have a clearer appreciation of the nature of alcoholics' dependency needs and major problems around self-esteem. In contrast to early psychotherapeutic models, more recent approaches have appreciated the importance of structure, continuity, activity, and empathy in engaging and retaining alcoholics in treatment (Chafetz et al., 1962; Silber, 1970, 1974; Krystal & Raskin, 1970; Khantzian, 1980).

For some, the initial work of therapy becomes that of gradually discovering and identifying states of anxiety and/or depression that have been relieved by drinking. For others, a gradual identification of the forms their dependency has taken, such as a denial of their needs or counterdependent attitudes, becomes important. In early phases of treatment there is a need for the therapist to be active, and to share openly his understanding of the alcoholic's problems, particularly how his use of alcohol has interacted with the particular ego and self disturbances that have been identified.

Some of the alcoholic's disturbances in identifying and experiencing his feelings and rigidly defending against affects have particular psychotherapeutic implications. Krystal has suggested that a "pre-therapy" phase of psychotherapy (personal communication) may be necessary with such patients to teach them about their feelings by helping them to identify and label them, particularly feelings of anxiety, fear, and depression. Krystal (1977) has also focused on alcoholics' use of splitting and other rigid defenses to wall off their ambivalent feelings. He has emphasized that effective therapy with such individuals hinges on helping them to master their fear of closeness with the therapist (related to reactivated childhood longings and feelings of aggression), to learn to grieve effectively, to take responsibility for their destructive feelings, and, perhaps most important, to overcome the barriers (i.e., rigid defenses) that prevent effective comforting of themselves. In my own work with alcoholics I have been impressed with how the affect disturbances significantly contribute to the self-care impairments of alcoholics and how necessary and useful it is to help such patients realize how feelings can be used as a guide for one's behavior and actions.

CASE 2

Psychotherapeutic interaction with a fifty-one-year-old man who had a combined alcohol-drug problem nicely demonstrated elements of such affect disturbance, and how such disturbances may be psychotherapeutically managed and brought into the patient's awareness. This patient also gave dramatic evidence of impairments in self-care and some of the more extreme and primitive defenses that are adopted in the absence of self-care, namely denial, counterphobia, and massive repression.

This man had achieved a significant amount of success in his life and his work despite an early childhood in which he suffered much traumatic neglect as a result of his mother's alcoholism and father's chronic depression and absorption with his wife's alcoholism.

Subsequent to the patient's eleven-year-old son's contracting a severe illness, the patient had recently become more withdrawn, depending increasingly on alcohol and drugs himself, and he had been mandated for treatment as a result of indiscriminate behavior at work as a result of his drug-alcohol use. The two most outstanding features of this man, not unrelated to each other, were (a) the direction his interests took starting in early adolescence, and (b) his almost total inability to talk about his feelings. Starting at around age ten he precociously and actively became sexually involved with the opposite sex. Early in his teenage years he turned to and became involved with hobbies that he has continued up until the present which have definite danger and/or violence associated with them. Except for his quick wit (sometimes biting) he displays very little emotion, usually appearing indifferent or apathetic in his facial expressions. Attempts to elicit or draw out feelings are met with either frank denial or, at best, tentative acknowledgment that he might be feeling something.

During one group therapy session the patient reviewed some of his recent indiscretions in his work situation that resulted in possibly jeopardizing his job. He went into great detail about the events, which could have resulted in harm to himself and others. He appeared to be strikingly devoid of feelings as he elaborated on his behavior. A group member immediately exclaimed, "Didn't you realize how vulnerable you were leaving yourself?" The patient insisted that he never gave the situation a thought and denied being fearful about dangerous consequences for himself or others. Other members of the group persisted in inferring an unconscious self-destructive motive. I chose to comment on the patient's insistence that he had neither thought about the danger nor experienced any fear in relation to his behavior. I shared with him and the group my sense of his reluctance and inability to "fuss" over himself or to admit to any worry or fear. I suggested that this difficulty was perhaps a reflection of insufficient "fussing" over him earlier in his life when his parents were too tied up with themselves and their own problems.

As the group meeting continued, a curious and revealing exchange developed between myself and the patient in which he gave further evidence of his deficiencies in signal affects (i.e., feelings in the service of mobilizing mechanisms of defense and/or restraint over impulses). This exchange also demonstrated the necessity for the therapist to be ready to use his/her own feelings and reactions with such patients as an object lesson in helping them to use feelings to better serve and care for themselves. The patient commented on and inquired about my seemingly gruff response in a recent individual psychotherapy hour when he had corrected me on some technicality. I hesitantly acknowledged that he might have been correct in his impression, and I indicated that I knew this was a trait of mine when I am worried and I believed it reflected my worrying about his problem. I subsequently offered that I was worrying for him when he was not sufficiently worrying about himself. He next disclosed to the group and myself how at times in our individual sessions he often deliberately "eyeballed" me and stared me down and that he was surprised that I repeatedly looked away, and again he asked why I reacted in that way. I was surprised again and somewhat caught off guard (perhaps I should not have been) that a man who was so unaware of his own reactions could be so fined tuned to my reactions. Pausing for a moment to get over my surprise, I answered him by acknowledging once again that he was most likely correct in his observation and that my reaction was probably a function of some self-consciousness as a result of his staring at me. I told him that I thought his puzzlement and surprise were some indication that he was unable to admit to any such part of himself, but that if he could continue to watch for other people's self-consciousness, especially in group therapy, he might better develop this in himself to his own benefit. I emphasized how my self-consciousness and others' can actually act as a guide and that being insufficiently self-conscious caused him to get into trouble. Toward the end of the group meeting he began mildly to taunt one of the patients on the number of cups of coffee he drank during the group meeting. Piecing this together with his uncharacteristic confrontations about my behavior, I interpreted his provocativeness to be a function of having overexposed himself and his behavioral difficulties early in the meeting. I pointed out that it was to his credit that he was courageous enough to share his problems with the group, but that I was also equally concerned that he might have overexposed himself; I told him that someone else might not have been as open and as explicit, leading to so much exposure, but that in his case he was not sufficiently self-conscious to protect himself from overexposure.

DURATION AND GOALS OF PSYCHOTHERAPY

Decisions about the duration and goals of psychotherapy with alcoholics should remain flexible and should be based on a consideration of the patient's wishes and a judgment by the therapist, weighing the indications and necessity for continued treatment against the hazards and risks. Many patients feel great relief and appreciation when they are able to control their drinking and know that someone who understands and accepts their problems is available. Such patients often decide for themselves that this is enough of a goal. If the patient is out of immediate danger, I often agree to stop, albeit my decision at times might be based as much on my clinical judgments about the patient as simply on what the patient wants to do, or even based more on my judgment. The following case illustrates how clinical judgments to stop treatment and what the patient wants are not mutually exclusive.

CASE 3

This patient, a forty-two-year-old, very intense and conscientious man, gave me good reasons pragmatically and clinically to take him seriously when he proposed that it was best to settle for the initial gains we had made and to discontinue his individual psychotherapy with me after a brief intervention that lasted about three months.

His initial meeting with me was prompted by a crisis that had been precipitated in his second marriage as a result of continued, recurrent alcoholic binges. He had recently remarried, entered into a new small business venture and relocated on the East Coast—all in an attempt to build a new life. He was originally from an extremely wealthy Midwestern family. After attending an exclusive college and doing a tour of duty as a jet pilot in the military, he joined his family's large corporate business. From his late college years and through the military he was a heavy social drinker. Upon joining the family business and over the subsequent ten years, his drinking became increasingly heavy, which ultimately led to a decline and deterioration in his social standing, his marriage, and his job.

By the time he came for his first interview he had rejoined Alcoholics Anonymous (he belonged once before) and was having some success in abstaining from alcohol. In the first visit with me he reviewed how success, ambition, and achievement had always been tremendously important. He went back and forth from examining my professional certificates on the wall to discussing his father's great business success (despite being an extremely heavy drinker himself) to his own lack of achievement and his alcoholic decline. He then went on to express in a most poignant way how there had been a lifelong strained relationship of aloofness and distance between his father and himself and how he had always longed for a better relationship. In this and subsequent interviews it was quickly evident that his longings for a closer relationship with his father coexisted with feelings of just as much bitterness and hatred. Strikingly and in contrast, during the same initial interview he reviewed with me some of his work in Alcoholics Anonymous and how it was helping him. He said the people there were "real—and seeking alternatives to destructiveness." He stressed how they were able to get into the issues of alcohol, and that the feelings of "warmness, camaraderie, and family" were very important to him. At the end of the first hour we agreed that there was a "cauldron of issues bubbling inside" with which he struggled, but that for a while we would focus on his marital problems and he would continue to work on his sobriety through Alcoholics Anonymous. He agreed to join a couples group in which a common denominator was that the life of one of the spouses in each couple had been affected by drug or alcohol dependence. He also agreed to see me for individual psychotherapy.

Over the next several months his ambivalence toward me became evident. On the one hand he admired my achievements and how I seemed to be able to understand him. However, he also regularly made it clear that psychiatrists understood little about alcoholism or alcoholics. In his first interview with me he said, "My [previous] psychiatrist never even asked about the alcohol—he gave me medicine saying it might help to deal with some of the underlying feelings so that I wouldn't have to use alcohol—and that when we got to the root of the problem, then maybe I wouldn't need to drink. I liked him, but I don't think he understood anything about alcohol." In subsequent visits he either would totally accept my clarifications and interpretations or just as arbitrarily would argue a point based on "strict principles" and a conviction that A.A. could serve him better, adding, furthermore, that it didn't cost anything.

After two months of individual and couples group meetings he became more clear and explicit about the reasons for his reluctance to continue in individual

symptoms such as sleeplessness, anorexia, and anergia is studied, in others whether abstinence is achieved, and in others overall improvement of depression. Reviews by Mottin (1973), Viamontes (1972), and Greenblatt and Shader (1973) are generally pessimistic about all classes of psychopharmacological agents in the treatment of alcoholism. Mottin is most negative with regard to drug therapy. Viamontes's review reveals that the majority of uncontrolled clinical trials using antidepressants, phenothiazines, and benzodiazepines are effective in the treatment of alcoholism. Mottin, Viamontes, and Greenblatt and Shader uniformly emphasize the methodological problems of clinical trials with these drugs and cite the lack of double-blind controlled studies that might better establish the efficacy of these drugs.

Notwithstanding these methodological inconsistencies and shortcomings, a number of carefully controlled and executed studies over the past decade have proved to be promising and hopeful with regard to the use of drug therapy in alcoholism. Bliding (1973) demonstrated the benzodiazepine oxazepam to be more effective than chlorprothixene or placebo in the treatment of chronic alcoholism. Kissin and Gross (1968) showed chlordiazepoxide combined with imipramine to be effective in controlling drinking behavior and furthering overall improvement. In studies by Butterworth (1971) and Overall et al. (1973), the use of tricyclic antidepressants and to a lesser extent phenothiazines has proved effective in relieving symptoms of underlying depression (also anxiety in the Overall et al. study). In another important study conducted by Quitkin et al. (1972) target symptoms of phobia and anxiety in a subsegment of alcoholics were dramatically relieved by imipramine with significant improvement of drinking behavior. More recently, reports by Wren et al. (1974), Kline et al. (1974), and Merry et al. (1976) suggest that lithium is effective in cases of alcoholism associated with depression.

What is to be made of these often confusing and contradictory findings? What should guide the practitioner in the decision to treat or not treat the alcoholic with these pharmacological agents? Do the findings of a dynamic approach that identifies structural impairments have any relevance to a descriptive approach that suggests such individuals might have pharmacologically treatable problems? Most if not all of the drug studies with alcoholics have been based on descriptive approaches in which target symptoms and psychopathology are identified. Nevertheless, I believe there is a basis for speculation that such target symptoms and psychopathology are the result of failures and deficits in ego and self structures, particularly those involving regulation of affects. I expect that these drugs work with alcoholics because they serve, support, and augment otherwise impaired ego capacities and disturbances in self-regulation.

The findings of descriptive psychiatry complement an approach aimed at identifying the ego and self disturbances in alcoholics. This is particularly so given recent trends in both descriptive psychiatry and psychoanalysis to state more explicitly the criteria for diagnosis and identify more precisely the nature of the psychopathology.* Such approaches are consistently demonstrating the ubiquity of depression, phobia, anxiety, and panic states in association with alcoholism (Weisman & Meyers, 1980; Weisman et al.; Winokur et al., 1970; Behar & Winokur, 1979; Klein, 1975; Quitkin et al., 1972). There is evidence that these conditions are as treatable in alcoholics as they are in other patients and that they are contributory to the alcoholism (Behar & Winokur, 1979; Klein, 1975; Quitkin et al., 1972). Although the incidence of depression in alcoholism has ranged from 3 to 98 percent in different studies, the application of precise diagnostic criteria for depression and phobic anxious states has produced more uniform results when attempts have been made more recently to identify these conditions in alcoholics (Weisman et al., 1980; Keeler et al., 1979). Moreover, when considered from a point of view taken by Klein (1975), where a more generic view of affective disturbance is considered symptoms of dysphoria, anergia, anxiety, and depression become interacting, overlapping, and on a continuum and seem more to be evidence of the "dysregulation of affects" and "disorders of activation" to which Klein refers.

In the first part of this chapter I explored how self-care disturbances and disturbances in affect regulation predisposed individuals to alcoholism. I speculated that in the absence of adequate self-care functions, the individuals' vague sense of vulnerability might contribute to phobias in alcoholics. I also suggested that because of developmental failures alcoholics either overregulated or underregulated their affects and depended on the effects of alcohol to release or submerge their "good and bad" feelings. In my estimation, many of the symptomatic features of alcoholics, including, for example, anxiety, depression, dysphoria, and sleeplessness, are indicators and the result of more fundamental and serious disturbances in the ego and self structures that are responsible for affect regulation and the achievement of subjective states of well-being, including the maintenance of self-esteem. These disturbances seriously incapacitate the alcoholic and are not easily or readily influenced by

*Editor's Note, *Archives of General Psychiatry,* 1979, *36,* 3.

psychotherapeutic interventions alone, especially early in treatment. It is exactly in this respect that many alcoholics need assistance with the intolerable and overwhelming feeling states with which they suffer and why psychopharmacological agents might be considered useful if not necessary.

The common and prevalent distrust of alcoholics' suitability for drug therapy is unwarranted, in my opinion. Much of the controversy over drug use in alcoholism stems from a misunderstanding of the alcoholic's dependency problems. When considering psychopharmacological treatment of the alcoholic, it is understandable that we remain apprehensive about the "regressive-oral" needs and inclinations of the alcoholic. However, when we consider the structural impairments with which alcoholics suffer, the use of psychoactive drugs becomes a logical alternative that should be seriously considered. In my own experience, using predominantly tricyclic antidepressants and/or benzodiazepines (particularly oxazepam), I have very rarely had patients abuse or misuse these drugs. On the other hand, I have seen several alcoholic patients in consultation who had overused prescribed benzodiazepines, and it has been my clinical impression that this was more likely to occur when they were prescribed in lieu of a treatment relationship that considered and tried to understand all aspects of the physiological and psychological disturbances associated with alcohol problems.

For some the duration of need for these psychopharmacologic agents is short, and for others the need continues for longer periods. For many others there is no need for medication at all. The timing, duration, and choice of these agents should be based on clinical observations and judgments about each patient as he or she gains or attempts to gain control over drinking. I believe the cases requiring no medication or only short-term use of medication are those in which the disturbances are less severe and/or the regression is more readily reversible. The more usual case in my experience involves situations where as control is gained over the drinking, depressive anxious syndromes, including phobias, surface, which are evident and are most often quite disabling. For some, the severity of these symptoms seems to be secondary and related to regressive states associated with protracted drinking, but the symptoms nevertheless respond to antidepressants and/or benzodiazepines. In my experience the decision as to which of the two drugs to use or whether to combine them should be based on clinical judgment as to the predominant symptomatology. Perhaps Klein has properly elaborated on what one rationale might be for using these drugs in combination, namely that the phobic and panic states often imvolved with alcohol problems respond to imipramine, but the anticipatory anxiety associated with the phobic states is unresponsive to this drug. The anticipatory anxiety does, however, respond to antianxiety drugs, and therefore these drugs might be indicated in alcohol problems associated with phobic states. In many instances the disturbances I have outlined are severe, ubiquitous, and persistent. The buffering, supporting action of these drugs in helping to manage affects is needed, and the need for a longer and more indefinite period of drug therapy is indicated. In those instances where the patient was slow to abstain or curtail his/her drinking, where all other efforts on the part of myself, A.A., the family, and others had failed, and where continued drinking threatened to be disastrous, I deliberately chose to initiate the use of antianxiety agents or antidepressants to help contain and cope with painful affects of anxiety and/or depression. This is admittedly risky, and I have in such cases involved family members for supervision and dispensed only small amounts of the medication. Fortunately these instances are rare.

In summary, I would suggest that it is often the combination of psychotherapeutic and psychopharmacologic interventions, especially early in treatment, that is critical in helping alcoholics overcome their dependence on alcohol and assisting them with their enormous problems with self-care and affect regulation. In some instances the psychopharmacologic intervention may be time-limited and an adjunct to psychotherapy and other approaches, but in other instances it may be a definitive treatment for identified target symptoms and psychopathology.

References

ABLON, J. Family structure and behavior in alcoholism: A review of the literature. In B. Kissin & H. Begleiter (Eds.), *The biology of alcoholism.* Vol. 4. *Social aspects of alcoholism.* New York: Plenum, 1976.

ABRAHAM, K. The psychological relation between sexuality and alcoholism. In *Selected papers on psychoanalysis.* New York: Basic Books, 1960. (Originally published, 1908.)

ADAMSON, J. A., & BURDICK, J. A. Sleep of dry alcoholics. *Archives of General Psychiatry,* 1973, *28,* 146–169.

ALBERT, M. S., BUTTERS, N., & LEVIN, J. Temporal gradient in the retrograde amnesia of patients with alcoholic Korsakoff's disease. *Archives of Neurology,* 1979, *36,* 211–216.

ALCOHOLICS ANONYMOUS. *Alcoholics Anonymous.* New York: Alcoholics Anonymous World Services, 1939 (1st ed.), 1976 (3rd ed.), & 1978 (4th ed.).

ALCOHOLICS ANONYMOUS. *As Bill sees it: The A.A. way of life.* New York: Alcoholics Anonymous World Services, 1967.

ALCOHOLICS ANONYMOUS. *Twelve steps and twelve traditions.* New York: Alcoholics Anonymous World Services, 1955 and 1977.

ALLMAN, L. R., TAYLOR, H. A., & NATHAN P. E. Group drinking during stress: Effects on drinking behavior, affect and psychopathology. *American Journal of Psychiatry,* 1972, *129,* 669–678.

ARMOR, D. J., POLICH, J. M., & STAMBUL H. B. *Alcoholism and treatment.* Santa Monica, Calif.: Rand Corporation, 1976.

ARMOTANG, J. D. The search for the alcoholic personality. *Annals of the American Academy of Political and Social Science,* 1958, *315,* 40–47.

BACON, S. D. The process of addiction to alcohol. *Quarterly Journal of Studies on Alcohol,* 1973, *34,* 1–27.

BAEKELAND, F. Evaluation of treatment methods in chronic alcoholism. In B. Kissin & H. Begleiter (Eds.), *The biology of alcoholism.* Vol. 5. *Treatment and rehabilitation of the chronic alcoholic.* New York: Plenum Press, 1977.

BAILEY, M. B., & LEACH, B. *Alcoholics Anonymous: Pathways to recovery—a study of 1058 members of the A.A. fellowship in New York City.* New York: National Council on Alcoholism, 1965.

BALES, R. F. Cultural differences in rates of alcoholism. *Quarterly Journal of Studies on Alcohol,* 1945, *6,* 480–499.

BALES, R. F. The "fixation factor" in alcohol addiction: An hypothesis derived from a comparative study of Irish and Jewish social norms. Unpublished doctoral dissertation. Cambridge, Mass.: Harvard University, 1944a.

BALES, R. F. The therapeutic role of Alcoholics Anonymous as seen by a sociologist. *Quarterly Journal of Studies on Alcohol,* 1944b, *5,* 267–278.

BALINT, M. *The basic fault.* London: Tavistock Publications, 1968.

BANDURA, A. Social learning and moral judgments. *Journal of Personality and Social Psychology,* 1969, *11,* 275–279.

BARRY, H. B., III. Psychological factors in alcoholism. In B. Kissin & H. Begleiter (Eds.), *The biology of alcoholism.* Vol. 3. *Clinical pathology.* New York: Plenum Press, 1974.

BASCH, M. The concept of affect: A reexamination. *Journal of the American Psychoanalytic Association,* 1976, *24,* 759–777.

BATESON, G. The cybernetics of "self": A theory of alcoholism. In *Steps to an ecology of mind.* New York: Ballantine Books, 1972, pp. 309–337.

BEAN, M. H. Alcoholics Anonymous: A.A. *Psychiatric Annals,* 1975, *5,* 3–64.

BEAN, M. H. Denial and the psychological complications of alcoholism. This volume.

BECKER, E. *The denial of death.* New York: Free Press, 1973.

BEHAR, D., & WINOKUR, G. Research in alcoholism and depression: A two-way street under construction. In R. W. Pickens & L. H. Heston (Eds.), *Psychiatric factors in drug abuse.* New York: Grune & Stratton, 1979.

BLANE, H. T. *The personality of the alcoholic: Guises of dependency.* New York: Harper & Row, 1968.

BLANE, H. T., OVERTON, W. F., & CHAFETZ, M. Z. Social factors in the diagnosis of alcoholism. *Quarterly J. of Studies on Alcohol,* 1963, *24,* 640.

BLIDING, A. Efficacy of anti-anxiety drug therapy in alcoholic post-intoxication symptoms: A double-blind study of chlorpromazine, oxazepam and placebo. *British Journal of Psychiatry,* 1973, *122,* 465–468.

BLUM, E. M. Psychoanalytic views of alcoholism. *Quarterly Journal of Studies on Alcohol,* 1966, *27,* 259–299.

BLUM, E. M., & BLUM, R. H. *Alcoholism.* San Francisco: Jossey-Bass, 1967.

BRENNER, C. On the nature and development of affects: A unified theory. *Psychoanalytic Quarterly,* 1974, *43,* 532–556.

BREWER, C., & PERRETT, L. Brain damage due to alcohol consumption: An air encephalographic, psychometric, and electroencephalographic study. *British Journal of Addictions,* 1971, *66,* 170–182.

BRILL, A. A. Alcohol and the individual. *New York Medical Journal,* 1919, *109,* 928–930.

BRILL, N. W., & BEEBE, G. W. *A follow-up study of war neurosis.* Washington, D.C.: U.S. Government Printing Office, 1955.

BURNETT, G. B. Common alcohol-related disorders: Recognition and management. *South Medical Journal,* 1978, *71,* 561–565.

BUTLER, S. *"Erewhon" and "Erewhon revisited."* New York: Modern Library, 1955. (Originally published, 1872 and 1901.)

BUTTERWORTH, A. T. Depression associated with alcohol withdrawal: Imipramine therapy compared with placebo. *Quarterly Journal of Studies on Alcohol,* 1971, *32,* 343–348.

CAHALAN, D., & CISIN, I. Drinking behavior and drinking problems in the United States. In B. Kissin & H. Begleiter (Eds.), *The biology of alcoholism.* Vol. 4. *Social aspects of alcoholism.* New York: Plenum Press, 1976.

CAHALAN, D., CISIN, I., & CROSSLEY, H. M. *American drinking patterns: A national study of drinking behavior and attitudes.* New Brunswick, N.J.: Rutgers Center of Alcohol Studies, 1969.

CAHALAN, D., & ROOM, R. *Problem drinking among American men.* New Brunswick, N.J.: Rutgers Center of Alcohol Studies, 1974.

CALDER, K. Psychoanalytic knowledge of group processes: Panel report. *Journal of the American Psychoanalytic Association,* 1979, *27,* 145–156.

CAMPS,, F. E., & DODD, B. E. Increase of the incidence of ABH blood group substances among alcohol patients. *British Medical Journal,* 1967, *1,* 30.

CANTER, F. M. The future of psychotherapy with alcoholics. In *The future of psychotherapy.* Boston: Little, Brown, 1969.

CAPELL,, H., & HERMAN, C. P. Alcohol and tension reduction: A review. *Quarterly Journal of Studies on Alcohol,* 1972, *33,* 33–64.

CHAFETZ, M., BLANE, H. T., ABRAM, H. S., et al. Establishing treatment relations with alcoholics. *Journal of Nervous and Mental Diseases,* 1962, *134,* 395–409.

CHAFETZ, M., & DEMONE, H. W., JR. *Alcoholism and society.* New York: Oxford University Press, 1962.

CHAFETZ, M., & YOERG, R. Public health treatment programs in alcoholism. In B. Kissin & H. Begleiter (Eds.), *The biology of alcoholism.* Vol. 5. *The treatment and rehabilitation of the chronic alcoholic.* New York: Plenum Press, 1977.

CHALMERS, D., & WALLACE, J. Evaluation of patient progress. In S. Zimberg, J. Wallace, & S. B. Blume (Eds.), *Practical approaches to alcoholism psychotherapy.* New York: Plenum Press, 1978.

COCHIN, J. The pharmacology of addiction to narcotics. In G. J. Martin & B. Kisch (Eds.), *Enzymes in mental health.* Philadelphia: Lippincott, 1966.

CRUZ-COKE, R. Colour blindness and cirrhosis of the liver. *Lancet,* 1964, *2,* 1064–1065.

CUMMINGS, N. W. Turning bread into stone: A modern anti-miracle. *American Psychologist,* 1979, *34,* 1119–1129.

DAVIES, D. L. Normal drinking in recovered alcoholic addicts. *Quarterly Journal of Studies on Alcohol,* 1962, *23,* 91–104.

DEWS, P. Comment on D. Robinson, The alcohologist's addiction: Some implications of having lost control over the disease concept of alcoholism. *Quarterly Journal of Studies on Alcohol,* 1972, *33,* 1045–1047.

DiCicco, L., UNTERBERGER, H., & MACK, J. E. Confronting denial: An alcoholism intervention strategy. *Psychiatric Annals,* 1978, *8,* 54–64.

DIESENHAUS, H. Current trends in treatment programming for problem drinkers and alcoholics. Unpublished paper prepared for the National Institute on Alcohol Abuse and Alcoholism, 1980.

DUDLEY, A., VERHEG, J., MASNOLA, M., MARTIN, C., & HOLMES, T. Long-term adjustment prognosis, and death in irreversible diffuse obstructive pulmonary syndrome. *Psychosomatic Medicine,* 1969, *31,* 310–325.

EDDY, N. B., HALBACK, H., ISBEL, H., & SEEVERS, M. H. Drug dependence: Its significance and characteristics. *Bulletin, World Health Organization,* 1965, *32,* 721–733.

EDWARDS, G., GROSS, M. M., KELLER, M., MOSER, J., & ROOM, R. (Eds.) *Alcohol-related disabilities.* Geneva: World Health Organization, 1977.

ERIKSON, E. H. Identity and the life cycle. [*Psychological Issues,* Monograph **1.**] New York: International Universities Press, 1959.

ERIKSON, E. H. *Identity: Youth and crisis.* New York: Norton, 1968.

EWING, J. A., ROUSE, B. A., & PELLIZZARI, E. D. Alcohol sensitivity and ethnic background. *American Journal of Psychiatry,* 1974, *131,* 206–210.

FRANKL, V. *Man's search for meaning.* New York: Pocket Books, 1959.

FREEDMAN, A. M., KAPLAN, H., & SADOCK, B. J. *Comprehensive textbook of psychiatry.* (2nd ed.) Baltimore: Williams & Wilkins, 1975. Chaps. 19.3 & 23.2.

FREUD, A. The ego and the mechanisms of defense. In *The writings of Anna Freud,* Vol. 2. New York: International Universities Press, 1966.

FREUD, S. An autobiographical study. In *Standard edition,* Vol. 20. London: Hogarth, 1959. (Originally published, 1925.)

FREUD, S. Civilization and its discontents. In *Standard edition,* Vol. 21. London: Hogarth, 1961. (Originally published, 1930.)

FREUD, S. The claims of psychoanalysis to scientific interest. In *Standard edition,* Vol. 13. London: Hogarth, 1955. (Originally published, 1913.)

FREUD, S. Fetishism. In *Standard edition,* Vol. 21. London: Hogarth, 1961. (Originally published, 1927.)

FREUD, S. The future of an illusion. In *Standard edition,* Vol. 21. London: Hogarth, 1961. (Originally published, 1927.)

FREUD, S. Group psychology and the analysis of the ego. In *Standard edition,* Vol. 18. London: Hogarth, 1955. (Originally published, 1921.)

FREUD, S. Inhibitions, symptoms and anxiety. In *Standard edition,* Vol. 20. London: Hogarth, 1959. (Originally published, 1926.)

FREUD, S. Instincts and their vicissitudes. In *Standard edition,* Vol. 14. London: Hogarth, 1957. (Originally published, 1915.)

FREUD, S. Introductory lectures on psychoanalysis. In *Standard edition,* Vol. 16. London: Hogarth, 1963. (Originally published, 1916-1917.)

FREUD, S. An outline of psycho-analysis. In *Standard edition,* Vol. 23. London: Hogarth, 1964. (Originally published, 1940.)

FREUD, S. Three essays on the theory of sexuality. In *Standard edition,* Vol. 7. London: Hogarth, 1955. (Originally published, 1905.)

FULTON, J., & BAILEY, P. Tumors in the region of the third ventricle. *Journal of Nervous and Mental Diseases,* 1969, *69,* 1-25, 145-164, 261.

GARDNER, H. *The shattered mind: The person after brain damage.* New York: Knopf, 1975.

GERARD, D. L., & SAENGER, G. *Outpatient treatment of alcoholism.* Toronto: University of Toronto Press, 1966.

GITLOW, S. Review of G. A. Marlatt & P. E. Nathan, (Eds.), Behavioral approaches to alcoholism. *American Journal of Psychiatry,* 1979, *136,* 1108-1109.

GLOVER, E. G. The etiology of alcoholism. *Proceedings of the Royal Society of Medicine,* 1928, *21,* 1351-1355.

GLOVER, E. G. On the etiology of drug addiction. *International Journal of Psycho-Analysis,* 1932, *13,* 298-328.

GOLDBERG, A., et al. (Eds.) *The psychology of the self.* New York: International Universities Press, 1978.

GOLDSTEIN, D. B., & GOLDSTEIN, A. Possible role of enzyme inhibition and repression in drug tolerance and addiction. *Biochemistry and Pharmacology,* 1961, *8,* 48.

GOLDSTEIN, K. The effect of brain damage on the personality. *Psychiatry,* 1952, *15,* 245-260.

GOMBERG, E. S. Etiology of alcoholism. *Journal of Consulting and Clinical Psychology,* 1968, *32,* 18-20.

GOODWIN, D. W. Is alcoholism hereditary? *Archives of General Psychiatry,* 1971, *25,* 545–549.

GOODWIN, D. W., & GUZE, S. B. Heredity and alcoholism. In B. Kissin & H. Begleiter (Eds.), *The biology of alcoholism,* Vol. 3. *Clinical pathology.* New York: Plenum Press, 1974.

GOODWIN, D. W., HILL, S. Y., & HOPPER, S. Alcoholic blackouts and Korsakoff's syndrome. In M. M. Gross (Ed.), *Alcohol intoxification and withdrawal: Experimental studies II.* New York: Plenum Press, 1975.

GOODWIN, D. W., SCHULSINGER, F., HERMANSEN, L., GUZE, S. B., & WINOKUR, G. Alcohol problems in adoptees raised apart from alcoholic biological parents. *Archives of General Psychiatry,* 1973, *28,* 238–243.

GOTTHEIL, E., ALTERMAN, A. I., SKOLODA, T. E., & MURPHY, B. F. Alcoholics' patterns of controlled drinking. *American Journal of Psychiatry,* 1973, *130,* 418–422.

GREEN, A. Conceptions of affect. *International Journal of Psycho-Analysis,* 1977, *58,* 129–156.

GREEN, J. R. The incidence of alcoholism in patients admitted to a medical ward of a public hospital. *Medical Journal of Australia,* 1965, *1,* 465–466.

GREENBLATT, D. J., & SHADER, R. I. *Benzodiazopines in clinical practice.* New York: Raven Press, 1973.

GRUNEBAUM, H., & SOLOMON, L. F. Toward a peer theory of group psychotherapy I: On the developmental significance of peers and play. *International Journal of Group Psychotherapy,* 1980, *30,* 23–49.

GUSTAFSON, J. The mirror transference in the psychoanalytic psychotherapy of alcoholism: A case report. *International Journal of Psychoanalytic Psychotherapy,* 1976, *5,* 65–85.

HABERMAN, P. W., & BADEN, M. M. Alcoholism and violent death. *Quarterly Journal of Studies on Alcohol,* 1974, *35,* 221–231.

HACKETT, T., & WEISMAN, A. Denial as a factor in patients with heart diseases and cancer. *Annals of the New York Academy of Sciences,* 1969, *164,* 802–817.

HAMM, J. E., et al. The quantitative measurement of depression and anxiety in male alcoholics. *American Journal of Psychiatry,* 1979, *136,* 580–582.

HARRIS, I. B., & WESTERMEYER, J. Chemical dependency education within medical schools: Supervised clinical experience. *American Journal of Drug and Alcohol Abuse,* 1978, *5,* 59–74.

HARTMANN, H. Ich-psychologie und das anpassungs problem. *Internationale Zeitschrift fuer Psychoanalyse,* 1935, *24,* 62–135. (Translated and condensed with comments by D. Rapaport in *Organization and pathology of thought.* New York: Columbia University Press, 1951. Pp. 363–396.)

HARTMANN, H. Technical implications of ego psychology. *Psychoanalytic Quarterly,* 1951, *20,* 31–43.

HARTOCOLLIS, P. Denial of illness in alcoholism. *Bulletin, Menninger Clinic,* 1968, *32,* 47–53.

HARTOCOLLIS, P. A dynamic view of alcoholism: Drinking in the service of denial. *Dynamische Psychiatrie,* 1969, *2,* 173–182.

HAZELDEN FOUNDATION. *Dealing with denial.* The Caring Community Series, No. 6. Center City, Minn.: Hazelden Foundation, 1975.

HELLMAN, A. D. *Laws against marijuana: The price we pay.* Urbana: University of Illinois Press, 1975.

HENDRICK, I. Work and the pleasure principle. *Psychoanalytic Quarterly,* 1943, *12,* 311–329.

HEYMAN, M. M. *Alcoholism programs in industry: The patient's view.* Monograph 12. New Brunswick, N.J.: Rutgers Center of Alcohol Studies, 1978.

HILL, M., & BLANE, H. T. Evaluation of psychotherapy with alcoholics: A critical review. *Quarterly Journal of Studies on Alcohol,* 1967, *28,* 76–104.

HOFFER, W. Theory of defense. *Psychoanalytic Study of the Child,* 1968, *23,* 178–188.

HOFFMAN, H., LOPER, R. G., & KAMMIER, M. L. Identifying future alcoholics with MMPI alcoholism scales. *Quarterly Journal of Studies on Alcohol,* 1974, *35,* 490–498.

HORTON, D. The function of alcohol in primitive societies: A cross-cultural study. *Quarterly Journal of Studies on Alcohol,* 1943, *4,* 199–230.

ILLIS, L. S. Regeneration in the central nervous system. *Lancet,* 1973, *1,* 1035–1037.

IMBER, S., SCHULTZ, E., FUNDERBURK, F., ALLEN, R., & FLAMER, R. The fate of the untreated alcoholic. *Journal of Nervous and Mental Diseases,* 1976, *162,* 238–247.

IMBODEN, J. B., et al. Alcoholism. Part 9 of the series Practical psychiatry in medicine. *Journal of Family Practice,* 1978, *6,* 685–686, 688, 691.

JACKSON, J. K. Alcoholism and the family. In D. J. Pittman & C. R. Snyder (Eds.), *Society, culture and drinking patterns.* New York: Wiley, 1962.

JACOBSON, E. Denial and repression. *Journal of the American Psychoanalytic Association,* 1957, *5,* 61–92.

JACOBSON, E. Depersonalization. *Journal of the American Psychoanalytic Association,* 1959, *7,* 581–610.

JELLINEK, E. M. *The disease concept of alcoholism.* New Haven, Conn.: College & University Press, 1960.

JELLINEK, E. M. Heredity of the alcoholic. *Quarterly Journal of Studies on Alcohol,* 1945, *6,* 105–114.

JELLINEK, E. M. Phases of alcohol addiction. *Quarterly Journal of Studies on Alcohol,* 1952, *13,* 673–684.

JONES, M. C. Personality correlates and antecedents of drinking patterns in adult males. *Journal of Consulting and Clinical Psychology,* 1968, *32,* 2–12.

KAISER, H. The problem of responsibility in psychotherapy. *Psychiatry,* 1955, *18,* 205–211.

KAMMEIER, M. L., HOFFMANN, H., & LOPER, R. G. Personality characteristics of alcoholics as college freshmen and at time of treatment. *Quarterly Journal of Studies on Alcohol,* 1973, *34,* 390–399.

KAPUR, N., & BUTTERS, N. Visuoperceptive defects in long–term alcoholics and alcoholics with Korsakoff's psychosis. *Quarterly Journal of Studies on Alcohol,* 1977, *38,* 2025–2035.

KAZIN, A. The giant killer: Drink and the American writer. *Commentary,* 1976, *61,* 44–50.

KEELER, M. H., TAYLOR, I. C., & MILLER, W. C. Are all recently detoxified alcoholics depressed? *American Journal of Psychiatry,* 1979, *136,* 586–588.

KELLER, M. Alcohol consumption. In *Encyclopaedia Britannica,* Vol. I. Chicago: Encyclopaedia Britannica, Inc., 1973.

KELLER, M. The definition of alcoholism and the estimation of its prevalence. In D. J. Pittman & C. R. Snyder (Eds.), *Society, culture and drinking patterns.* New York: Wiley, 1962.

KELLER, M. A lexicon of disablements related to alcohol consumption. In G. Edwards, M. M. Gross, M. Keller, J. Moser, & R. Room (Eds.), *Alcohol-related disabilities.* Geneva: World Health Organization, 1977.

KELLER, M., & McCORMICK, M. *A dictionary of words about alcohol.* New Brunswick, N.J.: Rutgers Center of Alcohol Studies, 1968.

KELLERMAN, J. L. *Alcoholism: A merry-go-round named denial.* New York: Alcoholics Anonymous Family Group Headquarters, Inc., 1969.

KENDALL, R. E., & STANTON, M. C. The fate of untreated alcoholics. *Quarterly Journal of Studies on Alcohol,* 1966, *27,* 30–41.

KERNBERG, O. F. *Borderline conditions and pathological narcissism.* New York: Aronson, 1975.

KERNBERG, O. F. Large group processes: Psychoanalytic understanding and applications. Paper presented at the panel on "Psychoanalytic knowledge of group processes," American Psychoanalytic Association, New York, Dec. 18, 1977.

KHANTZIAN, E. J. Some treatment implications of the ego and self disturbances in alcoholism. This volume.

KHANTZIAN, E. J. The alcoholic patient: An overview and perspective. *American Journal of Psychotherapy,* 1980, *34,* 4–19.

KHANTZIAN, E. J. The ego, the self and opiate addiction: Theoretical and treatment considerations. *International Review of Psycho-Analysis,* 1978, *5,* 189–199.

KHANTZIAN, E. J. Impulse problems in addiction: Cause and effect relationships. In H. Wishnie & J. Nevis-Olesen (Eds.), *Clinical approaches to impulsive patients.* New York: Plenum Publishing Corporation, 1979a.

KHANTZIAN, E. J. On the nature of the dependency and denial problems of alcoholics. *Journal of Geriatric Psychiatry,* 1979b, *11,* 191–202.

KHANTZIAN, E. J., MACK, J. E., & SCHATZBERG, A. F. Heroin use as an attempt to cope: Clinical observations. *American Journal of Psychiatry,* 1974, *131,* 160–164.

KISSIN, B. The pharmacodynamics and natural history of alcoholism. In B. Kissin & H. Begleiter (Eds.), *The biology of alcoholism.* Vol. 3. *Clinical pathology.* New York: Plenum Press, 1974.

KISSIN, B., & GROSS, M. M. Drug therapy in alcoholism. *American Journal of Psychiatry,* 1968, *125,* 31–41.

KLEIN, D. F. Psychopharmacology and the borderline patient. In P. Hartocollis (Ed.), *Borderline states in psychiatry.* New York: Grune & Stratton, 1975.

KLEINKNECHT, R. A., & GOLDSTEIN, S. Neuropsychological deficits associated with alcoholism: A review and discussion. *Quarterly Journal of Studies on Alcohol,* 1972, *33,* 999–1020.

KLEIN, N. S., WREN, J. C., COOPER, T. B., VARGA, E., & CANAL, O. Evaluation of lithium therapy in chronic and periodic alcoholism. *American Journal of Medical Science,* 1974, *268,* 15–22.

KNIGHT, R. P. The dynamics and treatment of chronic alcohol addiction. *Bulletin, Menninger Clinic,* 1937a, *1,* 233–250.

KNIGHT, R. P. Psychodynamics of chronic alcoholics. *Journal of Nervous and Mental Diseases,* 1937b, *86,* 538–548.

KOBLER, J. *Ardent spirits: The rise and fall of prohibition.* New York: Putnam, 1973.

KOFFEND, J. The case for alcohol. *Atlantic Monthly,* 1979, *244,* 66–70.

KOHUT, H. *The analysis of the self.* New York: International Universities Press, 1971.

KOHUT, H. Forms and transformations of narcissism. *Journal of the American Psychoanalytic Association,* 1966, *14,* 243–272.

KOHUT, H. Preface. In *Psychodynamics of drug dependence.* Research monograph 12. Rockville, Md.: National Institute on Drug Abuse, 1977a. Pp. vii–ix.

KOHUT, H. *The restoration of the self.* New York: International Universities Press, 1977b.

KOHUT, H., & WOLF, E. S. The disorders of the self and their treatment: An outline. *International Journal of Psycho-Analysis,* 1978, *59,* 413–426.

KOLB, L. C. *Modern clinical psychiatry.* Philadelphia: Saunders, 1973.

KOVAKS, M., & BECK, A. T. Maladaptive cognitive structures in repression. *American Journal of Psychiatry,* 1978, *135,* 525–533.

KROUT, J. A. *The origins of prohibition.* New York: Knopf, 1925.

KRYSTAL, H. Self- and object-representation in alcoholism and other drug dependence: Implications for therapy. In *Psychodynamics of drug dependence.* Research monograph 12. Rockville, Md.: National Institute on Drug Abuse, 1977. Pp. 88–100.

KRYSTAL, H., & RASKIN, H. A. *Drug dependence: Aspects of ego functions.* Detroit: Wayne State University Press, 1970.

KUBLER-ROSS, E. On death and dying. New York: Macmillan, 1969.

LAPLANCHE, J., & PONTALIS, J. B. *The language of psychoanalysis.* Translated by D. Nicholson-Smith. New York: Norton, 1973.

LEACH, B. Does Alcoholics Anonymous really work? In P. Bourne & R. Fox (Eds.), *Alcoholism: Progress in research and treatment.* New York & London: Academic Press, 1973.

LEACH, B., NORRIS, J. L., DANCEY, T., & BISSELL, L. Dimensions of Alcoholics Anonymous. *International Journal of the Addictions,* 1969, *4,* 507–541.

LEMERE, F. What happens to alcoholics? *American Journal of Psychiatry,* 1953, *109,* 674–682.

LESTER, D. A biological approach to the etiology of alcoholism. *Quarterly Journal of Studies on Alcohol,* 1960, *21,* 701–703.

LEVINE, J., & ZIGLER, E. (Eds.). Denial and self-image in stroke, lung cancer and heart disease patients. *Journal of Consulting and Clinical Psychology,* 1975, *43,* 751–757.

LINDEMANN, E. Symptomatology and management of acute grief. *American Journal of Psychiatry,* 1944, *101,* 141–148.

LISANSKY, E. Clinical research in alcoholism in the use of psychological tests: A re-evaluation. In R. Fox (Ed.), *Alcoholism: Behavioral research, therapeutic approaches.* New York: Springer, 1967.

LOEWALD, H. *Psychoanalysis and the history of the individual.* New Haven, Conn.: Yale University Press, 1978.

LOGUE, P. E., GENTRY, W. D., LINNOILA, M., & ERWIN, W. C. Effect of alcohol consumption on state anxiety changes in male and female nonalcoholics. *American Journal of Psychiatry,* 1978, *135,* 1079–1082.

LUDWIG, A. M. On and off the wagon: Reasons for drinking and abstaining by alcoholics. *Quarterly Journal of Studies on Alcohol,* 1972, *33,* 91–96.

MACK, J. Alcoholism, A.A., and the governance of the self. This volume.

MacKAY, J. R. Clinical observations on adolescent problem drinkers. *Quarterly Journal of Studies on Alcohol,* 1961, *22,* 124–134.

MADDOX, G. L. (Ed.) *The domesticated drug: Drinking among collegians.* New Haven, Conn.: College and University Press Services, 1970.

MARDONES, J. On the relationship between deficiency of B vitamins and alcohol intake in rats. *Quarterly Journal of Studies on Alcohol,* 1951, *12,* 563–575.

MATHEW, R. J., CLAGHORN, J. L., & LARGEN, J. Craving for alcohol in sober alcoholics. *American Journal of Psychiatry,* 1979, *136,* 603–606.

McCord, W., & McCord, J. *Origins of alcoholism.* Stanford, Calif.: Stanford University Press, 1960.

McLearn, G. E., & Rodgers, D. A. Differences in alcohol preferences among unbred strains of mice. *Quarterly Journal of Studies on Alcohol,* 1959, *20,* 691–695.

McLellan, A. T., Woody, G. E., & O'Brien, C. P. Development of psychiatric illness in drug abusers. *New England Journal of Medicine,* 1979, *301,* 1310–1314.

Meissner, W. W. Psychoanalytic aspects of religious experience. *Annual of Psychoanalysis,* 1978, *6,* 103–141.

Mello, N. K. Behavioral studies of alcoholism. In B. Kissin & H. Begleiter (Eds.), *The biology of alcoholism.* Vol. 2 *Physiology and behavior.* New York: Plenum Press, 1972.

Mello, N. K., & Mendelson, J. H. Drinking patterns during work: Contingent and non-contingent alcohol acquisition. *Psychosomatic Medicine,* 1972, *34,* 139–164.

Mendelson, J. H., LaDou, J., & Solomon, P. Experimentally induced chronic intoxication in alcoholics: Psychiatric findings. *Quarterly Journal of Studies on Alcohol,* 1964, *25,* 40–52.

Mendelson, J. H., & Mello, N. K. Biological concomitants of alcoholism. *New England Journal of Medicine,* 1979, *301,* 912–921.

Menninger, K. *Man against himself.* New York: Harcourt, Brace, 1938.

Merry, J., Reynolds, C. M., Bailey, J., & Coppen, A. Prophylactic treatment of alcoholism by lithium carbonate. *Lancet,* 1976, *2,* 481–482.

Mitscherlich, A. Psychoanalysis and the aggression of large groups. *International Journal of Psycho-Analysis,* 1971, *52,* 161–168.

Moore, B. E., & Rubenfine, D. L. The mechanism of denial. Monograph. *Kris Study Group of the New York Psychoanalytic Institute,* 1969, *3,* 3–57.

Moore, R. A. The problem of abstinence by the patient as a requisite for the psychotherapy of alcoholism. *Quarterly Journal of Studies on Alcohol,* 1962, *23,* 105–111.

Moore, R. A., & Murphy, T. C. Denial of alcoholism as an obstacle to recovery. *Quarterly Journal of Studies on Alcohol,* 1961, *22,* 597–609.

Mottin, J. L. Drug-induced attenuation of alcohol consumption. *Quarterly Journal of Studies on Alcohol,* 1973, *34,* 444–463.

Nathan, P. E., & Bridell, D. W. Behavioral assessment and treatment of alcoholism. In B. Kissin & H. Begleiter (Eds.), *The biology of alcoholism.* Vol. 5. *The treatment and rehabilitation of the chronic alcoholic.* New York: Plenum Press, 1977.

National Commission on Marihuana and Drug Abuse. *Drug use in America: Problem in perspective.* 2nd report of the Commission. Washington, D.C.: U.S. Government Printing Office, 1973.

NATIONAL COUNCIL ON ALCOHOLISM. *What are the signs of alcoholism?* New York: National Council on Alcoholism, 1975.

NATIONAL COUNCIL ON ALCOHOLISM, CRITERIA COMMITTEE. Criteria for the diagnosis of alcoholism. *American Journal of Psychiatry,* 1972, *129,* 127–135.

NOVICK, D. M., & YANCOVITZ, S. R. Library resources in alcoholism. *Annals of International Medicine,* 1979, *91,* 325.

ONIONS, C. T. (Ed.) *Shorter Oxford English dictionary on historical principles.* (3rd ed.) London: Oxford University Press, 1952.

ORFORD, J., & EDWARDS, G. *Alcoholism.* London: Oxford University Press, 1977.

OSLER, W. *Principles and practice of medicine.* New York: Appleton, 1928.

OVERALL, J. E., BROWN, D., WILLIAMS, J. D., & NEILL, L. Drug treatment of anxiety and depression in detoxified alcoholic patients. *Archives of General Psychiatry,* 1973, *29,* 218–221.

PAREDES, A. Denial, deceptive maneuvers and consistency in the behavior of alcoholics. *Annals of the New York Academy of Sciences,* 1974, *233,* 23–33.

PARSONS, O. Brain damage in alcoholics: Altered states of consciousness. In M. M. Gross (Ed.), *Alcohol intoxification and withdrawal: Experimental studies II.* New York: Plenum Press, 1975.

PARSONS, O., & FREUND, G. Chronic central nervous system toxicity of alcohol. *Annual Review of Pharmacology,* 1973, *13,* 217–227.

PATTISON, E. M. A critique of abstinence criteria in the treatment of alcoholism. *International Journal of Social Psychiatry,* 1968, *14,* 268–276.

PATTISON, E. M. The rehabilitation of the chronic alcoholic. In B. Kissin & H. Begleiter (Eds.), *The biology of alcoholism.* Vol. 2. *Physiology and behavior.* New York: Plenum Press, 1972.

PATTISON, E. M. Nonabstinent drinking goals in the treatment of alcoholism. *Archives of General Psychiatry,* 1976, *3,* 923–930.

PATTISON, E. M., SOBELL, M. B., & SOBELL, L. C. *Emergency concepts of alcohol dependence.* New York: Springer, 1977.

PEARLIN, L. E., & RADABAUGH, C. W. Economic strains and the coping functions of alcohol. *American Journal of Sociology,* 1976, *82,* 652–663.

PLUM, F., & POSNER, J. B. *The diagnosis of stupor and coma.* Philadelphia: Davis, 1966.

POKORNY, A., PUTNAM, P., & FRYER, J. Drug abuse and alcoholism teaching in U.S. medical and osteopathic schools. *Journal of Medical Education,* 1978, *53,* 816–824.

POPHAM, R. E. A critique of the genetrophic theory of the etiology of alcoholism. *Quarterly Journal of Studies on Alcohol,* 1947, *7,* 567–587.

QUITKIN, F. M., RIFKIN, A., KAPLAN, J., & KLEIN, D. F. Phobic anxiety syndrome complicated by drug dependence and addiction. *Archives of General Psychiatry,* 1972, *27,* 159–162.

RADO, S. The psychoanalysis of pharmacothymia (drug addiction). *Psychoanalytic Quarterly,* 1933, *2,* 1–23.

RANDOLPH, T. G. The descriptive features of food addiction: Addictive eating and drinking. *Quarterly Journal of Studies on Alcohol,* 1956, *17,* 198–224.

RANGELL, L. Discussion of the Buffalo Creek disaster: The course of psychic trauma. *American Journal of Psychiatry,* 1976, *133,* 313–316.

RANKIN, J. G. (Eds.) *Alcohol, drugs, and brain damage.* Toronto: Addiction Research Foundation of Ontario, 1975.

REDLICH, F., & FREEDMAN, D. *The theory and practice of psychiatry.* New York: Basic Books, 1966.

RICHTER, C. P. Loss of appetite for alcohol and alcoholic beverages produced in rats by treatment with thyroid preparations. *Endocrinology,* 1956, *59,* 472–478.

RIZZUTO, A-M. The patient as a hero. Unpublished manuscript, 1976.

ROBINS, L. N. *Deviant children grown up.* Baltimore: Williams & Wilkins, 1966.

ROBINS, L. N. *The Vietnam drug user returns.* Special Action Monograph, Series A, No. 2. Washington, D.C.: Special Action Office for Drug Abuse Prevention, May 1974.

ROBINS, L. N., BATES, W. M., & O'NEAL, P. Adult drinking patterns of former problem children. In D. J. Pittman & C. R. Snyder (Eds.), *Society, culture and drinking patterns.* New York: Wiley, 1962.

ROBINSON, D. The alcohologist's addiction: Some implications of having lost control over the disease concept of alcoholism. *Quarterly Journal of Studies on Alcohol,* 1972, *33,* 1028–1042.

RODGERS, D. A. Factors underlying differences in alcohol preferences among unbred strains of mice. *Psychosomatic Medicine,* 1966, *28,* 498–513.

ROIZIN, L., HALPERN, M., BADEN, M. M., et al. Neuropathology of drugs of dependence. In S. J. Mule & M. Brill (Eds.), *Chemical and biological aspects of drug dependence.* Cleveland: C.R.C. Press, 1972.

ROOM, R. Comment on D. Robinson, The alcohologist's addiction: Some implications of having lost control over the disease concept of alcoholism. *Quarterly Journal of Studies on Alcohol,* 1972, *33,* 1049–1059.

ROSENFELD, H. A. The psychopathology of drug addiction and alcoholism: A critical review of the psychoanalytic literature. In *Psychotic states.* London: Hogarth, 1965.

ROSETT, H. L. Alcohol, brain physiology and ego function: Implications for psychotherapy. Unpublished paper.

ROUECHÉ, B. *The neutral spirit: A portrait of alcohol.* Boston: Little, Brown, 1960.

SCHEIDLINGER, S. Identification: The sense of belonging and of identity in small groups. *International Journal of Group Psychotherapy,* 1964, *14,* 291–306.

SCHEIDLINGER, S. On the concept of the ''mother-group.'' *International Journal of Group Psychotherapy,* 1974, *24,* 417–428.

SCHUCKIT, M. A., GOODWIN, D. A., & WINOKUR, G. A study of alcoholism in half-siblings. *American Journal of Psychiatry,* 1972, *128,* 1132–1136.

SCHUR, M. *The id and the regulatory principles of mental functioning.* New York: International Universities Press, 1966.

SEEVERS, M. H. Psychopharmacological elements of drug dependence. *Journal of the American Medical Association,* 1968, *206,* 1263–1266.

SELIGMAN, M. E. P. *Helplessness: On depression, development, and death.* San Francisco: Freeman, 1975.

SEMRAD, E. The organization of ego defenses and object loss. In D. M. Moriarty (Ed.), *The loss of loved ones.* Springfield, Ill.: Charles C Thomas, 1967.

SHAPIRO, R. Psychoanalytic knowledge of group processes. Presented at the panel on ''Psychoanalytic knowledge of group processes,'' American Psychoanalytic Association, New York, Dec. 18, 1977.

SHIMANO, E. Y., & DOUGLAS, D. B. On research in Zen. *American Journal of Psychiatry,* 1975, *132,* 1300–1302.

SILBER, A. An addendum to the technique of psychotherapy with alcoholics. *Journal of Nervous and Mental Diseases,* 1970, *150,* 423–437.

SILBER, A. Rationale for the technique of psychotherapy with alcoholics. *International Journal of Psychoanalytic Psychotherapy,* 1974, *28,* 47.

SIMMEL, E. Alcoholism and addiction. *Psychoanalytic Quarterly,* 1948, *17,* 6–31.

SINCLAIR, A. *Prohibition: The era of excess.* Boston: Little, Brown, 1962.

SKINNER, H. A., JACKSON, D. N., & HOFFMAN, N. H. Alcoholic personality types: Identification and correlates. *Journal of Abnormal Psychology,* 1974, *83,* 685–696.

SMITH, J. W., JOHNSON, L. C., & BURDICK, J. A. Sleep, psychological and clinical changes during alcohol withdrawal in NAD-treated alcoholics. *Quarterly Journal of Studies on Alcohol,* 1971, *32,* 932–949.

SOLOMON, H. C. Foreword. In M. Chafetz & H. W. Demone (Eds.), *Alcoholism and society.* New York: Oxford University Press, 1962.

SPRUIELL, V. Three strands of narcissism. *Psychoanalytic Quarterly,* 1975, *44,* 577–595.

STEWART, D. A. The dynamics of fellowship as illustrated in Alcoholics Anonymous. *Quarterly Journal of Studies on Alcohol,* 1955, *16,* 251–262.

STRAUS, R. Alcohol abuse and physicians' responsibility. *Archives of Internal Medicine,* 1977, *137,* 1513–1514.

SUNDBY, P. *Alcoholism and mortality.* Oslo, Norway: Universitets-Forlaget, 1967.

SUTHERLAND, E. H., SCHROEDER, H. G., & TORDELLA, O. L. Personality traits of the alcoholic: Critique of existing studies. *Quarterly Journal of Studies on Alcohol,* 1950, *11,* 547–567.

SYME, L. Personality characteristics and the alcoholic: A critique of current studies. *Quarterly Journal of Studies on Alcohol,* 1957, *18,* 288–302.

TAMERIN, J. S. The psychotherapy of the alcoholic woman. In S. Zimberg, J. Wallace, & S. B. Blume (Eds.), *Practical approaches to alcoholism psychotherapy.* New York: Plenum Press, 1978.

TAMERIN, J. S., & MENDELSON, J. H. The psychodynamics of chronic inebriation: Observations of chronic alcoholics during the process of drinking in an experimental setting. *American Journal of Psychiatry,* 1969, *125,* 886–899.

TAMERIN, J. S., & NEUMAN, C. D. Psychological aspects of treating alcoholism. *Alcohol Health and Research World,* Spring 1974, Experimental Issue, 14–18.

TAMERIN, J. S., WEINER, S., & MENDELSON, J. H. Alcoholics' expectancies and recall of experiences during intoxication. *American Journal of Psychiatry,* 1976, *126,* 1697–1704.

TIEBOUT, H. M. Alcoholics Anonymous: An experiment of nature. *Quarterly Journal of Studies on Alcohol,* 1961, *22,* 52–68.

TIEBOUT, H. M. Therapeutic mechanisms of Alcoholics Anonymous. *American Journal of Psychiatry,* 1943–1944, *100,* 468–473.

TITCHENER, J. L., & KAPP, F. J. Family and character change at Buffalo Creek. *American Journal of Psychiatry,* 1976, *133,* 295–299.

TOMKINS, S. *Affects, imagery, and consciousness,* Vol. 1. New York: Springer, 1962.

Touch of Evil. Universal International. Alfred Zugsmith, producer, 1958.

TRICE, H. M. A study of the process of affiliation with Alcoholics Anonymous. *Quarterly Journal of Studies on Alcohol,* 1957, *18,* 39–54.

TRUNELL, E., & HOLT, W. E. The concept of denial or disavowal. *Journal of the American Psychoanalytic Association,* 1974, *22,* 769–784.

TUMARKIN, B., WILSON, J. D., & SNYDER, G. Cerebral atrophy due to alcoholism in young adults. *U.S. Armed Forces Medical Journal,* 1955, *6,* 67–74.

TWERSKI, A. J. Alcologia: A "logical" paralogia. *American Journal of Psychoanalysis,* 1974, *34,* 257–261.

UNTERBERGER, H. Personal communication, Aug. 14, 1978.

VAILLANT, G. E. *Adaptation to life*. Boston: Little, Brown, 1977.

VAILLANT, G. E. Adaptive ego mechanisms. *Archives of General Psychiatry*, 1971, *24*, 108.

VAILLANT, G. E. Alcoholism and drug dependence. In A. M. Nicholi (Ed.), *The Harvard guide to modern psychiatry*. Cambridge, Mass.: Belknap Press of Harvard University Press, 1978.

VAILLANT, G. E. Dangers of psychotherapy in the treatment of alcoholism. This volume.

VAILLANT, G. E. *The natural history of alcoholism*. In preparation, 1981.

VAILLANT, G. E. Natural history of male psychological health: V. The relation of choice of ego mechanisms of defense to adult adjustment. *Archives of General Psychiatry*, 1976, *33*, 535–545.

VAILLANT, G. E. Natural history of male psychological health: VIII. Antecedents of alcoholism and "orality." *American Journal of Psychiatry*, 1980, *137*, 181–186.

VAILLANT, G. E. Personal communication, April 1979.

VAILLANT, G. E. A twelve-year follow-up of New York narcotic addicts: III. Some social and psychiatric characteristics. *Archives of General Psychiatry*, 1966, *15*, 599–609.

VAN DIJK, W. K., & VAN DIJK-KOFFERMAN, A. A follow-up study of 211 treated alcohol addicts. *British Journal of Addictions*, 1973, *68*, 3–24.

VANICELLI, M. I. Mood and self-perception of alcoholics when sober and intoxicated. *Quarterly Journal of Studies on Alcohol*, 1972, *33*, 341–357.

VIAMONTES, J. A. Review of drug effectiveness in the treatment of alcoholism. *American Journal of Psychiatry*, 1972, 128, 1570–1571.

VICTOR, M., ADAMS, R. D., & COLLINS, G. H. *The Wernike Korsakoff syndrome: A clinical and pathological study of 245 patients, 82 with postmortem examinations*. Philadelphia: Davis, 1971.

VISCHI, T. R., et al. *Alcohol, drug abuse, and mental health national data book*. Rockville, Md.: Alcohol, Drug Abuse, and Mental Health Administration, 1980.

WAELDER, R. The principle of multiple function: Observations on overdetermination. *Psychoanalytic Quarterly*, 1936, *5*, 45–62.

WALDORF, D., & BIERNACKI, P. The natural recovery from heroin addiction: A review of the incidence literature. *Journal of Drug Issues*, 1979, *9*, 281–289.

WALLACE, J. Behavior modification as adjunct to psychotherapy. In S. Zimberg, J. Wallace, & S. D. Blume (Eds.), *Practical approaches to alcoholism psychotherapy*. New York: Plenum Press, 1978.

WALLER, J. A., & TURKEL, H. W. Alcoholism and traffic deaths. *New England Journal of Medicine*, 1966, *275*, 532–536.

WARREN, G. H., & RAYNES, A. E. Mood changes during three conditions of alcohol intake. *Quarterly Journal of Studies on Alcohol,* 1972, *33,* 979–989.

WEIL, A. T. *The natural mind.* Boston: Houghton Mifflin, 1972.

WEINSTEIN, B., & KAHN, R. *Denial of illness.* Springfield, Ill.: Charles C Thomas, 1953.

WEISMAN, A. D. *On dying and denying.* New York: Behavioral Publications, 1972.

WEISMAN, M. M., & MEYERS, J. K. Clinical depression in alcoholism. *American Journal of Psychiatry,* 1980, *137,* 372–373.

WEISMAN, M. M., MEYERS, J. K., & HARDING, P. S. The prevalence rates and psychiatric heterogeneity of alcoholism in a United States urban community. *Quarterly Journal of Studies on Alcohol,* 1980, *41,* 672–681.

WHITELOCK, P. R., OVERALL, J. E., & PATRICK, J. H. Personality patterns and alcohol abuse in a state hospital population. *Journal of Abnormal Psychology,* 1971, *78,* 9–16.

WIEDER, H., & KAPLAN, E. H. Drug use in adolescents: Psychodynamic meaning and pharmacogenic effect. *Psychoanalytic Study of the Child,* 1969, *24,* 399–431.

WIKLER, A. Conditioning factors in opiate addiction and relapse. In D. M. Wilmer & G. G. Kassenbaum (Eds.), *Narcotics.* New York: McGraw-Hill, 1970.

WILLIAMS, A. The student and the alcoholic patient. *Nursing Outlook,* 1979, *27,* 470–472.

WILLIAMS, A. F. The alcoholic personality. In B. Kissin & H. Begleiter (Eds.), *The biology of alcoholism.* Vol. 4: *Social aspects of alcoholism.* New York: Plenum Press, 1976.

WILLIAMS, R. B., RUSSELL, R. M., DUTTA, S. K., & GIOVETTI, A. G. Alcoholic pancreatitis: Patients at high risk of acute zinc deficiency. *American Journal of Medicine,* 1979, *66,* 889–893.

WILLIAMS, R. J. *Alcoholism: The nutritional approach.* Austin: University of Texas Press, 1959.

WILLIAMS, R. J. The etiology of alcoholism: A working hypothesis involving the interplay of hereditary and environmental factors. *Quarterly Journal of Studies on Alcohol,* 1947, *7,* 567–587.

WINOKUR, G., CLAYTON, P. J., & REICH, T. *Manic depressive illness.* St. Louis: Mosby, 1969.

WINOKUR, G., REICH, T., RIMMER, J., & PITTS, G. Alcoholism: III. Diagnosis and familial psychiatric illness in 259 alcoholic probands. *Archives of General Psychiatry,* 1970, *23,* 104–111.

WOLFF, P. H. Ethnic differences in alcohol sensitivity. *Science,* 1972, *175,* 449–450.

WOODRUFF, R. A., GUZE, S. B., CLAYTON, P. J., & CARR, D. Alcoholism and depression. *Archives of General Psychiatry*, 1973, *28*, 97–100.

WREN, J., KLINE, N., & COOPER, T. Evaluation of lithium therapy in chronic alcoholism. *Clinical Medicine*, 1974, *81*, 33–36.

WURMSER, L. *The hidden dimension: Psychodynamics in compulsive drug use.* New York: Aronson, 1978.

WURMSER, L. Psychoanalytic considerations in the etiology of compulsive drug use. *Journal of the American Psychoanalytic Association*, 1974, *22*, 820–843.

YORKE, C. A critical review of some psychoanalytic literature on drug addiction. *British Journal of Medical Psychology*, 1970, *43*, 141.

ZALEZNIK, A. Psychoanalysis and organization theory. Presented at the panel on "Psychoanalytic knowledge of group processes," American Psychoanalytic Association, New York, Dec. 18, 1977.

ZETZEL, E. R. Anxiety and the capacity to bear it. *International Journal of Psychoanalysis*, 1949, *30*, 1–12.

ZETZEL, E. R. On the incapacity to bear depression. In M. Schur (Ed.), *Drives, affects and behavior*, Vol. 2. New York: International Universities Press, 1965.

ZIMBERG, S. Psychiatric office treatment of alcoholism. In S. Zimberg, J. Wallace, & S. B. Blume (Eds.), *Practical approaches to alcoholism psychotherapy*. New York: Plenum Press, 1978a.

ZIMBERG, S. Treatment of socioeconomically deprived alcoholics. In S. Zimberg, J. Wallace, & S. B. Blume (Eds.), *Practical approaches to alcoholism psychotherapy*, New York: Plenum Press, 1978b.

ZINBERG, N. E. Alcohol addiction: Toward a more comprehensive definition. This volume.

ZINBERG, N. E. Alcoholics Anonymous and the treatment and prevention of alcoholism. *Alcoholism: Clinical and Experimental Research*, 1977, *1*, 91–101.

ZINBERG, N. E. Medical education and intoxicant use. In J. Lowinson (Ed.), Proceedings of National Drug Abuse Conference, New York, 1976.

ZINBERG, N. E., & BEAN, M. H. Introduction: Alcohol use, alcoholism, and the problems of treatment. This volume.

ZINBERG, N. E., & FRASER, K. M. The role of the social setting in the prevention and treatment of alcoholism. In J. H. Mendelson & N. K. Mello (Eds.), *The diagnosis and treatment of alcoholism*. New York: McGraw-Hill, 1979.

ZINBERG, N. E., & ROBERTSON, J. A. *Drugs and the public.* New York: Simon & Schuster, 1972.

ZUSKA, J. J. Beginnings of the Navy program. *Alcoholism: Clinical and Experimental Research*, 1978, *2*, 352–357.

Index

longings and needs. Empathically focusing on the patient's discomfort, shame, and embarrassment reactions allowed the therapist to analyze with the patient how he repeatedly and characteristically denied and avoided his wish for recognition and approbation. Taking such an approach also makes extreme and alternating patterns of self-indulgence and denial more understandable, and thus more controllable—patterns that are otherwise driven, repetitious, and self-defeating. Such reactions suggest the operation of narcissistic resistances analogous to neurotic transference resistances, and represent opportunities for the patient and therapist to understand together, in the treatment relationship, the nature and origins of core conflicts around need satisfaction and dependency problems.

Many of the defenses and reactive patterns of alcoholics, including those of the patient just reviewed, resemble aspects and features of borderline and narcissistic conditions described by Kohut and Kernberg. Although they differ in their theoretical understanding and clinical application of these problems, they have both implicated such processes in drug-alcohol problems, and certain of their observations and approaches to such patients seem worth considering. In my opinion it is not clear whether borderline and narcissistic conditions share in common with alcoholics processes that are similar though not necessarily the same, or whether borderline and narcissistic pathology is at the root of alcoholism. However, the more recent emphasis on treatment of the deficits and pathology in ego and self structures is a promising and hopeful development for alcoholism treatment. I also believe we are still in a discovery phase of understanding narcissistic pathology in general, and how such pathology and its treatment applies in cases of alcoholism.

IMPLICATIONS FOR PSYCHOPHARMACOLOGICAL TREATMENT

The use of psychotropic drugs has a legitimate place among the treatment alternatives for alcohol problems and alcoholism. However, the literature on the efficacy of psychotropic agents in the treatment of alcoholism is for the most part confusing and discouraging. Part of the problem in drawing conclusions from these reports is that few if any of the studies are comparable. First, standard criteria for diagnosis of the alcoholism or the presumed underlying condition which is being treated are lacking. Another problem is related to the fact that depending on the study, different facets of the problem are studied to judge the usefulness of various psychopharmacological agents. In some reports relief of target people. He gave the example of people in medicine professing a motive of wanting to help when he suspected the motive of wanting money and prestige. He went on to say that he became defensive when a consultant such as the attending physician "delivers on what I implicitly ask for—or want." He also indicated he felt the same with me when I delivered on what he wanted. Among the forms his "defensiveness" might take he listed cynicism, humor, and a "carping anger." He reflected that he might be self-defeating, for example with the attending physician at grand rounds, and he might become obsequious, and he then questioned whether there might be a parallel pattern with me. I gently confirmed that such alternating patterns had occurred with me.

After a slight pause he began quietly to review how he thought a lot went into his reactions. He said, "Part of me wants to make repair of the things that are bad; part of me wants to exaggerate and make too much or the most of things. Somewhere in here there is a part of me that emerges that I don't know very well—it reminds me of how I recently told you I didn't know what my father thought of me. I still wonder how people see me."

He then began to address himself more directly to me. "Although you don't see me in action, I think you know me pretty well and have a pretty fair idea of how I interact with people. But I don't know how you see me—so I wonder what I am." His mood shifted abruptly and with a hint of embarrassment and some more evident impatience with himself he protested, "This is getting too complicated for this hour of the morning." I told him that I thought he was talking about something important but that he became uncomfortable when he approached a part of himself that he watned me to know and understand better; he had become embarrassed as he did so, as was evident when he tried to dismiss his thoughts by commenting on the hour of the morning. He then associated to wanting to have children but returned to his embarrassment reaction and the wishes behind such reactions that I had been "able to pick up." He said, "You will think, how self-centered of me." I responded that he not only was embarrassed, but even more, he was ashamed of his wishes towards me. I suggested that he was experiencing in a small way with me the ways he got stuck in his life with his defensiveness, wherein he went from one extreme or the other, so that he couldn't allow himself anything he wanted or indulged himself too much. He quickly interjected that drinking was his main "self-indulgence" and then chastised himself, saying twice, "God, I wish I didn't drink!" He promptly qualified this, reassuring me and himself he had been doing better. He then just as promptly castigated himself for reassuring himself. I ended the hour by pointing out that he berated and put himself down for reassuring himself. I said that reassuring himself was important and that if he could not allow that kind of indulgence for himself it was understandable how he could continue to resort to more extreme, self-defeating indulgences.

This case demonstrates how certain patients adopt exaggerated postures of indifference and self-sufficiency to defend against their dependent become more apparent. Qualities and characteristics often emerge in the treatment relationship that are symptomatic of ego and self impairments and become the basis for judgments about continued, long-term treatment.

In some cases more definitive long-term analysis-treatment of the determinants of the ego and self disturbances is not only possible but indicated. In my experience there is no basis to conclude categorically that a person with an alcohol problem lacks the requisite ego strength and capacity for an alliance to do such psychotherapeutic work. In such cases it is important for the therapist to combine elements of empathy and ego analysis to help patients gain an understanding of their dilemmas, as the following case illustrates.

CASE 4

Taking such an approach with a twenty-nine-year-old resident internist was particularly useful. Worried that he might be prone to alcoholism, he described a drinking pattern that involved regular, daily consumption of moderate to heavy amounts of beer interspersed with periodic episodes of extremely heavy drinking at various social get-togethers in which he might become amnesic for part of or all the episode.

The developments over the course of a particular treatment hour demonstrated how empathy with the patient's embarrassment and shame over his need to be appreciated, reassured, and understood led to a better elucidation and understanding of certain ego traits (cynicism and suspiciousness) and the uneven and self-defeating ways in which he satisfied his dependency including his use of alcohol. At the beginning of the hour he mentioned that he had to present a problem case to a senior attending physician at grand rounds. With a certain degree of detachment he observed that it would be interesting to see what the attending physician had to say on the case. He quickly became aware of and commented on his own "cynicism" and then conceded that the attending physician might also feel under pressure to do a good job. He wondered out loud some more as to the meaning of his cynicism. He speculated that it had to do with feeling "on the outside" and trying to get "in" himself. In an aside he complained of feeling "hung over" from the previous evening, when he had drunk a considerable amount of beer. He then joked about a new symptom of bruxism and lightly reviewed in the same vein how he frequently washed his hands, drank a lot, and "twiddled" his fingers. At this point I observed that he began to be self-conscious and wonder about his own cynicism and then to make light of his symptoms at the point where he indicated his more sympathetic appreciation that both the attending physician and myself might feel pressure to do a good job. He quickly agreed and volunteered that he was quick to disbelieve the intentions of and ultimately group psychotherapy. He worried that his dependency on me and my ideas might be too consuming emotionally and financially (despite relatively unlimited financial backing from his family). References to competitive situations and stories where someone or an animal was killed or hurt only thinly masked concerns about his relationship with me. In one group meeting someone asked him about his tendency to avoid people with whom he identified. He responded that he tended to become anxious and then resort to "impulsive and compulsive behavior." About six weeks into the treatment (in association with a drinking setback) he sent a letter to me stating he would not see me anymore, indicating he did "not want to go back into the 'cauldron of issues' anymore." With one phone call from me he agreed to return, but he persisted in his ambivalence about continuing in individual psychotherapy. I told him I respected his wishes, and we met a few more times. In one of his final regularly scheduled meetings he once again spoke with concern about his tendency to adopt and depend upon others wholesale but said that he wanted and intended to continue group because he could "sample" other people's ideas and thoughts with "a little more protection." In this hour he made a reference to "symbiotic relationships" and commented on some stories about the Pharaoh and the "tooth scraper" and a crocodile who had a bird picking his teeth.

Considering that his drinking was under control, that he had by then joined several A.A. groups in which he felt comfortable, and the help obtained from the couples group, I decided that he had gained enough personal support and control over his drinking to stop his individual meetings. He also asked if he might periodically see me if he felt the need (which he has since done). I felt that the limited goals and involvement of obtaining support, clarification, and sobriety for this man were sufficient and outweighed the risks that were possible, given the intensity of his ambivalence toward me.

As the above case demonstrates, the risks of ongoing psychotherapy with certain alcoholics outweight the advantages that might be achieved, and limited goals of clarification and support are preferable. However, in many other cases disabilities and problems surface for which psychoanalytic psychotherapy should be considered, and in fact might be the treatment of choice. Many patients continue to evidence considerable impairment and vulnerability, and the constant threat of reversion to alcohol and other forms of impulsivity remains apparent. In still other instances, despite considerable stability and improvement the patient and the therapist begin to sense and identify the persistence of subtle indications that things are not right: dissatisfactions in relationships or feelings of loneliness, isolation, and unhappiness emerge; or vague feelings of tension, anxiety, and depression continue; or self-defeating personality characteristics continue to plague a person, and related complaints and conflicts previously masked by the alcohol and associated acting out